REFORMATION ANGLICANISM

Essays on Edwardian Evangelicalism

EDITORS

MARK EARNGEY & STEPHEN TONG

FOREWORD

PETER F. JENSEN

The Latimer Trust

Reformation Anglicanism: Essays on Edwardian Evangelicalism © Mark Earngey and Stephen Tong 2022. All rights reserved.

ISBN 978-1-906327-79-8 Published by the Latimer Trust March 2023.

The Latimer Trust (formerly Latimer House, Oxford) is a conservative Evangelical research organisation within the Church of England, whose main aim is to promote the history and theology of Anglicanism as understood by those in the Reformed tradition. Interested readers are welcome to consult its website for further details of its many activities.

The Latimer Trust
London N14 4PS UK
Registered Charity: 1084337
Company Number: 4104465
Web: www.latimertrust.org
E-mail: administrator@latimertrust.org
Views expressed in works published by The Latimer Trust are those of the authors and do not necessarily represent the official position of The Latimer Trust.

Here is a rich, well-written and intriguing account of aspects of the 16th Century Reformation of the Church of England. It includes the significance of such heroes as Bishops Hooper and Ponet, theologians Cranmer and Bullinger, and the important roles played by Catechisms, Homilies, Cathedrals, The Forty-Five Articles, and attempts at Church Discipline. The contributions are set in the context of the wider European Reformations, and of current diverse accounts of the English Reformation. It is full of fresh information and insights!

Peter Adam, served as Vicar of St Jude's Carlton and as Principal of Ridley College in Melbourne, Australia. He is the author of numerous articles and books.

This is a tremendously stimulating collection of essays by first-rate scholars examining the Anglican Reformers, their inspiring formularies, their enduring legacies, and the theological heartbeat of the Reformation under Edward VI, which rejoices in finding great treasure in some of the less well-trodden paths of recent scholarship and dives deeply into neglected but fascinating aspects of that crucial and formative period in church history.

Revd Dr Lee Gatiss, Editor of *The First Book of Homilies: The Church of England's Official Sermons in Modern English*, **and author of** *Light After Darkness: How the Reformers Regained, Retold, and Relied on the Gospel of Grace.*

There is an urgent need in our time to show, yet again and with new vigor, how rich and compelling is the actual faith, theology, and liturgy of the English Reformation. If heard well, the sophisticated, spiritually vibrant works of Bucer and Ponet, Cranmer and Hooper continue to hold the potential to transform these names from mere historical figures to what they are indeed--*luminaries*, who continue to illuminate faithful paths before us today. What a joy it is, then, to see their distinctive contributions given the weight and careful analysis exhibited in this book! Here is a book we've needed, where careful scholarship illustrates the authentic Reformed Anglicanism which is catholic but not Catholic, evangelical but not subjectivist, biblical but not biblicistic, tradition-rich but not mere traditionalism. This a collection of essays whose many virtues signal the longstanding and continuing critical role played by Moore College and the Latimer Trust in resourcing faithful Reformed Anglicanism, and Mark Earngey and Stephen Tong are to be thanked—congratulated, rather!—for this service to the Church near and far. My sincere hope is that this volume will serve not only as a corrective to misunderstandings and misrepresentations for those within and outside of the global Anglican fold, but will also provoke fresh, even courageous efforts to renew in our day the Church's embrace of the faith and life that distinguished our fathers in the Reformation. To do so is not merely to honor them, but to honor the same God at work in them who works among us.

Mark A. Garcia (Ph.D., Edinburgh) is President and Fellow of Scripture and Theology at Greystone Theological Institute and Associate Professor of Systematic Theology at Westminster Theological Seminary (PA, USA).

Contents Page

Foreword by Peter Jensen — i

Contributors — iii

Conventions — v

Acknowledgements — v

Writing the Reformation: An Introduction — 1
Mark Earngey and Stephen Tong

1. The Enduring Significance of 'A Fruitful Exhortation to the Reading and Knowledge of Holy Scripture' — 15
Mark D. Thompson

2. John Ponet's *Short Catechisme:* A Neglected Formulary? — 33
Mark Earngey

3. Cranmer's Forty-Five Articles of 1552: An Overlooked Reformation Text — 47
Tim Patrick

4. The Reformation of Church Discipline — 63
Gerald Bray

5. Bishop John Hooper: Maverick of Magisterial Reformer? 85
   Stephen Tong

6. Melanchthon, Oecolampadius, Cyril, and Cranmer on the Eucharist 99
   Ashley Null

7. Reformation Cathedrals: Anomalies or Opportunities? 123
   Edward Loane

8. Heinrich Bullinger's Influence on Edwardian England 141
   Joe Mock

9. *In memoriam Martini Buceri:* the contested afterlife of Martin Bucer in England 161
   N. Scott Amos

Appendix A – *A Fruitful Exhortation to the Reading and Knowledge of Holy Scripture* 183

Appendix B – *The Short Catechisme* 193

Appendix C – The Forty-Five Articles of Religion (1552) 225
Translated by Derek Scales

"Dearly beloved, although to lose life and goods, or friends, for the sake of God's gospel, may seem a bitter and sour thing ... let us with good cheer take the cup at his hand and drink it merrily."
(John Bradford)

"The Lord God, I acknowledge, has taken from me all that I had, which indeed was most ample. But why should he not? He who gave has taken away. But what? Worldly, earthly, perishable things: while he is intending, I hope, yea, I do not doubt, to bestow upon me things heavenly and imperishable."
(John Ponet)

"Now is the time of trial, to see whether we fear more God or man. It was an easy thing to hold with Christ while the prince and world held with him; but now the world hateth him, is the true trial who be his." (John Hooper)

"... embrace Christ's cross, and Christ shall embrace you."
(Hugh Latimer)

"... though my breakfast be somewhat sharp and painful, yet I am sure my supper shall be more pleasant and sweet."
(Nicholas Ridley)

"But yet one thing grieveth my conscience ... more than any thing that ever I did or said in my whole life, and that is the setting abroad of a writing contrary to the truth; which now here I renounce and refuse ... And forasmuch as my hand offended, writing contrary to my heart, my hand shall first be punished therefor; for, may I come to the fire, it shall be first burned."
(Thomas Cranmer)

Foreword

Looking back is not always a good thing. It can be a sort of refuge, to keep us safe from the anarchy of the present and to justify unsustainable conservatism.

For as long as I can remember, Moore College has treasured the Reformation, and especially the English Reformation. The riches of its Library bear witness to this, and so too does the fact that the study of church history and historical theology has centred first on the Patristic period, and then on the Reformation. The present volume, written by outstanding scholars testifies to the same commitment. But is this merely comfortable conservatism? Not so, for three reasons.

First, the reformation period laid the foundations of the modern world, even the postmodern world which we inhabit. Of course, much has occurred to change the world since those days. But to take one case, it is rightly thought that the rediscovery of biblical Christianity contributed decisively to the birth of modern science. The modern world is unthinkable without the Reformation.

Second, the reformation teachers spoke with an enduring power and effectiveness about the meaning of the Scriptures and the centrality of the gospel. No doubt each generation makes its own contribution to our understanding of Scripture, but no one can rob the sixteenth century reformers of the glory of those who so decisively re-discovered the doctrines of grace and so changed the world.

Third, the world of Anglicanism is large and significant within world Christianity. Within that world, exist approaches as distinct as strong Anglo-Catholicism, radical liberalism and contemporary Pentecostalism. But a large number of contemporary Anglican believers may fairly be described as Evangelical. By whatever means each strand of Anglicanism may trace its history and gain its identity, it is those who can with justice still claim the Book of Common Prayer and the Articles of Religion, who can still claim, in other words, to be the children of the sixteenth century English Reformation, who can with most justice claim the name of 'Anglican'.

But how can such conservatives survive in a world so different from that of the sixteenth century?

By being true to God's word written, with a hermeneutic which allows the word to speak with all its mighty power, and not be obscured by critical theories intent on making the reader into the author. What binds us together with the reformers and indeed with Christians since the beginning is the Bible, and we have the inestimable privilege of hearing the voices of those who have read the same Bible and declared its message also. We do not regard them as infallible – we do not become slaves of the Reformation – but we hear and respect their witness, so often sealed with their own blood.

Those who treat the Bible thus and acknowledge their debt to the Reformation are set free from, not shackled by, conservatism. For it is those who are clear on the basics who can be free to experiment for the sake of sharing the gospel. When we need to speak to this world, so unimaginably different from the reformation world, not to say the world of antiquity, we are free to use our own language to describe the realties taught to us by the Reformation.

That is what they did, and to be true to them we must do the same thing. But if we ever think that their witness no longer matters, we will be in danger of succumbing to this world and losing the gospel which they proclaimed with such authority.

Peter F. Jensen
Former Archbishop of Sydney

Contributors

Mark D. Thompson is the Principal of Moore Theological College, Sydney. He is the author of *The Doctrine of Scripture: An Introduction* (Crossway, 2022) and of numerous articles in Reformation theology and history. He is married to Kathryn and they have four young adult daughters.

Mark Earngey is the Head of Church History at Moore Theological College, Sydney. He is the co-editor of *Reformation Worship: Liturgies from the Past for the Present* (New Growth Press, 2018). He is married to Tanya and they have four young children.

Tim Patrick is the Principal of Bible College SA and has several publications in English Church history including *Anglican Foundations* (Latimer Trust, 2018) and *Establishment Eschatology in England's Reformation* (Routledge, forthcoming 2023). He is married to Cat and they have three children.

Gerald Bray is the Director of Research with the Latimer Trust, London and Research Professor of Divinity at Beeson Divinity School, Samford University, Birmingham, Alabama, USA. He is the author of many books, including most recently *The History of Christianity in Britain and Ireland* (2021).

Stephen Tong is a History Master at Sydney Grammar School. He is the author of the forthcoming *Building the Church: The Book of Common Prayer and the Edwardian Reformation*. He is married to Bettina and they have three young children.

Ashley Null is an independent scholar based in Berlin and a visiting fellow of the Cambridge Divinity Faculty. He is author of *Thomas Cranmer's Doctrine of Repentance* (OUP, 2000) and studies the private theological notebooks of Thomas Cranmer.

Edward Loane is an Anglican minister who is currently serving as Warden of St Paul's College, Sydney and lecturer at Moore Theological College. His academic writing includes books, chapters and articles on

Christian Theology and History. He is married to Jocelyn and they have five children.

Joe Mock is a Presbyterian minister who assists in the ministry at Gracepoint Presbyterian Church Lidcombe NSW. He is married to Mavis and they have two children and three grandchildren.

N. Scott Amos is Professor of History at the University of Lynchburg in Lynchburg, Virginia. He is the editor of *Joshua, Judges, Ruth. Reformation Commentary on Scripture* (2020), and the author of *Bucer, Ephesians, and Biblical Humanism: The Exegete as Theologian* (2015). He is married to Liesl, and they have two daughters, Miriam and Rachel.

Conventions

In order to aid readability, early modern English spelling has been modernised except in instances where discussion requires precision. However, in order to reflect sixteenth-century usage, we have retained the contemporary spelling of certain place names (e.g. Strassburg, Zürich, etc.).

Acknowledgements

The production of this book would not have been possible without the help of several people. We are indebted to them and wish to express our genuine gratitude. Our contributors have been more than patient with the editors as COVID temporarily paused this project. We thank them for the occasional emails and nudges to stay the course. Those who proofread chapters and ran an additional editorial eye across the volume – in particular Timothy Young, Alex MacDonald, and Jonathan Adams – have served us especially well. We are grateful to Mark Thompson, who as Principal of Moore Theological College, originally seeded the idea to host a Reformation Anglicanism conference from which these essays were gathered and expanded. We also owe a debt of gratitude to the Latimer Trust who supported this project and were patient enough to see it through to publication. Lastly, it is the Lord Most High, the source of inspiration for our contributors, and the focus of devotion and debate among the personalities of the Reformation, who deserves the highest honour. In the words of the service of Holy Communion, "It is very meet, right, and our bounden duty, that we should at all times, and in all places, give thanks to thee, O Lord Holy Father, Almighty Everlasting God."

Mark Earngey and Stephen Tong

Lent 2023

Non ego sed Christus

Writing the Reformation: An Introduction

Mark Earngey and Stephen Tong

> Tradition is the living faith of the dead; traditionalism is the dead faith of the living. And, I suppose I should add, it is traditionalism that gives tradition such a bad name. – Jaroslav Pelikan

> The longer I live the more I am thoroughly persuaded that the world needs no new Gospel, as some profess to think. I am thoroughly persuaded that the world needs nothing but a bold, full, unflinching teaching of the 'old paths'. – J.C. Ryle

The Reformation fascinates us. For Christians who hold to a solifidian theology, this fascination is grounded in the conviction that we are the heirs of that sixteenth-century movement. It is not a modern phenomenon. The writing of church history is often undertaken by those who claim to be able to draw a direct path from their own lives to the biblical ideas promised in the Jewish scriptures and fulfilled by Jesus Christ. This is because the people of God find their sense of identity in the history of the church throughout the ages.

The Reformation was no different. It was an attempt to revitalise and rejuvenate the Western Church by recentring its doctrine and practice upon the Bible. In doing so, it aimed to bring men and women into union and communion with God through personal faith in the Lord Jesus Christ. The reformers emphasised that it was the work of the Holy Spirit in conjunction with the Holy Scriptures – rather than holy priests, holy sacraments, or holy relics and pilgrimages – that brought people to a saving faith, gave them a right standing before God, and thus an assurance of eternal life after death.

These soteriological concepts (and many more) are now embedded in the various shades of Protestantism that have emerged since Martin Luther nailed his '95 Theses' to the door of the Castle Church in

Wittenberg (1517) and since Huldrych Zwingli was embroiled in the 'Affair of the Sausages' in Zürich (1522). Therefore, understanding the diverse personalities and themes within historic Protestantism helps explain both the dynamics that shape much of modern Christianity, and the way many Christians engage with the modern world. Perhaps our enduring fascination with the Reformation may be explained in part by the fact that it is more than a watershed cultural, theological, and political moment. The Reformation continues to have modern relevance.

Just as each new sunrise illuminates a landscape in a new and revealing way, so fresh examination of the past always casts new light on a moment, place, or person, however well known they may be. For the past 500 years, historians and theologians have grappled with how best to portray the Reformation, its actors, and its legacy. The present volume does not attempt to bring a neat conclusion to this discussion. Rather, it seeks to throw new light on an ostensibly familiar period. The focus is on the Anglican roots that were put down during the dynastic drama of Tudor England. The picture that emerges from these essays reflects the deep thought and commitment of several key reformers who applied the *norming norm* of Scripture to the theological and social issues of their day. What we will see, therefore, is an ecclesial movement driven by an evangelical mind and thoroughly imbued with an evangelical.

This has not always been recognised. Indeed, the term 'evangelical' requires definition before we move on. The term 'evangelical' refers to that group of believers who shaped and led the sixteenth-century English Reformation, and either 'traditionalist' or 'conservative' is used to denote their theological opponents. More than just a modern term of political or ecclesial identification, and more than a term characterising the Great Awakenings of the 18th century, 'evangelical' is an accurate historic term for the protagonists of the English Reformation. Ashley Null has helpfully provided a brief etymology of the word 'evangelical', tracing it from Luther's German word for the general Protestant movement (*evangelisch*) – a term derived in turn from the New Testament's word for 'good news' or 'gospel' (*euangelion*).¹ The term has now become commonplace within Reformation scholarship.² In fact, Diarmaid MacCulloch has powerfully demonstrated that 'evangelical' is the most accurate epithet to use when discussing the early sixteenth-century English reformers, since it best captures the original priorities of that movement. Indeed, 'evangelical' (or often 'gospeller') was a common term of self-identification for these reformers.³ Adopting this specific label is important for recognising the nature and legacy of the English Reformation, and thus for contemporary Anglicanism. Therefore, for our present purposes, the term 'evangelical' is used in the sense just outlined, while the term 'Protestant' is used more generally when discussing the broader pan-European movement of those who adopted doctrines and practices distinct from the Roman Catholic church of their day.

It is not an understatement to say that there have been massive movements in the historiography of the English Reformation during the last century. Indeed, until recently, it would have been difficult to find an historical textbook that dissented from the idea that the Reformation in England was a 'howling success'.⁴ From as early as the late-sixteenth century, the traditional narrative told a triumphant story of how Tudor politicians secured England as a Protestant kingdom against malevolent foreign Roman Catholic forces – Elizabeth's victory

---

[1] Ashley Null, 'Thomas Cranmer and Tudor Evangelicalism', in Kenneth J. Stewart and Michael A. G. Haykin (eds.), *The Emergence of Evangelicalism: Exploring Historical Continuities* (Nottingham: Apollos 2008), 228.

[2] Alec Ryrie, 'The Strange Death of Lutheran England', *Journal of Ecclesiastical History* (2002) 53(1), 64-92; Peter Marshall, *Religious Identities in Henry VIII's England* (Ashgate: Aldershot, 2006), 20; Maria Dowling, 'The Gospel and the Court: Reformation under Henry VIII', in Peter Lake and Maria Dowling (eds.), *Protestantism and the National Church in Sixteenth Century England* (Place?: Croom Helm, 1987), 40-2.

[3] Diarmaid MacCulloch, *Reformation: Europe's House Divided, 1490-1700* (London: Allen Lane, 2003), introduction; *Tudor Church Militant: Edward VI and the Protestant reformation* (London, 1999), 2; Catharine Davies, *A Religion of the Word: the Defence of the Reformation in the Reign of Edward VI* (Cambridge: CUP 2002), xx-xxii.

[4] Diarmaid MacCulloch, 'The Impact of the English Reformation', *The Historical Journal* 31/1 (1995), 152.

against the Spanish Armada in 1588 was a key moment in this story. At the same time, the runaway success of Foxe's *Actes and Monuments* (popularly known as the *Book of Martyrs* and first published in 1563) popularised the concept of an historic continuity and spiritual unity between contemporary evangelicals and Jesus' first disciples. The unification of England and Scotland in 1603 under a new dynastic family, the Stuarts, strengthened the evangelical character of the British Isles, in spite of the tumultuous century that followed, which saw the Puritan movement come into its own, remove monarchical rule and then relinquish political ascendancy a generation later.[5] Yet the Restoration still upheld an evangelical form of worship. Even if many saw this as a compromised situation, it meant that by the turn of the eighteenth century, there was a near-universal acceptance of Protestantism throughout the realm. Even if Ireland stood as an exception to prove this rule, the story of the successful Reformation in the British Isles has had an impact not only in the United Kingdom, but also in the many Anglophone speaking regions across the African continent, throughout the Americas, and within South East Asia down through the centuries.

In modern times, the prevalence of this traditional narrative of the English Reformation owes a great deal to the ground-breaking research of A.F. Pollard and G.R. Elton.[6] By surveying the letters and papers of King Henry VIII and the official legal records and writings of men such as Thomas Cromwell, the English Reformation was characterised as a movement dominated by the political circumstances of the times. As the winds of change blew through the corridors of power in the English court, the extent to which evangelicals were able to enact ecclesiastical change waxed and waned. Thus, the two giants of the Tudor dynasty,

---

[5] John Morrill, *Oliver Cromwell and the English Revolution* (London: Longmans, 1990);
Anthony Milton, *Catholic and Reformed: he Roman and Protestant Churches in English Protestant Thought, 1600-1640* (Cambridge: Cambridge University Press, 1995).

[6] For instance, A.F. Pollard, *Henry VIII* (London: Goupil, 1905) and *The History of England: From the Ascension of Edward VI to the death of Elizabeth (1547-1603)* (London: Longmans & Green, 1910); G.E. Elton, *The Tudor Revolution in Government: Administrative Changes in the Reign of Henry VIII* (Cambridge, CUP, 1953).

Henry VIII and Elizabeth I, emerged as essential partners in an unequal relationship of crown and church. Quite simply, without the backing of the monarch, any attempt to reform the church was dead in the water. The implementation of ecclesial reform was therefore presented as a 'top down' process in which the Reformation was imposed on the English population via royal injunctions and acts of parliament such as the Act of Supremacy and the Act of Uniformity. In fact, in Elton's view, it was the ingenuity of Thomas Cromwell which supplied King Henry with concrete ideas for the English ecclesiastical Brexit. This political interpretation of events has left a deep impression on the academic landscape.

While we should not discount the significance of political influence on the development of the English Reformation, trying to explain how the evangelical faith was accepted at the popular level demands that we look to other types of sources for answers. In 1964, when A.G. Dickens first published his landmark *The English Reformation,* he noticed that ordinary men and women tended to fall through the gaps between the study of rulers, religious leaders, and liturgical literature. Thus, a significant part of his research was concerned with the man on the street.[7] This was achieved through the study of material evidence (such as parish registers, churchwardens accounts, etc.) made recently available through the development of local historical societies and record offices. In Dickens' view, English Catholicism was in an irreparable condition and the almost inevitable Reformation was both rapid and highly successful. Thus, between Pollard and Elton's 'top-down' historical approach and Dickens' inclusion of 'bottom-up' factors, the traditional narrative of the unstoppable English Reformation was widely disseminated.

In addition to the availability of local archival material, the rise of 'new histories' in the 1960s witnessed the injection of psychology, economics, anthropology, and myriad other disciplines into the writing of the English Reformation. This led to the proliferation of new approaches and ideas that led historians working in the late 1970s and 1980s to revise the accepted narrative of the English Reformation. Spearheaded by Christopher Haigh and his focused study on *The*

---

[7] A.G. Dickens, *The English Reformation* (London: B.T. Batsford, 1964).

Reformation and Resistance in Tudor Lancashire (1975), a new wave of 'revisionist' historians highlighted the persistence of Roman Catholic devotion and practice in England in spite of the evangelical political ascendancy. Evidence for the existence of stubborn traditional belief in regions of early modern England allowed revisionists to question historical accounts which emphasised a widespread popular appeal of the evangelical movement. This revisionist approach is exemplified by J.J. Scarisbrick's *The Reformation and the English People* (1984) which cast the Reformation as a state imposition upon an unwilling people, and Haigh's *Reformation Revised* (1987), a collection of essays that inserted Catholicism back into the Reformation narrative as much as it took the Protestantism out.

It did not take long before the form of public worship – the primary site of popular religion – came under the microscope. The unambiguously evangelical *Book of Common Prayer*, which underwent three editions in the Tudor era, fundamentally altered the way English parishes approached God as a corporate body. However, this new liturgy, it was argued, also unravelled the very fabric of English society.[8] Eamon Duffy's *Stripping of the Altars* (1993) appeared as the pinnacle of the revisionist movement. It used intricate detail and thick description to reveal a pre-Reformation world of sincere Roman Catholic faith that was best expressed through the late-medieval liturgy, which gave a defined shape and rhythm to the lives of English folk. Naturally, evangelicalism was seen as an incursion into this idyll. For Duffy and other revisionist historians, the evangelical movement was disruptive – even subversive – and therefore viewed as a largely unwanted intrusion into the flourishing traditional religion of the English people. In fact, upon reading some revisionist accounts of this supposedly unwanted evangelicalism, one could reasonably ask why was there any Reformation at all. It was no coincidence that one prominent revisionist scholar was publicly accused of writing Catholic history rather than a history of Catholicism – not a mild academic charge.

From this revisionist turn, several fundamental questions emerged about Dickens' thesis. Can the English Reformation really be

---

[8] John Bossy, 'The Mass as a Social Institution, 1200-1700', *Past and Present* 100 (1983), 29-61.

considered a largely unified and rapidly successful movement? Or is it better to see the development of Protestantism in England as a series of semi-detached reformations? If the second proposition was accepted, then, how many reformations were there, and how long did 'the' English Reformation last?

All of these questions, and more, were taken up by so-called 'post-revisionist' historians from the 1990s onwards. Rather than seeing the English Reformation as a series of conjoined moments, researchers paid more attention to the ways in which Protestantism was promoted and accepted. Periodisation was replaced by an interest in processes. Hence historians focused increasingly on a broader range of sources. As they looked at images, fashion, architecture, household objects, and even the natural landscape, a rich visual and material culture emerged that indicated a much deeper and more complex acceptance of Protestantism.[9] In many ways, post-revisionists have advanced the revisionist attempt to rehabilitate 'the view from the pew' by considering the various ways those outside of the political elite embraced, enabled, and engaged with Protestantism.[10] Ethan Shagan's *Popular Politics and the English Reformation* (2002) nuanced the traditional narrative of the English Reformation by arguing that it was only possible for reformation doctrine and practice to be woven into the fabric of society through the co-operation of local authorities and lay folk. Post-revisionists have portrayed the English Reformation not as an unwelcome imposition of royal authority intruding into the lives of otherwise content subjects, but rather as a two-way conversation between ruler and ruled so that the Reformation's final acceptance was amicable, and even one in which the lowest ranks of society were given a degree of agency to determine its course. This goes some way in helping to explain why the destructive iconoclasm associated with the earlier reform movement was joined with such enthusiasm. More

---

[9] Ulinka Rublack, *Dressing Up: Cultural Identity in Renaissance Europe* (Oxford: Oxford University Press, 2010); Tara Hamling, *Decorating the 'godly' Household: Religious Art in Post-Reformation Britain* (London: Paul Mellon Centre for Studies in British Art, 2010); Alex Walsham, *Reformation of the Landscape: Religion, Identity, and Memory in Early Modern Britain and Ireland* (Oxford: Oxford University Press, 2012).

[10] Christopher Marsh, "'Common Prayer' in England 1560-1640: The View from the Pew', *Past and Present* 171 (2001), 69-94.

recently, Alexandra Walsham's *Charitable Hatred: Tolerance and Intolerance in England 1500-1700* (2006), and Alec Ryrie's *Being Protestant in Reformation Britain* (2013) have encouraged us to take seriously the applied theology of layfolk. While many early modern men and women accepted evangelical doctrine, they adapted official forms of faith through the lens of their own experience and context. We must also remember that the Reformation converged with other intellectual, political, and cultural developments, which helped stimulate conditions for substantial structural, doctrinal, and ecclesial change.[11] What has emerged is a richer and more complex, and probably more accurate, understanding of how the collective consciousness of England's society and politics have been imbued with a Protestant ethic.

A notable historiographic trend within 'post-revisionism' is the renewed emphasis on understanding the Reformation as an intellectual movement. Historians are increasingly taking the reformers on their own terms and accepting the sincere beliefs of evangelicals as legitimate epistemes. It is ironic that in a world that is increasingly less inclined to believe in the reality of spiritual powers, there has been a recent move to pay closer attention to the complex theology developed by reformers and to engage with it in a serious manner. Early signs of this trend were detected in Patrick Collinson's *Elizabethan Puritan Movement* (1979). More recently, Diarmaid MacCulloch's superb *Thomas Cranmer* (1996) and Ashley Null's *Thomas Cranmer's Doctrine of Repentance* (2000) have reminded scholars that we must give due credence to the evangelical belief system that motivated the reformers, even if we do not share that same belief. This growing interest in the intellectual nuances and application of evangelical theology has yielded some important fruit. An excellent example of this is Alec Ryrie's essay, 'The Strange Death of Lutheran England' (2002), which demonstrated the decline of Lutheran theological distinctives and the rise of Reformed doctrines towards the end of Henry VIII's reign.[12] Another example is MacCulloch's recent *Thomas Cromwell* (2018) which not only reconnected Lollardy with

---

[11] Alexandra Walsham, 'The Reformation and 'The Disenchantment of the World' Reassessed', *The Historical Journal*, 51/2 (2008), 497-528.
[12] Alec Ryrie, 'The Strange Death of Lutheran England', *Journal of Ecclesiastical History*, 53/1 (2002), 64-92.

important strands of the early English Reformation but demonstrated the evangelical – and indeed Swiss – influences upon and impulses behind vicegerent Cromwell's religious outlook.

Coupled with this revival of theological investigation has been the rediscovery of the pan-European flow of ideas which affected the English Reformation. The work of Andrew Pettegree, for example, sheds new light upon the migration and community life of both English and foreign persecuted Protestants; Anne Overell and others have illuminated the importance of Italian reform upon the English Reformation; and Torrance Kirby, Carrie Euler, and a rising chorus of scholars continue to demonstrate the influence of Zürich upon the English Reformation.[13] The very Victorian idea of a discrete English Reformation separate from the Reformation on "the Continent" is no longer academically tenable, and Reformation historians now speak of the European Reformation which involves those small but significant islands known as the British Isles. Indeed, the Anglo-Catholic historiographical myth of the Church of England as a peculiar *via media* between Rome and the Reformed is thankfully a thing of the past. The English Reformation may have had an idiosyncratic phase under Henry VIII; it may even have had a short but significant Lutheran episode. But it was undoubtedly a Reformed Reformation with a robust relationship with the theologians of Strassburg and Zürich.

In terms of current scholarship, the harvest of this post-revisionist research into the English Reformation is perhaps best presented in Peter Marshall's *Heretics and Believers: A History of the English Reformation* (2017). With a masterful grasp of the primary and secondary sources related to the English Reformation, Marshall manages to combine the major themes and personalities with poignant examples while keeping the pace of the narrative flowing along

---

[13] Andrew Pettegree, *Foreign Protestant Communities in Sixteenth-Century London* (Oxford: Clarendon Press, 1986); Torrance Kirby, *The Zurich Connection and Tudor Political Theology* (Leiden: Brill, 2007); Carrie Euler, *Couriers of the Gospel: England and Zurich, 1531-1558* (Zurich: Theologischer Verlag Zurich, 2006); Anne Overell, *Italian Reform and English Reformations, c.1535–c.1585* (Aldershot: Ashgate, 2008).

buoyantly. It is undoubtedly the English Reformation lecturer's best book recommendation for the curious student. However, one of the shortcomings of Marshall's otherwise erudite treatment of the English Reformation is the relatively slim coverage of the reform during the reign of King Edward VI. Many of the significant aspects of the Edwardian Reformation are covered by Marshall but the extent to which he treats religious life on the eve of the Reformation and the dynamics of the Marian Counter-Reformation is not matched in his treatment of the significant evangelical efforts under Edward VI – the main focus of this publication.

With one exception, the essays in this volume were delivered at the Reformation Anglicanism Symposium held at Moore Theological College in 2019. Although located in the distant antipodes, Moore College has a long and illustrious tradition of hosting papers delivered by world leading scholars and this event was no exception. Each of the main presenters very kindly expanded their papers out to form the essays before you (and very patiently waited for this publication to come to fruition). Thus, the following essays provide insights into various aspects of the sixteenth-century English Reformation that gave birth to the Anglican Church. Some of these aspects of Reformation Anglicanism are well-known, others are less so. Together, these essays serve as a window into the wide-ranging means by which the Reformers sought to reclaim the authority of Scripture as the plumbline of authentic Christianity, both in a public and private sense.

The first half of this volume examines some foundational documents of the English Reformation. Mark Thompson reminds us of the importance of Word-based preaching in public worship. By taking a close look at the *Book of Homilies* (1547), Thompson reveals how Archbishop Cranmer put preaching at the heart of the English Church during the reign of Edward VI (1547-1553). While some may blanch at the thought of 'preaching' from an extrabiblical set text, the *Homilies* were a necessary corrective to the theological vagaries of late medieval sermons. Moreover, the *Homilies* inculcated English congregations with solifidian soteriology. That is to say, these homilies not only extolled the virtues of salvation by God's grace alone but they also explained how salvation was attained by faith in Christ alone. In doing so, the *Homilies* provided an important theological foundation upon which reformed public worship could be built.

Theological education was not isolated to the pulpit, however. As Mark Earngey shows, regular catechesis further enhanced the reformers' ability to embed biblical doctrine in the hearts and minds of their contemporaries. Taking the biblical injunctive to foster the faith in the next generation seriously, reformers produced various catechisms for use in schools and local congregations. Earngey's essay focuses on Bishop John Ponet's *Short Catechisme* (1553) to help illuminate our understanding of how the Christian faith is for all people, regardless of age, gender, and financial situation. Though the polymath Ponet and his catechism are both little known today, Earngey demonstrates that this much neglected reformer and his catechism supply an important foundational document for the English Reformation – indeed, one of the best commentaries on the official Reformed theology of the English Church in King Edward VI's reign.

In addition to reshaping the forms of worship, the English Reformation also codified their doctrinal outlook. Tim Patrick's essay investigates the doctrinal character of the English Church by reconsidering Cranmer's *Forty-Five Articles* (1552). This is an important investigation into the origins of the *Forty-Two Articles of Religion* which were first published as an appendix to Ponet's *Short Catehisme* and which were eventually consolidated into the *Thirty-Nine Articles of Religion* (1571) that continue to regulate Anglican theology today. As Patrick argues, a close examination of this document reminds us that official evangelical doctrine was not formulated hastily, but a product of careful research, thought, and discussion. This doctrinal development may also be observed in Gerald Bray's essay on the *Reformatio legum ecclesiasticarum* (1553), which reveals the immensely significant proposed changes to canon law developed during the Edwardian Reformation. This great 'What if' of the English Reformation elucidates the reformers' theological breadth and depth and the importance of canon law in their program of reform. Both the *Forty-Five Articles* and the *Reformatio* are under-studied documents, and considering them further is extremely helpful in understanding the impulses and intended direction of the English Reformation. These two essays, therefore, provide fresh insights into the period. They especially highlight how English reformers sought to create an institutional bulwark against heresy in order to protect the evangelical identity of the Church of England.

The second half of the book focuses on foundational people and places. In a departure from the usual line up of the evangelical "Who's Who," the essays in this volume focus on churchmen and theologians who were very influential, but in ways not often considered. For instance, John Hooper, the evangelical firebrand who is most famously associated with the Edwardian vestments controversy, and generally seen as an antecedent of the non-conformist movement, is recast by Stephen Tong as a willing supporter of the institutional reforms that were enacted in the period. Although he had a different understanding of *adiaphora* compared to Cranmer and Ridley, Hooper's overriding concern was ensuring that the form and content of institutional reform aligned with Scripture. Ashley Null then takes us on a rich exploration of Cranmer's eucharistic theology. Through a close examination of Cranmer's commonplace notebooks, Null demonstrates that the archbishop sharpened his theology by interacting with his contemporaries on the continent as well as building on the inheritance of Church Fathers. This is a salient lesson for our times, and a helpful allegory for the Christian walk. Although one's faith is personal, we are encouraged and strengthened through the communion we share with our spiritual brothers and sisters.

The next two essays throw a different light on the English Reformation by considering how two non-English reformers played significant roles in the evangelical movement. Joe Mock examines the underappreciated influence of Heinrich Bullinger, the Swiss reformer who helped to develop Zürich as a leading Reformation city after Zwingli's death. Although Bullinger never set foot on English soil, Mock shows us that he had direct and intimate contact with senior figures within the English establishment. These connections allowed Bullinger to stimulate the English scene from afar, and thus helped to significantly enrich the English evangelical movement. Martin Bucer was another European reformer who had an enormous influence on the shape of the English Church, most notably via his critique of the first *Book of Common Prayer*; his suggestions which were integrated into subsequent editions of the prayer book. Although Bucer died in 1551, he left an enduring legacy, which Scott Amos helpfully explores here.

Bucer's changing public image after his death reflected the mutations in the confessional identity of those in power. This essay is therefore a reminder of confessional memories and the ways in which histories are muted or made for posterity. Taken together, these two essays point to the significance of Edwardian England in the minds of mid-sixteenth- century reformers. Clearly, the investment of such internationally recognised theologians suggests that the development of the Edwardian Reformation held importance across the Protestant world.

In some respects, the final essay in this collection brings us full circle. Having begun with the *Homilies* that overlay the traditional practice of preaching with evangelical characteristics, the last essay considers how another iconic element of the past was transformed for evangelical purposes. Ed Loane brings our attention to the ways in which cathedrals were deliberately reconstituted and reformed. Although many consider the retention of cathedrals as an anomaly, these buildings actually had the potential to express the Reformation spirit quite thoroughly. While these architectural relics offered tangible links to the past, they were also transformed into beacons of light in the most evangelical of senses. Once again, cathedrals remind us of the transmutation of tradition which occurred during the English Reformation, and remain as physical evidence of historical change and continuity.

The Reformation *should* continue to fascinate us, not least because it helps explain the dynamics that helped shape the modern churches we see around us. The old paths of the Reformation provide stability for new steps. It is our hope that this collection of essays will, on the one hand, help to ward off the kind of 'traditionalism that gives tradition such a bad name', and on the other, that it would commend 'the living faith of the dead' upon whose giant shoulders we now stand.

The Enduring Significance of 'A Fruitful Exhortation to the Reading and Knowledge of Holy Scripture'

Mark D. Thompson

In the contemporary struggles over Anglican identity, an often-neglected resource are the *Homilies*. Alongside the *Thirty-nine Articles of Religion*, the *Book of Common Prayer,* and the *Ordinal*, these two books of model thematic sermons are part of the Anglican foundational documents, the formularies of the Church of England. That fact is remarkable in itself. As Gerald Bray remarked, 'the Church of England ... was the only branch of Christendom that incorporated sermons into its statements of faith'.[14] They represented an attempt to expound in more detail the theology and principles of reform adopted by the Church of England and expressed in the Articles. Article 35 (a revision of Article 34 in the original 42 Articles) speaks of them as containing 'a godly and wholesome Doctrine, and necessary for these times' and encourages them 'to be read in Churches by the Ministers, diligently and distinctly, that they may be understanded of the people'. In other words, the Homilies were part of a wider program of disseminating reformed doctrine and pastoral practice throughout the realm. If we are to recover the theological perspective of reformation Anglicanism, then, the Homilies are most certainly worthy of our attention.

The first book of homilies is in fact only mentioned in passing in the Articles of Religion. While Article 35 explicitly highlights the second book, published in Elizabeth's reign and most probably edited by Bishop John Jewel, it does include the first book in the assessment when it says 'as doth the former book of Homilies, which were set forth in the time of Edward the Sixth'. In fact, it seems that the first book was prepared in 1543, during Henry VIII's reign, but was sidelined by the manoeuvrings of some of the conservatives in the Canterbury

---

[14] G. L. Bray (ed.), *The Books of Homilies: A Critical Edition* (Cambridge: James Clarke & Co, 2015), ix.

convocation, including, especially, the Bishop of Winchester, Stephen Gardiner.[15] It became, then, 'the first work pertaining either to the public worship or to the teaching of the Church of England that was put forth in the reign of Edward VI',[16] published merely six months after Edward's accession, and, as Ashley Null puts it, 'designed to be a manifesto of the regime's theological agenda *and* the means of its revolutionary implementation'.[17] The original published title was *Certayne Sermons, or Homelies, Appoynted by the Kynges Majestie to Be Declared and Redde by all Persones, Vicars, or Curates every Sondaye in their Churches where they have Cure* and they were accompanied by a royal injunction that they should be read through to parishioners again and again 'until the king's pleasure should be further known'.[18] It appears to have been a popular work. We have evidence of at least nine editions in 1547 alone, though it is difficult to determine the size of each of these.[19] However, even widespread availability did not guarantee they were used as they were intended. In some parishes, the clergy were so illiterate this was impossible. In others, the Homilies were met with resistance from the congregation. Hugh Latimer complained in a sermon before King Edward VI, delivered on 15 March 1549, that 'though the priest read them never so well, yet if the parish like them not, there is such talking and babbling in the church that nothing can be heard; and if the parish be good and the priest naught, he will so hack it and chop it, that it were as good for

---

[15] Bray's brief survey of the historical context of the Homilies is helpful in this connection: Bray, xi–xix. It would seem that on 16 February 1543 Cranmer 'presided over the formal presentation of several homilies in convocation …[and] in the spring of 1547 he wrote letters describing his intention to act on the homilies agreed to in convocation years before'. J. A. Null, 'The Official Tudor Homilies', pp. 348–365 in H. Adlington, R. McCollough & E. Rhatigan (eds), *Oxford Handbook of the Early Modern Sermon* (Oxford: Oxford University Press, 2011), 350.
[16] J. Griffiths, 'Editor's Introduction', in J. Griffiths (ed.), *The Two Books of Homilies Appointed to be Read in Churches* (Oxford: Oxford University Press, 1859), vii.
[17] Null, 'Homilies', 348 (emphasis added).
[18] Griffiths, viii. See Injunction 32 in G. L. Bray (ed.), *Documents of the English Reformation* (Minneapolis: Fortress, 1994), 256.
[19] Griffiths, ix (esp. fn. h).

them to be without it, for any word that shall be understood'.[20] The lesson was yet to be learned that, especially in matters of religion, you can lead the horse to water, you can even provide the trough and fill it to the brim, but you cannot make it drink.

A number of the sermons in this collection were composed by Thomas Cranmer himself, including the first, on reading and understanding the Bible. It is possible to see a pattern in the collection, with six doctrinal homilies (which are nevertheless richly pastoral) followed by six pastoral homilies (which are nevertheless anchored in the teaching of Scripture). The doctrinal homilies expound the doctrine of the church while the pastoral homilies apply that doctrine to the circumstances and conditions of sixteenth century England. Notwithstanding that distinction, the commonality of purpose in the entire collection is clear when we turn to the preface composed in 1547:

> The king's most excellent majesty ..., that all curates, of what learning soever they be, may have some godly and fruitful lessons in a readiness to read and declare with their parishioners for their edifying, instruction and comfort; hath caused a book of homilies to be made and set forth, wherein is contained certain wholesome and godly exhortations, to move the people to honour and worship Almighty God, and diligently to serve him, everyone according to their degree, state and vocation.[21]

It is not without significance that the very first homily in the first book of Homilies concerns the reading and knowledge of Holy Scripture. Cranmer's commitment to the authority and efficacy of Scripture is evident not only in the Articles he helped draft and the homily he authored, but also in his personal research notes, known as 'Cranmer's Great Commonplaces'.[22] It is in these notes that he remarked

---

[20] H. Latimer, 'The Second Sermon Preached before King Edward' in J. Watkins (ed.), *The Sermons and Life of the Right Reverend Father in God, and Constant Martyr of Jesus Christ, Hugh Latimer, some time Bishop of Worcester* (London: Aylott & Son, 1858), 106–7.
[21] Bray, 3–4.
[22] J. A. Null, 'Thomas Cranmer and the Anglican Way of Reading Scripture', *Anglican and Episcopal History* 75/4 (2006): 488–526 (493–4).

'Scripture comes not from the church, but from God and has authority by the Holy Spirit' and the 'authority of the Scriptures is from God, the author, not from man'.[23] Biblical texts he looked to for support of such propositions included 2 Peter 1:21, 2 Timothy 3:16, 1 Corinthians 11:23, Galatians 1:11–12, and Deuteronomy 4:2.[24] Furthermore, the shape and content of the *Book of Common Prayer*, with the prominent place it gives to the reading of Scripture and a lectionary that provided for the Book of Psalms to be read through once a month, most of the Old Testament once a year, and most of the New Testament three times a year, further reflects Cranmer's understanding of how God changes lives, how people are 'moved' to 'honour and worship Almighty God'. In this a slight difference of emphasis can be discerned when compared with the liturgies produced by other European reformers. Luther's attention to the preached word *and* the sacrament, and Calvin's attention to the importance of preaching, were in no way antithetical to what was going on in England. Indeed, Luther and Calvin had very small domains of liturgical responsibility compared to Cranmer, who had to contend with thousands of English churches served by traditionalist clergy disgruntled by the reformation and who had been inadequately trained for a preaching ministry. Cranmer did not deny the importance of either the sermon or the sacrament. Yet for theological reasons, and not just the ecclesiastical and historical exigencies of the time, Cranmer saw the public and private reading of Scripture as the engine of change.[25]

Cranmer could have begun this collection with the homily on salvation. After all, at the heart of the Protestant movement was a recovery of the biblical gospel: that we have been saved by God's grace not our merit, that its basis is Christ's full and sufficient atonement for sinners on the cross, and that the instrument by which God draws us into this salvation and sets us right before him is faith. Starting there would have been entirely appropriate. Or else he could have begun, as a way

---

[23] 'Cranmer's Great Commonplaces', British Library MS 7.B.XI, 8^v, 32^v. These are cited in Null, 493.
[24] 'Cranmer's Great Commonplaces', 8^v-9^r; Null, 493.
[25] Architecturally Cranmer's church would have neither altar nor pulpit as the centre of attention but instead the lectern, to which the Bible was chained and from which the Bible was read.

of locating all that he wanted to say within the orthodoxy of ancient creeds, with an exposition of the nature and character of God. If, as Aquinas had pointed out centuries before, theology is talk about God and about all things in relation to God, then this too would have been entirely appropriate.[26] Another possibility would have been to invert what became the final order of the collection, especially given the 'established' character of the English church and the political concern for civil obedience. That would have put the 'Sermon against Contention and Brawling' up front. Slightly odd, to be sure, but it would not have been impossible to justify given royal and episcopal concern for peace, good order, and a 'godly commonwealth'. Yet the collection begins with the homily on Scripture, reflective of Cranmer's conviction that the instrument the Spirit of God will use to make a difference in the hearts of men and women, and so in the life of the nation, is the word of God written.

What I am proposing to do in this chapter is not to provide an account of the doctrine of Scripture generally accepted in the early English Reformation. I do not even propose to provide an account of Thomas Cranmer's doctrine of Scripture. That has been more than ably done by others.[27] Instead, I have the much more manageable aim of spending some time with this first of the homilies, a vehicle by which Cranmer hoped that many in the churches of England would be convinced of the proper authority and right use of the Bible.

The architecture of the homily

The *Fruitful Exhortation to the Reading and Knowledge of Holy Scripture* is not a 'theological account of the nature of Scripture' as may be found in the first book of Calvin's *Institutes* or even the first three sermons of Bullinger's *Decades*. Cranmer's emphasis is on the *use* of Scripture, its place and its impact in the Christian life. It is one of the doctrinal homilies, but as we have noted it is richly pastoral. It is

---

[26] T. Aquinas, *Summa Theologiae,* trans. T. Gilby et al (60 vols; London: Eyre & Spottiswoode, 1963), I:15 (*ST* Ia, 1. 3).
[27] Null, 'Thomas Cranmer'. However, see M. D. Thompson, 'Sola Scriptura', in M. Barrett, *Reformation Theology: A Systematic Summary* (Wheaton: Crossway, 2017), 180–185.

genuinely an exhortation, an encouragement to those who will hear this homily to read the Bible and so to know God and his will, as well as their own office and duty.[28] Recent Cranmer scholarship has characterised him as an 'affective theologian', concerned with the transformation of the believer's affections as a way of bringing about genuine and lasting change in behaviour, and influenced in this by both Erasmus and Melanchthon.[29] In Ashley Null's words, 'what the heart loves, the will chooses and the mind justifies'.[30] This is an immensely productive insight which helps us to understand Cranmer's larger reforming agenda and role that a regular and extensive exposure to Scripture plays in that agenda. More than that, though, it is reflected quite explicitly in this homily. Cranmer wrote, 'This Word, whosoever is diligent to read and in his heart to print that he readeth, the great affection to the transitory things of this world shall be minished in him, and the great desire of heavenly things that be therein promised of God, shall increase in him'.[31] An affection for this world and what it offers is 'overcome by a more vehement affection' (to use Melanchthon's expression) for Christ and all in him presented to us in the Scriptures.[32] This is why, for Cranmer, the continual, diligent and meditative reading of Scripture (he exhorts the congregation to 'ruminate and, as

---

[28] From this point the text of the homily will be cited with short title and the page number in Bray's critical edition. So, 'A Fruitful Exhortation', 7.
[29] J. A. Null, *Thomas Cranmer's Doctrine of Repentance* (Oxford: Oxford University Press, 2000), 100–101. Null, 'Thomas Cranmer', 240.
[30] http://acl.asn.au/resources/dr-ashley-null-on-thomas-cranmer/ (accessed 24 August 2019). '... Melanchthon argued that the affections were located in the heart and that they determined both the choices of the will and the reasoning of the mind. For what the heart loved, the will would inevitably choose, and the mind would then defend.' Null, 'Homilies', 353. 'The supernatural redirection of human affections through encountering Scripture lay at the very heart of Cranmer's understanding of the Christian life'. Null, 'Thomas Cranmer', 513.
[31] 'A Fruitful Exhortation', 9.
[32] Null, *Repentance,* 100. See Melanchthon on this dynamic as expressed in the story of Paris, who was overcome with a 'more vehement affection' (*uictus reuera uehementiore adfectu*) for Helen of Troy. P. Melanchthon, *Commonplaces: Loci Communes 1521* (trans. C. Preus; St Louis: Concordia, 2014), 34. Centuries later, Thomas Chalmers would write of the same dynamic in his *The Expulsive Power of a New Affection* (London, 1861).

it were, chew the cud, that we may have the sweet juice')[33] will transform the affections of the believer in a way that has profound consequences: 'his heart and life altered and transformed into that thing which he readeth'.[34]

The homily falls into two halves. The first part treats the nature and purpose of Holy Scripture: what Scripture is and what it is designed to do. The second part is largely taken up with overcoming popular arguments against the reading and knowledge of Scripture. The overall effect of this arrangement is to base encouragement to read and persevere in reading the Bible upon God's goodness in giving it to us. 'Let us be glad to revive this precious gift of our heavenly Father', he wrote near the very end of the sermon.[35] Scripture is God's 'great and special gift, beneficial favour and fatherly providence'.[36] The homily involves a movement, as all good preaching does, from an advance in our knowledge of God and his purposes, to rich corporate and personal application. It is an exhortation, as the title suggests, but not a bare exhortation that would amount to little more than a new pietistic legalism. Rather, it is meant as a *fruitful* exhortation because it is anchored in the benevolence of God and his continued active involvement in the lives of those he has redeemed.

The text of the homily is littered with biblical language and allusion but with surprisingly few direct quotations. It is clear that Cranmer wants to anchor his exhortation about the nature and use of Scripture in Scripture itself. Yet he also makes use of the select church fathers. He cites Chrysostom, Fulgentius or Ruspe, and, of course, Augustine. Its style is richly hortatory, evidencing again and again the pastoral concern (and not just a political agenda) which drove the reformation. That is clear from the very first line:

> Unto a Christian man there can be nothing either more necessary or profitable than the knowledge of Holy

---

[33] 'A Fruitful Exhortation', 13.
[34] 'A Fruitful Exhortation', 9.
[35] 'A Fruitful Exhortation', 13.
[36] Ibid.

Scripture, forasmuch as in it is contained God's true Word, setting forth his glory and also man's duty.[37]

Scripture is to be valued because it is 'that fountain and well of truth',[38] 'the food for the soul',[39] 'the well of life' contrasted with 'the stinking puddles of men's traditions',[40] 'the heavenly meat of our souls',[41] 'a light lantern to our feet',[42] 'a constant and perpetual instrument of salvation',[43] and 'the words of eternal life'.[44] The preacher's concern here is for more than the embrace orthodox belief: it is for the transformed life, life transformed by the word God — '...turned into it... inspired with the Holy Ghost...in his heart and life altered and transformed into that thing which he readeth'.[45]

Null has helpfully pointed us to the structure of the Homilies, both as a collection and individually. Cranmer broke with the standard pattern of sermons following the medieval liturgical calendar, but also with Archbishop John Peckam's catechetical approach — a 'formulaic rota of quarterly addresses' on the Decalogue, the seven sacraments, and the Creed (together with the Lord's Prayer and the Ave Maria)[46] — instead following Erasmus' advice to organize the biblical material under topics or 'commonplaces', 'using scripture to interpret scripture on ... key doctrines of Christian theology'.[47] To this was added the emphasis he found in Melanchthon on not simply moral application but on a reorienting of affections in the light of God's goodness and grace. In the collection as a whole, then, this is reflected in six sermons describing 'the fundamentals of the way of salvation' followed by six

---

[37] 'A Fruitful Exhortation', 7.
[38] Ibid.
[39] Ibid.
[40] Ibid.
[41] 'A Fruitful Exhortation', 8.
[42] Ibid.
[43] Ibid.
[44] Ibid.
[45] 'A Fruitful Exhortation', 9.
[46] S. Wabuda, *Preaching During the English Reformation* (Cambridge: Cambridge University Press, 2002), 34–35.
[47] Null, 'Homilies', 353.

sermons addressing 'important aspects of Christian living'.[48] In the Homily on Scripture, it is seen in the movement from the provision of Scripture to the profit of Scripture via its 'power to convert through God's promise' and 'be effectual through God's assistance'.[49] To unpack this further, let us turn in more detail to the Homily itself.

The first part: what Scripture is and how it functions

The homily begins with the dual purpose of Scripture: to set forth God's glory and the duty of his human creatures. Without Holy Scripture, persons can 'neither know God and his will, neither their office and duty'.[50] The language of 'office' and 'duty' is strange in the twenty-first century. The concept of 'a position or place to which certain duties are attached' or of 'an action or behaviour due by moral or legal obligation' (OED) clashes with the egalitarian spirit of our age. Yet the concept and language of office and duty was very much alive in the sixteenth century (as it is in the New Testament, see Luke 17:10 or Acts 1:20). To live in God's world generates certain obligations. There is an appropriate response to grace that is not just a matter of personal preference. But how is one to know what that is and what in particular is expected of each Christian in their very different circumstances of life? The homily's answer is that in such matters Holy Scripture is not only necessary but profitable, indeed, nothing can be either 'more necessary or profitable than the knowledge of Holy Scripture'. For Cranmer as his theology found expression in this homily and elsewhere, the nature of Scripture is not an abstract consideration. The nature of Scripture and its use are inextricably tied together. God has given us his word for this purpose. It wonderfully fulfils this purpose because it is this word. Woven throughout this first section, then, are these twin themes of 'nature' (what Scripture is) and 'use' (what Scripture does).

So, we are told, 'in Holy Scripture is fully contained what we ought to do and what to eschew, what to believe, what to love and what to look for at God's hands at length' — the proper objects of faith, hope, and

---

[48] Null, 'Homilies', 354.
[49] 'A Fruitful Exhortation', 8.
[50] 'A Fruitful Exhortation', 7.

love.⁵¹ With perhaps an echo of those words that famously began even the very first (1536) edition of Calvin's *Institutes,* we are told that in these books 'we may learn to know ourselves, how vile and miserable we be, and also to know God, how good he is of himself, and how he communicateth his goodness unto us'.⁵² Of course, that does not mean that Scripture tells us everything. The preacher makes clear that we know God's will and pleasure 'as much as for this present time is convenient for us to know'.⁵³ Yet, nevertheless—and here the quotation from Chrysostom (perhaps Pseudo-Chrysostom as Gerald Bray suggests) makes clear where this language comes from—, 'Whatsoever is required to the salvation of man is fully contained in the Scripture of God'.⁵⁴ Scripture is not pre-eminently or even properly the source of abstract yet erudite speculations about the divine substance. It is rather a book intended for us as 'words of eternal life for they be God's instrument, ordained for the same purpose'.⁵⁵ Cranmer will not separate out revelation and salvation without insisting that the words God has given to us were given to us for a purpose: they are 'a constant and perpetual instrument of salvation'. The influence of Melanchthon, and through him Luther, is evident at this point. We know God as Saviour or not at all. We know Christ as Saviour or not at all. And Scripture is the instrument he uses to bring us to that Saviour and the salvation he has secured for us.

The power of Scripture to effect change is a major theme in this first half of the homily. This book is not simply a human artefact. It is God's instrument, it is his Word, and he attends the faithful, humble reading of it. The words of Scripture 'have power to convert, through God's promise and they be effectual through God's assistance, and being

---

⁵¹ Ibid. The very next line points to another triad, the blessed Trinity: 'In these books we shall find the Father from whom, the Son by whom and the Holy Ghost in whom all things have their being and conservation, and these three persons be but one God and one substance.
⁵² 'A Fruitful Exhortation', 8. J. Calvin, *Institutes of the Christian Religion: 1536 Edition* (trans. F. L. Battles; Grand Rapids: Eerdmans, 1975), 15.
⁵³ 'A Fruitful Exhortation', 8.
⁵⁴ Pseudo-Chrysostom, *Hom. in Matthaeum,* 41. Yet the expression is found in what is undoubtedly Chrysostom, namely his *Hom. in 2 Timotheum,* 9.
⁵⁵ 'A Fruitful Exhortation', 8.

received in a faithful heart they have ever an heavenly spiritual working in them'.[56] It is the Scripture that does it. These words have that 'power to convert'. Yet in the most proper perspective it is God who does it: 'they be effectual through God's assistance'.[57] Ultimately Cranmer, like Tyndale before him, saw no dichotomy here. God's word is God at work. 'God is but his word'.[58] That is why he insists,

> there is nothing that so much establisheth our faith and trust in God, that so much conserveth innocency and pureness of heart, and also of outward godly life and conversation, as continual reading and meditation of God's Word.[59]

There is an important note to be struck at this point. Cranmer is at pains to insist he is talking, not of a simple chance encounter with Scripture but with the 'perpetual', 'diligent', 'continual' reading of Scripture. It is this regular, repeated exposure to the God's Word which will change people by realigning their affections—giving them a greater love for God than for the world—directing their wills and shaping their thinking. It is no surprise, then, that Cranmer should produce a liturgy and lectionary 'which is plain and easy to be understood; wherein (so much as may be) the reading of holy scripture is so set forth, that all things shall be done in order, without breaking one piece from another'.[60] No surprise, then, either that, years before, he should, in his preface to the Great Bible, invoke the

---

[56] 'A Fruitful Exhortation', 8–9.
[57] 'A Fruitful Exhortation', 9.
[58] W. Tyndale, *The Obedience of a Christian Man,* repr. in H. Walter (ed.), *Doctrinal Treatises* (Cambridge: Parker Society, 1848), 146. 'William Tyndale did not think that he was translating a book about God or a mere fallible witness to God, but the very word of God itself and a word so closely and rightly identified with God that by the Spirit it conveys the Word of God to the soul.' P. F. Jensen, 'God and the Bible', pp. 477–496 in D. A. Carson (ed.), *The Enduring Authority of the Christian Scriptures* (Grand Rapids: Eerdmans, 2016), 496.
[59] 'A Fruitful Exhortation', 9.
[60] 'Concerning the Service of the Church', the preface to the 1549 Book of Common Prayer, in *The First and Second Prayer Books of King Edward VI* (London: J.M. Dent & Sons, 1910), 4.

example of John Chrysostom, who encouraged his hearers to read the Scriptures between sermons and even gave them notice of what he would preach on next so that they might prepare by reading ahead: 'that you yourselves in the mean days may take the book in hand, read, weigh, and perceive the sum and effect of the matter, and mark what hath been declared and what remaineth yet to be declared, so that thereby your mind may be the more furnished to hear the rest that shall be said'.[61] Cranmer understood that a transformed heart, will, and mind took time and prolonged, repeated engagement with this powerful gift God has given us.

Cranmer's homily shows no interest in a detached and academic engagement with Scripture, pontificating on which parts are acceptable and which parts are not, or simply remaining at a distance from its comfort, challenges and admonitions. In one of its memorable turns of phrase this first part of the homily concludes with, 'And in reading of God's Word he not always most profiteth that is most ready in turning of the book, or in saying of it without the book, but he that is most *turned into it,* that is most inspired with the Holy Ghost, most in his heart and life altered and transformed into that thing which he readeth ...'[62] It is that changed life that is the proper fruitfulness of Scripture-reading according to Cranmer.

The second part: the exhortation to read

The entire homily is an exhortation to the reading of Scripture, yet the first part concentrated on the ground of that exhortation, the nature and usefulness of Scripture. In the second part of the sermon the preacher turns the screws a little and challenges his hearer's reluctance to take up the Bible and read it for themselves. 'How can any man', Cranmer asks, 'then say that he professeth Christ and his religion if he will not apply himself as far forth as he can or may conveniently, to read and hear, and so to know the books of Christ's gospel and doctrine?'[63] Even more pointedly, 'What excuse shall we therefore

---

[61] Cranmer's preface to the 1540 edition of the 'Great Bible' online at http://www.bible-researcher.com/cranmer.html
[62] 'A Fruitful Exhortation', 9.
[63] 'A Fruitful Exhortation', 10.

make at the last day, before Christ that delight to hear men's fantasies and inventions more than his most holy gospel?'[64] The proper nature of the Christian life involves a devotion to the Word.

Here, in a richly pastoral tone, Cranmer addresses what he calls 'two vain and feigned excuses', two reasons why Christian people might be reluctant to read the Scripture for themselves. The first is the danger of falling into error and the second is the difficulty of Scripture. Starting with Prierias' first reply to Luther in 1521, arguments against the Reformation doctrine of Scripture had repeatedly used these reasons to demonstrate that Christians need the magisterial guidance of the church in understanding Scripture. What is striking is how the homily gently encourages its hearers in the face of these false arguments and fears.

Are you afraid of falling into error? Well, ignorance is the chief cause of error and familiarity is its antidote. In fact, all of us were at one time or other ignorant and it is only through familiarity with the word that this error was overcome. Don't be paralysed by the fear of making a mistake, Cranmer insists. Think about it for a minute: if you never left home for fear you you fall into the mire, if you never ate meat because you were afraid of turning into a glutton, if you never went about your daily work because of the risks associated with it, then you would do nothing. And so, the preaching pastor says,

> And if you be afraid to fall into error by reading of Holy Scripture, I shall show you how you may read it without danger of error. Read it humbly, with a meek and lowly heart, to the intent you may glorify God and not yourself, with the knowledge of it; and read it not without daily praying to God that he would direct your reading to good effect, and take upon you to expound it no further than you can plainly understand it ... Presumption and arrogancy is the mother of all error and humility needeth to fear no error.[65]

---

[64] Ibid.
[65] 'A Fruitful Exhortation', 11.

The stance of the reader or hearer of Scripture is critical. 'The humble man', Cranmer went on to say, 'may search any truth boldly in the Scripture, without any danger of error'.[66] But he does not leave it at that. He fills out what such humility looks like and the five strategies by which it will avoid error: pursue the truth, compare passages with one another, pray, ask others, and wait (don't rush ahead with an explanation that betrays ignorance rather than knowledge). In his words,

> For humility will only search to know the truth; it will search and will confer one place with another, and where it cannot find the sense it will pray; it will inquire of others that know and will not presumptuously and rashly define anything which it knoweth not.[67]

With such strategies the reader of Scripture can confidently proceed. Interestingly, at this point Cranmer moves in exactly the opposite direction to Luther on the relative value of hearing and reading. While Luther insisted that there was a special value in *hearing* the word, aligned with his assertion that 'the ears alone are the organ of a Christian man', Cranmer writes 'a man may profit only with hearing, but he may much more profit with both hearing and reading'.[68] What are we to make of that? Well to start with, the dichotomy is artificial, especially in a world with a continuing level of illiteracy. What is more, Luther was quite obviously committed to reading the word as well as preaching the word and in one of his very last treatises against the pope wrote 'He who wants to hear God speak should read Holy Scripture'.[69] The point Cranmer is making, though, is that these two activities — hearing the word and reading the word — reinforce each other, much along the line of argument that led Chrysostom to his practice of encouraging reading ahead in Constantinople 1200 years before.

---

[66] Ibid.
[67] Ibid.
[68] M. Luther, 'Lectures on Hebrews' (1517–8) *Luther's Works,* 29:224 (*WA* 57/3:222.7). 'A Fruitful Exhortation', 11.
[69] He went on to say 'He who wants to hear the devil speak should read the pope's decretals and bulls'. M. Luther, 'Against the Roman Papacy, An Institution of the Devil' (1545) *Luther's Works* 41:332 (*WA* 54:263.14–16).

The second 'feigned excuse' Cranmer addresses is the difficulty of Scripture. There are parts of it that are hard to understand. Here Cranmer's remedy echoes again what he had written earlier in his preface to the Great Bible. Arguments mounted in the past by Augustine and Gregory the Great — Scripture as a full of low valleys as well as high mountains, a river shallow enough that a lamb might find a footing and deep enough for an elephant to swim, in the easier passages the Holy Spirit relieves our hunger and in the more obscure he drives away our pride — provide a critical backdrop and Cranmer quotes Chrysostom at length.[70] Just as God sent Philip to the Ethiopian Eunuch, he may send those who can help us when we struggle with the meaning of a particular piece of Scripture. However, the fundamental 'resource' of the Christian reader is the Holy Spirit himself, 'who inspireth the true sense unto them that with humility and diligence do search therefore'.[71] Our reading, like everything else in the Christian life, is undertaken in an attitude of humility and dependence upon God rather than our own resources or those others we might marshall in an effort to extract meaning from a difficult text. What is more, no individual text exists in a vacuum, and the comparison of one text with another is the single most important strategy in overcoming difficulty, since the entire Scripture is from God and his eternal consistency and therefore the coherence of the Scriptures should be assumed. In Cranmer's words, 'Although many things in the Scripture be spoken in obscure mysteries, yet there is nothing spoken under dark mysteries in one place, but the selfsame thing in other places is spoken familiarly and plainly, to the capacity of both the learned and the unlearned'.[72] His final advice is not to let the difficulty of a part prevent the reading of the whole.

Ultimately, Cranmer returns to the simple fact that Scripture is given to us by a God who is for us. It his 'great and special gift, beneficial favour and fatherly providence'. It has been given to us as an instrument of salvation, a 'comfortable medicine' as well as a stinging challenge.

---

[70] Augustine, *On Christian Doctrine*, II.6 (8). Gergory, *Moralia in Iob* (ad Leander I.v). 'A Fruitful Exhortation', 11–12.
[71] 'A Fruitful Exhortation', 12.
[72] Ibid.

An Anglican peculiarity?

This emphasis on the power of God's word to transform corporate and individual life was something Cranmer shared with the European Reformers. Nevertheless, it had a particular consequence in the shape of reformation Protestantism in England. The lectionary devised by Cranmer for use with the *Book of Common Prayer* is an expression of this. The 'unadorned' reading of the Scriptures, sequentially, repeatedly, with the goal of a kind of immersion in the word of God, was a feature of the Edwardian vision for the Church of England. The lectern became a most significant piece of church architecture. It stood in the middle of the chancel displaying the Great Bible, which was chained to the lectern to prevent its removal, so that the Word of God was simultaneously visible and accessible to all. Encouragement to read privately as well as to hear Scripture read publicly was explicit. In the decades that followed, aids to reading became popular among those who were literate.[73] Thomas Greshop's preface to the 1560 edition of the Geneva Bible, a table outlining 'How to take profit by reading of the holy Scriptures', is just one example. The Geneva Bible also included thousands of marginal cross-references as an aid to Bible study.

Personal reading was encouraged with plans that assisted regular (daily) reading. Andreas Hyperius' *Course of Christianitie: or, as touching the dayly reading and meditation of the holy Scriptures,* was translated into English by John Ludham in 1579. At the turn of the next century (1613), John Waymouth produced *A Plaine and easie table, whereby any man may bee directed how to reade over the whole Bible in a yeere.* Personal engagement with the Bible, a desire to be shaped and directed by its teaching, was not a later Puritan phenomenon nor was it simply a legacy of the eighteenth-century Evangelical Revival. It was a feature of Anglicanism from the beginning.

A fascinating footnote to this discussion on the content and trajectory of the first of the homilies is the debate between Richard Hooker and the Puritan Thomas Cartwright later in the century. Amongst the other

---

[73] See H. Hamlin, 'Reading the Bible in Tudor England', published November 2015 in *Oxford Handbooks Online* at https://www.oxfordhandbooks.com/view/10.1093/oxfordhb/9780199935338.001.0001/oxfordhb-9780199935338-e-77

issues of dispute was the place of preaching, and in particular what we might call the supremacy of preaching in the church. Thomas Cartwright had insisted that 'the *ordinary* and especial means to work faith by is preaching and not reading ... it is the excellentest and most *ordinary* means to work by in the hearts of the hearers ... the *ordinary* ways whereby God regenerateth his children is by the word of God which is preached'.[74] Hooker fired back, in defence of the reading of Scripture and not just the preaching of Scripture, 'whatsoever fit means there are to notify the mysteries of the word of God, whether publicly (which we call Preaching) or in private howsoever, the word by *every such mean* even 'ordinarily' doth save, and not only by being delivered unto men in Sermons. Sermons are not the only preaching which doth save souls'.[75] He went a step further just a page later, 'the external administration of his word is as well by reading *barely* the Scripture, as by explaining the same when sermons thereon be made'.[76] The unadorned reading of the word of God, confident that the God who has given it to us is able to bring it by his Spirit to hearts of those who come in humble faith and a willingness to listen — Hooker was, in an important sense, echoing the teaching of the earliest English reformers embodied in the Homily on Scripture, the *Book of Common Prayer* and the *Articles*.

This legacy of the English Reformation, its commitment to the untrammelled authority of Scripture with its supreme focus on Christ and the salvation he has secured, is something under threat in many areas of Anglicanism today. It needs to be recovered. But so too does the stance before Scripture that this homily typifies so well — the humble, contrite heart which trembles at God's word (Isa. 66:2). Which is why it is fitting to conclude with Cranmer's collect for the Second Sunday in Advent:

> Blessed Lord, which hast caused all holy Scriptures to be written for our learning; grant us that we may in such wise

---

[74] T. Cartwright, *A replye to an ansvvere made of M. Doctor VVhitgifte Against the admonition to the Parliament* (Hemel Hempstead?: John Stroud?, 1573), RSTC 4712, 159.
[75] R. Hooker, *The Laws of Ecclesiastical Polity* (Every Man's Library 202; London: J. M. Dent & Sons, 1907), 78–79 (V.xxi).
[76] Ibid. (p. 80)

hear them, read, mark, learn, and inwardly digest them; that by patience, and comfort of thy holy word, we may embrace, and ever hold fast the blessed hope of everlasting life, which thou hast given us in our saviour Jesus Christe.

John Ponet's *Short Catechisme:* A Neglected Formulary?

Mark Earngey

A Catechism Among the Formularies?

What is Anglican doctrine? This important question has, of course, prompted numerous debates and publications over the course of the last five hundred years. Readers will be glad to know that this chapter does not seek to resolve the matter. However, in what follows, I want to suggest John Ponet's *Short Catechisme* (1553) – a little-known document written by a little-known English reformer – is essential for comprehending the theological roots of Reformation Anglicanism.[77] To support the surprising nature of this thesis, the following essay will outline three surprising facts about the *Short Catechisme.* Firstly, I will demonstrate that it was written by one of the leading English reformers at the height of the Edwardian church. Secondly, I will establish that it possessed an extraordinary degree of intellectual, ecclesiastical, and political authority. And thirdly, I will outline some of the reformed theology embedded within it, noting a few of its unusual theological features. Having discussed these three facts, we should be able to see how the *Short Catechisme* provides an informative window into the official theological stance of the Church of England at the end of Edward VI's reign. This in turn should enable us to answer the question of whether the *Short Catechisme* should be considered a neglected formulary.

John Ponet and the Origins of the Short Catechisme

Let us begin with another subject of neglect: Bishop Ponet himself. Born in the county of Kent in the year 1516 and dying in city of Strassburg in the year 1556, John Ponet lived during the exact forty years "in which", according to Sir Marcus Loane, "the English

---

[77] The entire catechism is printed in the Appendix of this book.

Reformation was cradled and nurtured for the glory of God."[78] Ponet embodied these exciting years of evangelical progress and was an extraordinary ecclesiastical leader of the English reformation. He was one of the leading intellectuals in his generation at the University of Cambridge, alongside Thomas Smith and John Cheke (two similarly neglected intellectual giants of the reformation). Ponet shortly thereafter became chaplain to Archbishop Thomas Cranmer and King Henry VIII. Under Edward VI, he was rapidly promoted to the bishopric of Rochester and was then elevated to the important see of Winchester, where he worked closely with Ridley in London and Cranmer in Canterbury. After the accession of Queen Mary and his subsequent ejection from Winchester, he was intimately involved in Wyatt's Rebellion, and afterwards went into exile in Strassburg, where he died the most senior ranking clergyman among the English exiles. Throughout his lifetime he advanced the study of Greek linguistics, made marvellous astronomical devices, actively promoted evangelical reform among his dioceses, and authored important theological treatises. At the apex of the Edwardian Reformation he was the youngest among Cranmer's bench of bishops (in fact, he was the youngest man made bishop in the whole Tudor period), and he was one of the most important intellectuals among the English reformers. Indeed, according to John Bale, he was the Archbishop's faithful *Achates,* who always provided him with excellent advice in theological matters.

At heart, Ponet was an educator. After completing his B.A. at Queens' College, Cambridge, he was elected fellow (1532), and after a short stint teaching philosophy, he rapidly assumed one of the most important teaching positions in Cambridge: University Greek Lecturer. Indeed, this was a plum position for the aspiring humanist scholars of Cambridge during the late 1530s, and was first held by Nicholas Ridley before being assumed by Ponet in 1537 who taught until 1541.[79] From this position Ponet enthusiastically taught the 'New Pronunciation' of the Greek language, which he, Thomas Smith, and John Cheke had

---

[78] Marcus Loane, *Masters of the English Reformation* (Edinburgh: Banner of Truth Trust, 2005 [repr. 1954]), xvii
[79] In 1538 this position was held by Roger Ascham, while Ponet – as Senior Bursar – attended to the acquisition of the adjacent Carmelite friary (former home to John Bale) and also taught Greek to the students of Queens' College.

recently developed and disseminated through lectures and through dramatic performances of Greek comedies and tragedies. This discovery – a symbol of the 'New Learning' – was rapidly absorbed by the eager Cambridge evangelical tribe, which included such future luminaries as William Cecil, James Pilkington, John Aylmer, Walter and James Haddon, Edwin Sandys, and Edmund Grindal – a number of whom Ponet would teach, alongside Peter Martyr Vermigli and Jerome Zanchi, at the end of his life during exile in Strassburg.

In the 1540s, Ponet was recruited by Archbishop Thomas Cranmer, and though he was thoroughly preoccupied with ministerial duties, he did not lose his enthusiasm for the theological education of students. In Lent 1550, this enthusiasm was evident during a sermon preached before the King and Privy Council at Westminster (the Lenten series of sermons featured talented other evangelical preachers such as Hugh Latimer, Thomas Lever, and John Hooper). The subject of Ponet's sermon series was the Lord's Supper, and after a lengthy exposition of the Scriptural teaching on the sacrament, he detailed a number of strategies to combat the 'setting up again of the doctrine and kingdom of the Romish Antichrist'. The strategy which Ponet dedicated the most space towards was the education of youth in the schools throughout the country. 'Oh what hurt these popish Schoolmaster doth', preached Ponet, 'They will scarcely suffer any good doctrine to be talked on in their Schools. ... They mar all, most noble prince, poisoning the children's ears with popery in their youth'. And with that, Ponet turned, and petitioned King Edward directly:

> For redress whereof I would wish (most noble prince) that there might be a Catechism made in the Latten tongue, which should be read by commandment in all grammar Schools throughout your noble realm, and so should the brood of this most noble realm, not be brought so popishely up as they be. ... The good education of them in true religion, shall be a fortress to all your graces proceedings. The evil education of that brood of England in popery and superstition shall in conclusion be an overthrow to all your graces most godly proceedings. Wherefore for God's love and the wealth of this your realm

most noble prince. I wish that they should be remembered.[80]

Catechising the 'brood' had been an ancient concern for the Christian church: Moses taught God's people to impress God's law on their children (Deut. 6:7), the Apostle Paul exhorted the fathers of the Ephesian church to bring up their children in the discipline and instruction of the Lord (Eph. 6:4), and the example of Timothy, who knew the Scriptures from his infancy, was held up as a timeless example of the importance of catechesis (2 Tim. 3:15). Taking their cues from these verses of Scripture, the reformers of the Church of England made concerted catechetical efforts to nurture the renewed faith which had recently broken free from the Bishop of Rome. Indeed, the years between the 1530s through to 1553 witnessed what Philippa Tudor has described as 'an ambitious programme of religious instruction for children and adolescents ... planned on a nation-wide basis in England'.[81] The ambition for catechetical instruction during the reign of Edward VI, in particular, is evident from the various authors and styles of catechisms produced. These catechisms – just as with the Primers and Catechisms of the pre-reformation Church – uniformly expounded the Decalogue, the Apostles' Creed, and the Lord's Prayer. What set these Edwardian catechisms apart was the reformational content, often involving lengthy expositions. Edmund Allen's different catechisms are a good example of this variety: his evangelical productions of 1548, 1550, and 1551 varied in length and complexity, but they traversed the same three theological building blocks, and they used the typical 'master' and 'scholar' form of question and answer:[82]

---

[80] John Ponet, *A notable sermon concerninge the ryght vse of the lordes supper and other thynges very profitable for all men to knowe ...* (London: Mierdman for Gwalter Lynne, 1550), RSTC 20177, Gi^v-iii^r.

[81] Philippa Tudor, 'Religious Instruction for Children and Adolescents in the Early English Reformation', *JEH* 3/35 (1984): 391-392; see also, Ian M. Green, *The Christian's ABC: Catechisms and Catechizing in England c. 1530-1740* (Oxford, 1996): 59-60.

[82] Edmund Allen, *A catechisme, that is to saie, a familiar introduccion and trayning of the simple ...* (London, 1548), RSTC 359; *A shorte catechisme A briefe and godly bringinge vp of youth ...* (Zürich, 1550), RSTC 361; *A cathechisme that is to say a christen instruccion ....* (London, 1551), RSTC 360.

M: Why do we call him Jesus?
S: Because he is an helper and saviour, which saveth and helpeth the children of god from sin and from all kind of evil.

M: Why do we call him Christ?
S: Because he is the anointed king of God, which governeth the children of God unto everlasting life.[83]

Archbishop Cranmer himself prioritized the catechising of youth and published an extensive catechism in 1548 entitled the *Catechismus*. In the prefatory dedication to Edward VI, he declared his desire that, 'the youth & tender age of your loving subjects, may be brought up and traded in the truth of God's holy word'.[84] This *Catechismus* was largely Thomas Becon's translation from Justus Jonas' German catechism, and unfortunately contained some embarrassing Lutheran aspects of eucharistic theology which would later haunt the now-Reformed Archbishop. Cranmer's more determined program for evangelical youth ministry was set forth in the 1549 *Book of Common Prayer*, which contained a rubric stating that curates ought to catechise candidates for confirmation at least once every six weeks (this became a weekly catechism class under the 1552 revision of the Prayer Book). This prayerbook catechism could be regulated through use of episcopal visitation articles which examined clergy on their adherence to the Prayer Book, for example:

> Norwich (1549): Item, whether once in six weeks at the least your ministers do hear some children say the Catechism openly in the church of the holy-day at afternoon before Evensong.[85]

> Lincoln (1552): Whether your curate once in six weeks at the least upon some Sunday or Holy Day before Evensong

---

[83] Allen, *A catechisme,* f.iiii[r-v].
[84] Thomas Cranmer, *Catechismus, that is to say, a shorte instruction into Christian religion ...* (London, 1548). RSTC 5993, (?), iii[r].
[85] Church of England, *Articles to be inquired of in the visitation to be had in the byshopricke of Norwyche* (London: Wolfe, 1549), RSTC 10285, sig. A.iv[r].

do openly in the church instruct and examine children not confirmed, in some parts of the catechism.[86]

Gloucester & Worcester (1552): Item, that the Catechism be read and taught unto the children every Sunday and festival day in the year, at one or two of the clock after dinner, and that they may be thereof duly examined one after another by order; and that all other elder people be commanded to be present at the same.[87]

John Ponet was an enthusiastic advocate for Cranmer's catechetical vision, and during his episcopal ministry at Winchester, he made heavy use of the consistory courts for the prosecution of catechetical negligence. Though we have lost the visitation articles, John Bale's description of the 'Winchester sessions' throughout 1551-1552 details their extensive and intensive nature, and indicates that they were almost as comprehensive as John Hooper's use of the consistory court in Gloucester.[88] However, one of the major differences between Hooper's and Ponet's use of the church courts during this same period (1551-1553) is that whereas Hooper's comprehensive examinations appear not to have focused upon catechesis, Ponet's less comprehensive examinations do.[89]

All of this is to say that Ponet was a serious supporter of catechetical ministry – his request to King Edward during the Lenten sermon of 1550 must be read in that context. But what is striking about Ponet's sermonic supplication was the call for a royally enforced Latin

---

[86] Church of England, *Articles to be enquired of, in the visitacion, of the ryght reuerende father in God, Ioh[a]n Bysshop of Lyncol[n]n* (London: Wyer, 1552), RSTC 10228, sigs. A.iii^v-A.iv^r.

[87] Charles Nevinson (ed.), *Later Writings of Bishop Hooper* (Cambridge: CUP, 1852), 126.

[88] John Bale, *An Expostulation or Complaynte agaynste the Blasphemyes of a Franticke Papyst of Hamshyre* (London, 1552), RSTC 1294. Compare the summary above, with Barrett Beer's summary of Hooper's activity in Gloucester as described in 'Episcopacy and Reform', 242-244

[89] See F. D. Price, 'Gloucester Diocese under Bishop Hooper, 1551-3', Transactions of the Bristol and Gloucestershire Archaeological Society 60 (1938): 51-151.

catechism for every single grammar school in the realm. There had been royally approved catechisms before, and there had been catechisms used in grammar schools also, but nothing of this rigour had ever been attempted on this scale.

As a short postscript to this point, it is worth noting the historiographical tradition that refers to this catechism as *King Edward's Catechism of 1553*.[90] This ascription of the catechism to King Edward rather than John Ponet rightly captures the kingdom-wide significance of the *Short Catechisme*. However, it wrongly assumes that while the Bishop of Winchester was the driving force behind the catechism, there are insufficient grounds to prove his authorship of the same. The flaw behind this position lies in its overreliance upon secondary sources, rather than original documentation. There is, however, clear evidence of his authorship in the State Papers held at the National Archives, various manuscripts in the British Library, the *Greyfriars Chronicle*, the *Stationers' Register*, and even in Sir John Cheke's enthusiastic letter to Heinrich Bullinger shortly after its publication: '[the King] has lately recommended to the schools by his authority the catechism of John, bishop of Winchester'.[91]

The Creation and Authority of the Short Catechisme

Though Ponet raised the idea in 1550, the *Short Catechisme* was only published sometime around May 1553. However, it was not simply his energetic efforts, nor the King's will, which were wholly responsible for bringing the *Short Catechisme* into being. Its creation was a complex process, and understanding the twists and turns of its production is important for our understanding of its authority. Let us consider who else was involved in its production besides Ponet and the King. Firstly,

---

[90] J. Ketley (ed.), *The Two Liturgies, with other Documents Set Forth by Authority in the Reign of King Edward VI* (Cambridge, 1844).
[91] Lord President Northumberland to William Cecil, 7 September 1552: "After my hertie commendacions, for asmoche as the byschope of winchester hathe taken grete labor and travaylle partlie at my requeste to sette forthe a Catechisme bothe in Lattyne and englishe, for the better erudistion of lerners and schollers, aswelle in grammar scolles as others", TNA SP 10/15, 5^r; John Cheke to Heinrich Bullinger, 7 June 1553, *OL* 1:150. See below for further explicit references to Ponet's authorship.

the King's own printed prefatory note reveals that it was debated and diligently examined by 'certain Bishops, and other learned men, whose judgement we have in great estimation'.[92] So, in addition to Ponet and the King, we now have unnamed bishops and learned men – probably Thomas Cranmer, Nicholas Ridley, Peter Martyr Vermigli, and others – involved in its production. Secondly, in a letter to William Cecil, dated 7 September 1552, Lord President Northumberland revealed that after 'great labour and travail', Ponet had completed both Latin and English versions of the catechism, 'partly at my request'.[93] So, we can add Northumberland himself to the list of luminaries.

With so many parties involved, and with such a financial windfall to be had from such a big project, the publication arrangements became the bone of some contention. In the aforementioned letter of September 1552, Northumberland requested that John Day, 'this poor man, who hath been always a furtherer of godly things', should receive an exclusive license to publish Ponet's catechism.[94] Then less than a week later, Day obtained the royal licence in answer to this request, not simply for the English publication, but also for the Latin version.[95] However, Day's licence eventually hit a snag, as Cranmer's favourite printer Reyner Wolfe had also been granted the privilege of printing the Latin version, sometime before October 1552.[96] After the mediation of Cecil during the following months, it was decided in March 1553 that Wolfe would retain the rights to the Latin publications, and Day would have the lucrative English version, with the added compensation of the

---

[92] *Short Catechisme*, A.ii^v.
[93] TNA SP 10/15, 5^r, as printed above.
[94] SP 10/15, 5^r: "... I haue thoughte good to requier yt to be meane for the kinges maiesties lycens for the printinge of the same, and that this pore man, who hathe byn allwaies a furderer of godlie things, may by his highnes gracuis goodnes be auctorised for the onlie printinge of the same for a certein <*uncertain word?*> soche as shalbe thought mete by his maiestie, wherin the poore man shalhaue caus to pray for his highness."
[95] BL Royal MS 18 C XXIV, 254^v.
[96] Peter W. M. Blayney, *The Stationers' Company and the Printers of London 1501-1557*, 2 vols. (Cambridge, 2013), 2:735; Diarmaid MacCulloch, *Thomas Cranmer: A Life* (New Haven, 1996), 524; Elizabeth Evenden, *Patents, Pictures and Patronage: John Day and the Tudor Book Trade* (Aldershot, 2008), 25-26.

monopoly of printing all the works of both Ponet and Thomas Becon.[97] This contention dealt with, on 20 May 1553, King Edward VI commanded by royal injunction that all schoolmasters and teachers of youth within the realm ought to teach Ponet's advanced catechism immediately after the basic *A,B,C. Catechisme*.[98] The *Short Catechisme* was thus printed in English and Latin, with Michelangelo Florio's Italian translation — the first Italian book printed in England — briefly appearing in the short and chaotic period after the death of Edward VI.[99]

The degree of intellectual and political authority supporting Ponet's *Short Catechisme* was extraordinary. It was authored by one of the foremost reformed theologians of the period, driven by the impetus of King Edward and the Lord President of the Council, the product of various bishops and divines, and imprinted under the royal seal. Ponet was not simply the author of the catechism, but – as T.H.L. Parker right points out – he was speaking as the mouthpiece of Cranmer's circle of reformers.[100] Inevitably, since the *Short Catechisme* represented an indispensable part of the doctrinal stance of the Edwardian evangelicals, it became a priority target of the conservative strategy to unravel the reformation under the Marian regime. Edmund Bonner attacked it in his own catechism for schoolmasters, Richard Smith cited whole swathes of it disparagingly, and James Brooks preached against it at Paul's Cross.[101]

---

[97] 20 March 1553, Chancery Patent: BL MS Royal C XXIV, 318^v; 22 March 1553: Warrant, TNA C 82/962/23; 25 March 1553: Patent Roll, *CPR* 1553, v, 43; letters patent to John Day in *Short Catechisme*, Aiiii^v-Av^r.
[98] *Short Catechisme*, A.ii^{r-v}.
[99] Michelangelo Florio, *Cathechismo, cioe forma breue per amaestrare i Fanciulli* ... (London, 1553), RSTC 4813; Michael Wyatt, *The Italian Encounter with Tudor England: A Cultural Politics of Translation* (Cambridge, 2005), 185; Frances A. Yates, *John Florio: The Life of an Italian in Shakespeare's England* (Cambridge, 1934), 11.
[100] T.H.L Parker, *English Reformers* (London, 1966), 147-152.
[101] Edmund Bonner, *An honest godlye instruction and information for the tradynge, and bringine vp of children* ... (London, 1555), RSTC 3281; Richard Smith, *A bouclier of the catholike fayth of Christes church* ... (London, 1554),

Thus, with respect to the authorities associated with its production, it was very much like the other key formularies of the reformed English church. Indeed, although the *Forty-two Articles of Religion* were sometimes printed as a standalone document by Richard Grafton, they were ordinarily appended to both the English and Latin editions of Ponet's *Short Catechisme*.[102] The combined publication was the principal version (probably on account of its size), and the whole book was commonly understood as the book of the catechism (rather than the book of the articles). This can be seen in the *Greyfriars Chronicle*, which recorded that when Cranmer presented 'the new book that the Bishop of Winchester, Powny [Ponet], made' to convocation on 27 May 1553, there were 'diverse that denied many of the articles'.[103] This opposition to the combined book, spearheaded by conservative cleric Hugh Weston, carried over into the Marian reign. During the first convocation under Queen Mary, which met on 18 October 1553, Weston railed against 'a book of late set forth, called the catechism' and then proceeded to attack 'the articles of the catechism'.[104] Similarly, it was Weston who challenged Cranmer at his Oxford disputation for having 'set forth a Catechism' – meaning the book of the catechism.[105] This latter point is important, for sundry scholars have wrongly taken Cranmer's reference to be to his own *Catechismus* rather than the book of the catechism comprised of Ponet's *Short Catechism* appended with the *Forty-two Articles*.

It is important to understand the proper relationship between the articles and the catechism itself, and their combined role in the Edwardian church. While the articles received the name of the catechism, the catechism received the character of the articles.[106] In

---

RSTC 22816; James Brooks, *A sermon very notable, fruictefull, and godlie made at Paules crosse ...* (London, 1553), RSTC 3838.

[102] Compare *Short Catechisme* with *Articles Agreed on by the Bishoppes* (London, 1553), RSTC 10034; 10034.2. Florio's Italian edition does not contain the Articles of Religion.

[103] John Gough Nichols (ed.), *Chronicle of the Grey Friars* (London, 1852), 77-78.

[104] Robert Eden, *The Examinations and Writings of John Philpot*, BCL (Cambridge, 1842), 179-180.

[105] Thomas Cranmer, *Writings and Disputations of Thomas Cranmer*, John Edmund Cox (ed.), (Cambridge, 1844), 422.

[106] Parker, *English Reformers*, 149.

fact, the *Short Catechisme* complemented the *Forty-two Articles* – we might even say that we may not expound one place of the 'book of the catechism', that it be repugnant to another. Therefore, just like the articles, the teaching of the catechism was representative of the Church of England at the height of the Edwardian period. This was the view of Ponet himself, who in the context of the debate over clerical marriage, wrote in 1555:

> Our whole doctrine wherein we consented touching fasting, prayer and marriage etc. is plainly and fully set forth in the books of common prayers, the Homilies, the Catechisms and the Articles whereupon the whole realm concluded. …. Our doctrine was not kept so secret but that it was not only preached but also printed & so printed that it hath the testimony of the whole realm.[107]

And although the status of the *Shorte Catechism* as an authoritative formulary of the Church of England has escaped the attention of modern scholars, it has been rightly noted by others, such as Bishop Randolph in the nineteenth century:

> …a Catechism published in the time of king Edward VI and was the last work of the reformers of that reign; whence it may fairly be understood to contain as far as it goes their ultimate decision, and to represent the sense of the Church of England as then established.[108]

The Theology of the Short Catechisme

Thirdly and finally, the significance of Ponet's *Short Catechisme* also lies in its typically reformed theological features. His Christology retained thoroughly reformed features ('our everlasting and only High Bishop, our only attorney, only mediator, only peacemaker between God and man'). His doctrine of justification ('we are made righteous and saved by faith only') is thoroughly solifidian. On predestination, Ponet remarked that the faithful are those who "were forechosen, predestinate, & appointed out to everlasting life, before the world was

---

[107] John Ponet, *Apologie*, L
[108] John Randolph, *Enchiridion Theologicum; or, a Manual, for the use of Students in Divinity*, 2 vols. (Oxford, 1825), 1:vi.

made'. We may detect an infralapsarian position in Ponet's view, when he states that the context for predestination was the 'goodness and love of God'. Indeed, it was this goodness and love of the electing God which provided the context for Ponet's pastorally articulated description of the order of salvation.

Despite the presence of standard reformed theological features, Ponet's *Short Catechisme* reveals some important and perhaps surprising doctrinal features. His theology of the presence of Christ in the Lord's Supper gains theological mileage from the analogy of the sun and its rays. This articulation of the presence of the ascended Christ may appear strange to modern readers, but it summarises Ponet's own private and public writings on the subject, and almost precisely mirrors Archbishop Cranmer's eucharistic theology as articulated in the *Defence* and *Answer*.[109] His eschatology might appear less strange for modern readers, but actually reflects something of an unusual position among his contemporaries. Noticeable is his willingness to discuss eschatological continuities and discontinuities between this creation and the next, but unwillingness to speculate beyond what the Bible teaches. His ecclesiology examines the relationship between the whole and particular churches, and articulates a standard reformed view of the invisible and visible aspects of the church. However, when it comes to the marks of the church, Ponet identifies four: the pure preaching of the Gospel, brotherly love, upright and uncorrupted use of the Lord's Sacraments, and brotherly correction or excommunication. Thus, it cannot be argued that the Church of England differed from the church in Geneva on account of the marks of the church alone.

Due to its reformed credentials, the *Short Catechisme* became one of the heavily debated reformation texts in the seventeenth-century theological debate between William Prynne and Peter Heylin over Calvinism and Arminianism, and in the eighteenth-century tract war between Augustus Toplady and Thomas Nowell over the same. Toplady was a great admirer of the *Short Catechisme* ('this excellent prelate's *Catechism*'), whereas Nowell held it in contempt ('excellent only for its

---

[109] See especially Ashley Null's chapter in this volume.

Absurdity').[110] Indeed, Nowell believed that the *Short Catechisme* came into being because '*some rigid Calvinists in Power*, had imposed upon that good young King, and made use of his Authority to impose their Notions upon the Church'.[111] It would be rather anachronistic to posit Ponet as a defender of Calvinism. However, Toplady was correct to assert that Ponet's catechism was undoubtedly reformed in its theology. Nowell had no reply of any substance, and was reduced to screeching at Toplady, that the 'Catechism, which you call A valuable Monument of good old Church Doctrine' contained less 'sound Divinity than the old Koran of Mahomet'.[112] Whatever Ponet might have thought about being identified so closely to the theology of John Calvin, he assuredly would have been more comfortable with Toplady's 'Calvinism' than Nowell's scurrilous remarks.

Indeed, the delicious irony of the debate between Toplady and Nowell over Ponet's supposedly 'Calvinist' catechism was that Nowell seemingly had no awareness (or was perhaps too embarrassed to reveal?) that a possible relative of his, Dean Alexander Nowell of St. Paul's Cathedral, had copied and pasted from the catechisms of both John Ponet and John Calvin to produce his own — more influential and more 'Calvinistic' — catechism under Elizabeth's reign in 1570.[113] In fact, Nowell's catechism – which came in shorter and longer varieties – was wildly popular during the latter half of the sixteenth century and into the seventeenth century. So popular, in fact, that Canon 79 of the 1604 Canons required that all schoolmasters should teach, in English or Latin, either of Nowell's shorter or longer versions. Thus, both the spirit and the letter of John Ponet's *Short Catechisme* was eventually enshrined in Church of England canon law.

---

[110] Augustus Toplady, *The Church of England Vindicated from the Charge of Arminianism* (London, 1769), 42; Thomas Nowell, *The Church of England Vindicated from the Charge of Absolute Predestination* (London, 1771), 53. Capitals and italics retained.
[111] Nowell, *The Church of England Vindicated from ... Predestination*, 53. Capitals and italics retained.
[112] Nowell, *The Church of England Vindicated from ... Predestination*, 53.
[113] Alexander Nowell, *A Catechisme, or First Instruction and Learning of Christian Religion* (London, 1570), RSTC 18708.

Conclusion

John Ponet's *Short Catechisme*, penned at the height of the Edwardian Reformation, should no longer be considered a neglected formulary. The preceding discussion has demonstrated that it was authored by John Ponet, that it carried the same – if not more – authority as the *Forty-two Articles of Religion*, and that its contents are of an impeccably – if not progressively – reformed nature. On this basis, I conclude that it is inadequate to conceive of the original Anglican formularies as only three documents: the *Book of Common Prayer*, the *Thirty-nine Articles of Religion*, and the *Ordinal*. Rather, since the *Short Catechisme* represents one of the most reformed positions that the Church of England has ever officially taken, the study of Ponet's work is essential for understanding the roots of Reformation Anglicanism.

CRANMER'S FORTY-FIVE ARTICLES OF 1552: AN OVERLOOKED REFORMATION TEXT

Tim Patrick

with an English Translation of the Forty-Five Articles by Derek Scales

Introduction

The final and enduring version of the Church of England's *Articles of Religion* was ratified by Queen Elizabeth I in 1571. Presenting thirty-nine separate articles of doctrine, this formulary was the end product of drafting and revisions conducted over two decades. The history of the evolution of the *Articles* from May 1553 onwards is well known, and requires only the shortest summary here. A set of *Forty-Two Articles* was published just prior to the death of Edward VI, but was not promulgated during the reign of Mary I and remained untouched until four years after the accession of Elizabeth I. Then, in the 1563 convocation, the *Articles* were heavily reworked with eight articles removed, five new articles added, and many of the other articles reworked—in some cases substantially—such that the resultant set of thirty-nine articles was approximately 25% different to the earlier *Forty-Two*.[114] Following the convocation, two changes were made, possibly by Elizabeth. First was an addition to the then twentieth article and second was the removal of the then twenty-ninth, the latter having potential to negatively impact diplomatic relations with the Germans.[115] This was hugely significant theologically, as the rejected article had ensured that the Church of England did not allow a Lutheran view of the Lord's Supper; something that had become possible by the very heavy reworking of the previous article in the convocation. Perhaps because of these tensions, the Queen did not ratify the *Articles* in 1563. That

---

[114] Patrick, T. *Anglican Foundations: A Handbook to the Source Documents of the English Reformation* (London: The Latimer Trust, 2018), 20–21.
[115] Horie, H. 'The Lutheran Influence on the Elizabethan Settlement 1558–1563', *The Historical Journal*, 34 (3), 1991, 519–537.

only happened after the convocation of 1571 when the diplomatic issue was no longer pressing and so the missing article could be returned to the set. Some other minor amendments and tidying up also occurred at this time, but in large part the *Thirty-Nine Articles* of 1571 were the same as those of 1563.

Charles Hardwick's *A History of the Articles of Religion* remains the best historical investigation into the *Articles*, with many of the more recent studies ultimately referring back to this work.[116] But Hardwick not only gives a detailed and well-researched account of the history sketched above, he also discusses an earlier history and an earlier extant draft of the *Articles*; a collection of forty-five separate articles which was produced around six months before the *Forty-Two Articles* and which has received almost no attention from scholars of the English Reformation.[117] In an appendix to the third edition of his work (1876), Hardwick includes a complete transcription of the *Forty-Five Articles* in their original Latin, and this may be the only place it has ever been fully reproduced.[118] In the footnotes of his appendix, Hardwick flags a number of the differences between the *Forty-Five* and *Forty-Two Articles*, but neither there, nor in his main text, does he enter into any discussion of these changes, of their impact on the doctrine of the *Articles*, or of the reasons that the changes were made. Instead, Hardwick states that the *Forty-Five Articles* are 'not in substance very different from the final issue' (ie. the *Forty-Two Articles*), and it was perhaps that conviction which somewhat justified

---

[116] Hardwick, C. *A History of the Articles of Religion*, Third Edition (London: George Bell & Sons, 1876).

[117] A draft set of articles was sent from Archbishop Cranmer to William Cecil and John Cheke on 19 September 1552 (Cox, J.E. (ed.) *Miscellaneous Writings and Letters of Thomas Cranmer* (Cambridge: Cambridge University Press, for the Parker Society, 1846), 439-440 (Letter CCCV)). On 21 October next, the Privy Council sent the articles to the royal chaplains and then, with the chaplains' signatures, back to Cranmer on 20 November (Dasent, J.R. (ed.) *Acts of the Privy Council of England, Volume 4, 1552-1554* (London: Her Majesty's Stationery Office, 1892), 148, 173). This is the manuscript of the *Forty-Five Articles* and is now held in The National Archives in London as part of the Edwardian domestic state papers, SP 10/15/28.

[118] Hardwick, *Articles*, 278–288.

his, and subsequent scholars', limited engagement with the *Forty-Five*.[119]

But despite Hardwick's assessment, there are, in fact, several differences of real substance between the *Forty-Five* and *Forty-Two Articles*, and it is a key purpose of this study to bring these to light and thereby to establish the *Forty-Five Articles* as a text that demands the attention of students of English theological history.[120] The basis for this study is a full English translation of the *Forty-Five Articles* noting every point at which it differs from the Latin and English fair copies of the *Forty-Two*.[121] This new translation has been made by Dr Derek Scales, and I am not aware of any other full English translation. It is now presented as an appendix.

Major Differences Between the Forty-Five and Forty-Two Articles

There are a large number of minor and superficial differences between the *Forty-Five* and *Forty-Two Articles*. For example, *ac* is substituted for *et* in Article 1 and *illius* for *eius* in Article 2, the word *inquam* is dropped from Article 7 as are the two parenthetic comments from Article 17, and the order of *rationem in sese* is switched to *in sese rationem* in Article 8 while *in gratiam eius* is reordered to *in ejus gratiam* in Article 13. These sorts of changes have been judged as immaterial to the meaning of the articles and therefore they will not be commented on in this chapter. They are, however, all noted in the appendix. In addition, what might seem to be the largest change, the reduction from forty-five to forty-two separate articles, is also not given any attention as it is simply the result of the four separate articles on the Lord's Supper in the *Forty-Five Articles* being combined into a single article of four separate paragraphs in the *Forty-Two*.

---

[119] Hardwick, *Articles*, 74.
[120] Cf. Lorimer, P. *John Knox and the Church of England* (London: Henry S. King & Co., 1875), 126 who says" The differences of substance [between the *Forty-Five* and *Forty-Two Articles* in every case are not without some importance, either in a doctrinal or ecclesiastical point of view".
[121] The *Forty-Two Articles* of 1552/3 were printed in English and Latin, the *Thirty-Eight Articles* of 1562/3 were printed in Latin, and the *Thirty-Nine Articles* of 1571 in English. Hardwick, *Articles*, 289–353 supplies all of these in parallel.

The articles that were materially changed are considered sequentially below where they are referred to by the numeration of the *Forty-Five Articles*. Where the numeration in the *Forty-Two Articles* is different (ie. from Article 30 onwards), this is given in parentheses.

Article 3, Of the going down of Christ into Hell.

This article is comprised of three statements in the *Forty-Five Articles*. The first simply repeats what is asserted in the Apostles' and Nicene Creeds: that just as Christ died and was buried, so too he descended to hell. The second statement elaborates that Christ's body remained in the tomb until his resurrection, and that his Ghost departed to the prison of hell, as testified by Peter (1 Pt 3:19). This statement thus enters into a contemporary Christo-anthropological debate and takes up the classic view, in contrast to the Lutheran, which claimed that the entire person of Christ descended.[122] The third statement goes further and claims that while in hell, Christ did not liberate anyone from imprisonment or torture. This is in direct opposition to medieval Catholic beliefs about the harrowing of hell. These maintained that the purpose of Christ's descent was to release God's faithful old covenant people—including the patriarchs and Moses—from the *limbus patrum*, that outer tier of hell that served as their temporary holding cell, as they awaited the Messiah who would rescue them, lead them to heaven and unlock its gates for them.[123] It was in contrast to this view that Calvin wrote that Christ descended to hell in Spirit not to liberate saints, but to proclaim victory over Satan. Interestingly, one place that

---

[122] Solid Declaration of the Formula of Concord, IX. Christ's Descent to Hell, *https://www.bookofconcord.org/sd-descent.php*, Accessed 16 December 2019. See also Turner, R.V. 'Descendit Ad Inferos: Medieval Views on Christ's Descent into Hell and the Salvation of the Ancient Just', *Journal of the History of Ideas*, 37 (2), 1966, 173–194.

[123] Eg. Aquinas, T. *Summa Theologiae*, Bk 3a, Qn 52. See also Marshall, P. "The Map of God's Word': Geographies of the Afterlife in Tudor and Early Stuart England' in Gordon, B. & Marshall, P. (eds) *The Place of the Dead: Death and Remembrance in Late Medieval and Early Modern Europe* (Cambridge: Cambridge University Press, 2000), 110–130.

Calvin expressed this conviction was in his commentary on 1 Peter, which he dedicated to Edward VI in 1551.[124]

The third statement is missing from the *Forty-Two Articles*, meaning that this later set of articles pulls back from a clear rejection of the medieval Catholic position. While the direction of this change may be somewhat surprising, the fact that there was a change is not, given the unsettledness of views on the post-mortem states in the early 1550s.

During the revision of 1563, bishop Alley of Exeter sought for resolution to the ambiguity of this article because of the conflict it was causing.[125] However, the debates of convocation resulted in the opposite and the second statement also being removed, leaving the final form of the article as nothing more than a completely unexpanded reproduction of a line in the creeds, open to an even greater range of interpretations, and somewhat redundant given the article affirming The Three Creeds.[126]

Article 8, Of original or birth sin.

This article has been quite heavily reworked in the *Forty-Two Articles*, although this has not affected any significant theological change, but rather just improved the expression of the doctrine as found in the *Forty-Five*. In both cases there is a rejection of the Pelagian notion that original sin is to do with a person's actions, and an affirmation that it is to do with their inherent evil nature, or concupiscence, which in itself has the nature of sin and so attracts God's condemnation.

Interestingly, while all the Latin versions of 1552, 1553, 1562/3 and 1571 include *propter Christum* to explain the grounds for believers being free from condemnation, all the English versions of 1553, 1563 and 1571 leave this phrase out. The consistency is likely due to the fact that the scribes based their work on earlier standard texts as a way of preserving as much as possible between each generation of articles. (A standard

---

[124] Calvin, J. *Commentaries on the Catholic Epistles*, (trans. and ed. Owen, J., Grand Rapids: Baker Book House, 2005), xi–xx.

[125] Strype, J. *Annals of the Reformation, Volume 1, Part 1*, New Edition (Oxford: Clarendon Press, for the Parker Society, 1824), 518–519.

[126] Patrick, T. 'The Purging of Purgatory and the Exclusion of the Apocrypha during England's Reformation', *Churchman*, 134 (2), 2020, 125–141.

practice also adopted for the translation presented in the appendix; see below.)

Article 12, Works before Justification.

In the *Forty-Two Articles*, the emphasis of this article is shifted marginally such that instead of speaking of works done before justification, it engages them as works done 'before the grace of Christ and the inspiration of his Spirit'. The doctrine of justification was, of course, being expounded at length during the Reformation years, including in England.[127] The minor change here may be an attempt to distance any ideas of works from justification and to focus instead on the influence of the Spirit on Christian activity.

Article 16, Blasphemy against the Holy Ghost.

There are two noteworthy differences between this article as it appears in the *Forty-Two Articles* and the *Forty-Five*. Both versions state that the blasphemy against the Holy Ghost is unpardonable, but the earlier article underscores this by further asserting that even repentance is ineffective for this sin. The revised article replaces that assertion by one simply explaining that those who blaspheme the Spirit 'entangle themselves with a most grievous and heinous crime'.

The second difference is in the structure and function of these two different statements. In the earlier article, the statement about the sinner being beyond repentance is given as the consequence of falling under God's curse as a result of their blasphemy: because they blasphemed, they are cursed and therefore beyond any restoration. In the later article the ideas are reversed: because they are under God's curse, they have become entangled with the most grievous and heinous crime of blasphemy. Thus, while the revision does not change the primary teaching of the article, there is a shift in the nuance of the underlying theology.

The article was obviously the subject of further considerations in the 1563 convocation when it was removed altogether.

---

[127] Eg. Knox, D.B. *The Doctrine of Faith: in the reign of Henry VIII* (London: James Clarke & Co. Ltd., 1961).

Article 20, Of the Church.

The interest in Article 20 is not because of any substantial differences between its appearances in the *Forty-Two* and the *Forty-Five Articles*, but rather because of a correction made to the manuscript of the *Forty-Five* itself. A small paper tab has been pasted over part of a line of the article's text, effectively deleting a phrase. Intriguingly, the phrase lies in between the two marks of the visible church as they were commonly understood among the different Protestant groups: the pure word of God is preached, and the sacraments are duly ministered.[128] Three obvious possibilities regarding the substance of the deletion follow. The first is simply that it was a copyist's error that has been removed. The second is that it was a phrase that modified 'the pure word of God is preached', just as 'the sacraments be duly ministered' is moderated by 'according to Christ's ordinance'. The third is that it was another mark of the church. Almost a century later, the Westminster Confession would make public worship the third mark of a true church, but in the Edwardian period, it was more likely to have been discipline, as it also was in the 1563 Homily for Whitsunday.[129] If it was indeed a third mark of the church, the question of why it was removed so late cannot be easily answered, but Archbishop Thomas Cranmer's desire to align the doctrines of the English Church as far as possible with its reforming continental cousins may have been one factor.

Article 22, Of the authority of general Councils.

Two paragraphs make up this article in the *Forty-Five Articles* and the second of these—a single extended sentence—is completely removed from the *Forty-Two*. The first paragraph makes plain that general councils may only be called by princes, that they can, and have, erred, and that the councils may require nothing for salvation beyond that

---

[128] Cf. The Augsburg Confession of 1530, The Gallican Confession of 1559, and The Second Helvetic Confession of 1566, Schaff, P. *The Creeds of Christendom, Volume 3: The Evangelical Protestant Creeds*, Sixth Edition (Grand Rapids: Baker Book House, 1931), 11–12, 275, 375.

[129] Bray, G.L. (ed.), *The Book of Homilies, A Critical Edition* (Cambridge: James Clarke, 2015), 443. Thanks to Derek Scales for alerting me to this point. Cf. Schaff, *Creeds*, 658 cf. 419–420.

which is found in Scripture. The brief second paragraph then goes on to state

> When the judgement or calling of general councils is not expected, kings and godly magistrates can, in their own commonwealth, settle matters of religion according to the word of God.

Thus, the article includes a declaration of the power of monarchs with regard to matters of doctrine. Negatively, it ensures that the general councils of the church do not arrogate those powers or go beyond biblical limits in their determinations. Positively, it explicitly claims the right of the prince to rule over the church in matters spiritual as well as temporal. This is similar to Article 39 (which was also heavily reworked; see below) although that article emphasises the king's position rather than his powers.

Interestingly, although the second paragraph was lost in 1553, it was a near-equivalent of this that was returned after the 1563 convocation to the start of Article 21 (then Article 20) at the same time that the article which would protect the church against Lutheran eucharistic theology was excluded, as noted above. The difference at that point was that the change claimed the power to determine rites and ceremonies, and to decide theological controversies, for the church, not for the monarch. However, given the doctrine of Article 39 (Article 37 in the *Thirty-Nine Articles*), this ultimately amounted to much the same thing.

Article 23, Of Purgatory.

In Article 23, prayer for the dead is removed from the list of practices connected to the Roman doctrine of the afterlife denounced as 'a fond thing vainly feigned and grounded upon no warrant of Scripture, but rather repugnant to the word of God'. This is a very peculiar and most unexpected change.

In the first place, the practice of praying for the dead would seem to be thoroughly intertwined with the other practices listed in the article: 'pardons, worshipping and adoration as well of images as of relics, and also invocation of saints'. To remove one while retaining the rest suggests a particularly fine theological distinction within the developing Protestant theological system. However, it may indeed be that, for a time, such a distinction was made. One of the strong criticisms of the first *Book of Common Prayer* (1549) offered by Martin Bucer in his *Censura* was that prayers for the dead were retained in the communion and burial services, even as other parts of the beliefs around the afterlife were excluded.[130] This is some evidence that Cranmer still kept room for some form of prayers for the dead in his theology even into Edward's reign.

However, this is very difficult to reconcile after 1552 when the second *Book of Common Prayer* was printed, now with the prayers for the dead removed. Although the revised article in no way endorses prayer for the dead, it needs to be admitted that it moved in the opposite direction to the *Prayer Book* on this practice.

Article 26, Of the Sacraments.

This article has had the final sentence of its first paragraph in the *Forty-Five Articles* greatly shortened in the *Forty-Two*. The excluded section highlighted that there were only two sacraments and that each only has a material substance. These beliefs were absolutely core to the English Protestants—especially in light of Henry VIII's *Assertio Septem Sacramentorum* of 1521 that won him the title *Fidei Defensor* from Leo X—and their removal from this article would be quite remarkable were they not well established in the subsequent articles. This instance of trimming down then would not seem to be in order to affect a change in the overall theological position of the collection of articles, but rather to more sharply focus the teaching of this particular article on the *nature* of the sacraments. Having noted this, it does need to be flagged that in 1563, the article was re-modified to again make plain that there are only two sacraments.

---

[130] Whitaker, E.C. *Martin Bucer and the Book of Common Prayer* (Great Wakering: Mayhew-McCrimmond Ltd, 1974), 50–53, 126–129. Cf. Ketley, J. (ed.) *The Two Liturgies, A.D. 1549. and A.D. 1552* (Cambridge: Cambridge University Press, for the Parker Society, 1844), 88, 145–147.

Article 31, On the bodily presence of Christ in the Lord's Supper.

(Article 29, paragraph 3 in the Forty-Two Articles*)*

There has been a slight filling out of the anti-ubiquitarian language in the *Forty-Two Articles* compared with the *Forty-Five*. While the change is not very significant in itself, it is a portent of the extended debates that would take place during Elizabeth's reign. Indeed, this article would be the most heavily reworked in the 1563 convocation, and the heresy of ubiquitarianism—which was ultimately seen to compromise the integrity of Christ's resurrection body—would repeatedly arise as one of the strong Protestant arguments against transubstantiation, especially as voiced by Zwingli.[131] This anti-ubiquitarian teaching of the *Forty-Two Articles* was also introduced into the 1552 *Book of Common Prayer* as part of the underpinning argument of the lately added Declaration of Kneeling, or so called 'Black Rubric'.[132]

Article 33, Of the perfect oblation of Christ made upon the cross.

(Article 30 in the Forty-Two Articles*)*

In the *Forty-Two Articles*, an extra clause has been added in to explain the intended purpose and effect of the Roman masses: to have remission of pain or sin. This is nothing more than would have been assumed in the earlier *Articles*, but it does clarify that the rejected ritual was not only directed towards satisfaction in a mechanistic or forensic sense, but also addressed the experiential consequences of sin.

Article 34, The state of single life is commanded to no man by the word of God.

(Article 31 in the Forty-Two Articles*)*

This article is longer in the *Forty-Five Articles* than in the *Forty-Two* as the earlier version not only declared that clergy were not required to be celibate as was the case in the Roman Church, it also released serving clergy from any of their standing vows of celibacy, declaring this sort

---

[131] Eg. Bromiley, G.W. (ed.) *Zwingli and Bullinger* (Philadelphia: The Westminster Press, 1953), 212–222.
[132] Ketley, *Two Liturgies*, 283.

of vow to be repugnant to the word of God. This change may simply be an example of trimming down for the sake of brevity, and because the need for a statement of release from these vows would not be required for any future generations of clergy who would never have made them at their ordination.

Article 35, Excommunicate persons are to be avoided.

(Article 32 in the Forty-Two Articles*)*

While the *Forty-Two Articles* retains the penalty for the open denunciation of the Church as excommunication, the *Forty-Five* supplies a little more justification for this sentence by categorising the behaviour among the 'deadly offences'.

Article 38, Of the book of Ceremonies of the Church of England.

(Article 35 in the Forty-Two Articles*)*

In the *Forty-Five Articles*, this article approves of not only the doctrine of the church's new *Book of Common Prayer*, but also of its ceremonies. In the *Forty-Two*, the two references to the ceremonies are removed from the body of the article, while the title is expanded to say 'Prayers and Ceremonies'. In itself, these changes may not appear to be as significant as many of the others that were made at the same time. However, in his 1875 volume *John Knox and the English Church*, Peter Lorimer strongly argues that these changes are, in fact, the most significant of all those made in 1553.[133] In one of the very few historical studies to engage the *Forty-Five Articles*, Lorimer tracks Knox's objection to the practice of kneeling at communion and claims that the call for a review of these *Articles* in October 1552 was largely motivated by the desire to remove their implicit support of this particular 'ceremony'.

There are a number of significant problems with Lorimer's case. One is that the change made in this article did not directly identify the issue of kneeling in communion, despite the fact that this was done explicitly elsewhere, most famously in the aforementioned Declaration on

---

[133] Lorimer, *Knox*, 126.

Kneeling that was inserted into the *Book of Common Prayer* in the very same month, a development that Lorimer is probably correct in attributing to Knox.[134] Another problem is that the change in the article does not bring any additional clarity to the English Church's position on any ceremonies, either positive or negative. Rather, it just establishes a silence on the matter. Next is the fact that the title of the revised Article does not do away with the word 'ceremonies'. And finally, despite the alterations, the article continues to strongly endorse the *Book of Common Prayer*, which was, after all, a book of formal liturgies that included its own defence of the church's ceremonies in Cranmer's famous essay that was moved to its beginning in 1552. Even if the change was precipitated by Knox's agitations, overall, it seems hard to regard it as among the most significant of differences between the *Forty-Five* and *Forty-Two Articles*.[135]

Article 39, Of civil magistrates.

(Article 36 in the Forty-Two Articles*)*

This article is shorter in the *Forty-Two Articles* than in the *Forty-Five* owing to the abbreviation of two sentences. The first removes a significant amount of text, but does not affect a material change to the teaching or theology. It could be well understood as the deletion of redundant material that does not make any new point. The second change, however, is quite significant as it removes the claim that subjects may not deny the monarch's right to collect tolls and tribute for the protection and conservation of the kingdom. The issue of taxation was very contentious during the Tudor period, and the church gave considerable time to dealing with the crown's requests for revenue. The removal of this part of the article did not mean that the issue was no longer important, but does seem to recognise that the matter is not most appropriately addressed in a document offering a summary of doctrine.

---

[134] Lorimer, *Knox*, 110.
[135] MacCulloch, D. *Thomas Cranmer: A Life*, Revised Edition (New Haven & London: Yale University Press, 2016), 528–529, 529n29 also has disagreement with Lorimer's interpretations.

In 1563, this article was very heavily reworked such that it read less like a listing of the monarch's secular powers, and more as a theological presentation of the balance of power between church and state, a change that makes sense given the different political context of the Elizabethan church when compared to the Edwardian.

Article 43, The souls of them that depart this life do neither die with the bodies, nor sleep idly.

(Article 40 in the Forty-Two Articles*)*

The *Forty-Two Articles* expand on the *Forty-Five*, to explain that when word 'sleep' is metaphorically applied to the dead, it refers to them 'being without all sense, feeling, or perceiving'.

Doctrines of the intermediate state were very strongly contested during the Reformation, as the Protestants sought to re-understand what happened between death and resurrection once they had rejected belief in purgatory. Calvin's first theological work, entitled *Psychopannychia* addressed the question and the development of thought in England can be traced quite clearly through the writings of the sixteenth century.[136] A sharpening refinement at this point is therefore not unexpected.

Analysis of Changes

Having noted the major differences between the *Forty-Five* and *Forty-Two Articles of Religion*, the first conclusions that can be immediately drawn are that the changes to around twenty percent of the articles cannot be considered insubstantial and that they do have some real bearings on theology. This means that the *Forty-Five Articles* ought no longer to be overlooked by historians of the Edwardian Church on the understanding that they are essentially the same as the *Forty-Two*. Rather, they should be included in any consideration of the developments of the Church of England's doctrinal positions during the Reformation years. Moreover, there needs to be a clear recognition that during Cranmer's arch-episcopate in the early 1550s, it was not only the doctrines found in the *Book of Common Prayer* that were being revised, but also those in the *Articles of Religion*. Indeed, most

---

[136] Patrick, *Purging of Purgatory*, 125–141.

of the formularies of the English Reformation underwent multiple revisions, highlighting the fact that Protestant doctrine was not quickly formulated as a complete package with obvious content, but was developed over a protracted period as the reformers wrestled with their context, the Bible, and the alternate theological systems of Rome, fellow reformers and the various radical groups.

Following this determination, an important question to ask is whether or not the changes introduced into the *Forty-Two Articles* share any common threads, and thus potentially trace an overarching theological shift or trend in England even over the short six month period between production of the two documents. While there does not appear to be any obvious theological theme unifying the changes outlined above, there is perhaps an overall slight move away from doctrinal rigidity and towards a marginally more generous inclusivism.[137] For example, the amendment to Article 3 allows for more Catholic doctrine and Article 12 removes the term 'justification', despite its priority among Protestants, Article 16 removes the explicit determination that there can be no effective repentance for blasphemy against the Spirit, Article 20 had already limited the marks of the church to just two, Article 26 does not declare that there are only two sacraments, contrary to Rome's seven, and Article 38 (Article 35 in the *Forty-Two Articles*) may relieve the Church of some of its commitment to ceremonies. In addition to the marginal increase in theological breadth is the slight loosening of state power over the church, as seen in the removal of the power of princes in Article 22 and the avoidance of any discussion of taxation in Article 39 (Article 36 in the *Forty-Two Articles*). If this overall broadening and lightening is real, it foreshadows more changes in a similar direction in the revision of 1563. However, in the opposite direction, Article 31 of the *Forty-Five* (Article 29, paragraph 3 in the *Forty-Two Articles*) is more explicit in its presentation of the anti-ubiquitarian conviction. While this much can be suggested, overall it is probably unwise to insist that all of the changes be viewed through a single controlling filter, and better to simply recognise that the various doctrinal shifts were one product of the Church being in a period of great flux.

---

[137] Cf. Lorimer, *Knox*, 126.

Who Made the Changes?

Changes to working statements of doctrine are very significant because they can represent changes and/or clarifications within the church's developing theology and within those tasked with espousing it. However, in many cases, alterations to the doctrinal productions of a whole church reflect attempts at compromise or political contingencies or doctrinal uncertainty, rather than any great sharpening up of conviction or better presentation of a well-considered view. Furthermore, revisions were often made by committees or other groups of people working together and not by a single known theologian whose wider views can be interrogated. In the case of the revisions that reshaped the *Forty-Five Articles* into the *Forty-Two*, a small amount of information tracks some of the progress, but much of the detail remains unknown.

When Archbishop Cranmer received the signed fair copy of the *Forty-Five Articles* from the Privy Council on 20 November 1552, there was a recognition that it was still in need of 'perfecting'.[138] When he returned the *Articles* on the 24th, Cranmer sent with them his own schedule for their last revision but this has unfortunately been lost.[139] It may be that the schedule accompanied the *Forty-Five Articles* into the convocation of March 1552/3 where the final changes resulting in the *Forty-Two Articles* were made.[140] Sadly, no records of this convocation have

---

[138] Dasent, *Privy Council*, 173 whose transcription of the Privy Council minute says the *Articles* had been 'all tried', contra Lorimer, *Knox*, 124 who puts that they had been 'altered'. Lorimer's reading of the ambiguous word is probably better, given the context. In full the minute reads "A lettre to the Archebusshop of Cauntorbury, with the articles heretofore drawen and delivered by hym to the Kinges Majestie, which being sence that tyme considered be certeine of his Highnes Chaplenes and others, ar in summe part [all tried / altered], and therefore returned to hym to be considered, so as after the perfecting of them ordre may be given for the putting the same in due execution." Dasent's marginal comment also mistakenly reports this minute as referring to changes in the Prayer Book.
[139] Strype, J. *Memorials of Archbishop Cranmer, Volume 2* (Oxford: Oxford University Press, for the Parker Society, 1848), 669 (App. LXIV).
[140] Cf. Todd, H.J. *The Life of Archbishop Cranmer, Volume 2* (London: C.J.G & F. Rivington, 1831), 290–291. Burnet, G. *The History of the Reformation of*

survived but both Wolfe and Grafton's notices on their licensed printings of the *Forty-Two* indicate that this is the place where the *Articles* received their final approval, and the detailed accounts of work on the *Articles* in the 1563 convocation shows that one purpose of these gatherings was exactly this kind of work.[141] Given this, we might fairly conclude that the revisions to the fair copy of the *Forty-Five Articles* were made in and around the convocation on 1552/3 and that Cranmer, as archbishop and primary contributor to the project would have continued to have an influence at this point, even if his voice was only the lead among many.

---

the Church of England, Volume 3, New Edition (Oxford: Clarendon Press, 1816), 362 gives arguments against the Articles having been presented to the whole convocation, and for them going only to the upper house, which would be in line with the preface to Wolfe's printing of the *Forty-Two Articles* (Hardwick, *Articles*, 289).

[141] Hardwick, *Articles*, 75, 289.

The Reformation of Church Discipline

Gerald Bray

The laws of the Church

Any institutional Church rests on three essential pillars. The first of these is doctrine, the substance of what we believe and teach. If a Church believes the wrong things or fails to teach what is right, it cannot survive as a credible witness to Christ. The formation of the New Testament canon, the emergence of the classical Creeds and the proliferation of numerous confessions in the sixteenth and seventeenth centuries, as well as more recently, all bear witness to this. The second pillar is devotion. If we do not realise that our beliefs are primarily an introduction to the right worship of God, we are wasting our time. Having a system of belief without acting upon it is rather like having a road map without going anywhere. It may be perfectly accurate and a pleasure to contemplate, but if we do not follow it, it is of little practical use.

The third pillar on which the Church is built is discipline. If the trumpet makes an uncertain sound, we cannot prepare ourselves for battle, and confusion is liable to result. If we are not headed in the same direction it matters little if we believe the same things. Prayer is vitally important, but if we are not clear about what we are praying for or how we should go about it, it hardly matters. Discipline is the key that holds doctrine and devotion together, the essential ingredient that binds the body of Christ into a single, effective unit. The Apostle Paul knew this, and in his advice to the Corinthians he laid stress on it. He even told the more spiritually-minded brethren that they were to restrain themselves in public worship, allowing no more than two or three prophecies at any one time and making sure that they were understood by the congregation. Let all things be done decently and in order was his advice, since otherwise the witness of the Gospel would be compromised and the world would hear only a message of incoherence and indecision (1 Corinthians 14:40).

The English Reformers were well aware of the threefold foundation on which their reformed Church would have to be built. Archbishop Thomas Cranmer set himself the task of working out what that Church's doctrine should be. He and his colleagues began this shortly after the break with Rome in 1534 and they made their way gradually from Ten Articles in 1536 to Forty-two in 1553, and after extensive revision, to Thirty-nine ten years later. Similarly, Cranmer and his colleagues did not neglect the devotional life of the Church. Here they proceeded more cautiously, beginning with an English translation of the Bible before experimenting with a translated litany. This was then followed by the production of a series of sermons, or homilies, designed to convey the Church's doctrine in the course of public worship, and finally by a Book of Common Prayer that was intended to shape the spirituality of the entire Church. As with doctrine, the establishment of devotion went through a number of phases, the most important of which occurred almost immediately, as the 1549 Book of Common Prayer gave way to that of 1552. Subsequent developments were really just modifications and additions to that second Book, culminating in what proved to be the definitive edition of 1662.

Discipline, however, was another matter, and one of particular importance in the circumstances. After all, the English Reformation had begun as a contest over Church discipline more than anything else. When Henry VIII sought to annul his marriage to Catharine of Aragón few people in England were concerned with the Church's doctrine and even fewer questioned its pattern of devotion. What concerned them, or more especially what concerned the king, was Church discipline and how it applied to holy matrimony, which was universally regarded as the sacrament of the laity. Matrimony did not directly concern the clergy but it was of great importance to the lay members of the Church, because irregularities in the way it was celebrated and observed could have very serious negative effects on their families, and therefore on their legacy to the next generation on which the future prosperity of society rested. That was certainly in the forefront of Henry VIII's mind as he contemplated the succession to his crown and the future stability of his kingdom. He was not too bothered about justification by faith, nor did he question the propriety of praying to God in Latin. His main concern was whether he could produce a credible heir, and it was his apparent failure in this regard that led to the series of events that produced the Reformation.

Henry's solution to his dilemma was to procure the annulment of his marriage, an operation that turned out to be more difficult than he had anticipated. It did not help that a quarter of a century before, his father had petitioned the papacy for a dispensation to allow his son to marry Catherine in the first place, since she was his dead brother's widow and therefore within the prohibited degrees of affinity. Nor did the fact that Catherine's nephew was Charles V, the Holy Roman Emperor who had just invaded Rome and was keeping the pope under lock and key do much to assist his case, which was not strong to begin with. Henry VIII discovered the hard way that the canon law was against him, and that he would have to do something about it if his plans were ever to come to fruition. In the end, the only way he could get what he wanted was to break with the papacy, which he did in 1534.

This date traditionally marks the beginning of the Reformation in England, but the only real change that occurred was that the faculties of canon law in Oxford and Cambridge were abolished. Something had to take their place, of course, and to this end Henry set up a commission to examine what the law was and report back to him, presumably as a preliminary to serious reform. A document that we call the Henrician Canons was composed, but what happened to it is something of a mystery. All that survives now is a single manuscript, written in a fair hand on high-quality parchment, which suggests that it was intended as a presentation copy for the king. However, it is incomplete, breaking off in mid-sentence, which probably means that it was shelved before anything could be done with it. There must have been a rough draft from which the fair one was drawn, but it seems to have disappeared. Even the copy we now have vanished from sight sometime in the sixteenth century and was not rediscovered until 1974 or edited until 2000. It is still not widely known and has not been studied in any depth, so both its original purpose and its possible influence on later developments remain unclear.

What we can say is that the Henrician Canons did not follow the traditional order of presentation, which can be traced back to the thirteenth century, if not earlier. This order had divided the canon law into five sections or books, which were dedicated to the judges (*iudex*), the judicial procedures (*iudicium*), the clergy (*clerus*), matrimony (*connubium*) and infractions (*crimen*). Elements of all five were retained, but of the thirty-six extant titles, only two (22-23) deal with matrimony. The procedural section is also very short, but as it is there that the manuscript breaks off, we may assume that there was more on the subject that has now gone missing. Given that matrimony was the cause of the initial attack on the canon law, this is surprising, but perhaps it was an example of cautionary wisdom on the part of the compilers, since we can probably assume that the more the canons said on that subject the less the king would have liked it.

The compilers of the Henrician Canons adopted an order that made it clear that they were largely confined to purely in-house matters. Four sections survive, the first dedicated to the clergy and their discipline, the second to the clergy and their ministry, the third to parochial administration and the fourth, which is incomplete, to the ecclesiastical courts. Interestingly, the titles on matrimony and divorce were included in the second section, the one devoted to the clergy and their ministry, since in 1536 matrimony was for other people, not for them.

Why the Henrician Canons were set aside is unknown, but in 1544 a new commission was set up with the express purpose of composing a set of canons for the reformed Church. The commission never got going and it lapsed when Henry VIII died on 28 January 1547. It then had to be re-constituted, a process that was not complete until 1 February 1550, when parliament passed a bill that stated that the commission was expected to review the canon law and report back within three years. Further delays ensured that nothing much was done until the end of 1551, and even then it was several months before the commission set to work. In the circumstances it is remarkable that it was able to produce a draft document in time for parliament's meeting in March 1553, but that draft was rejected by the House of Lords and never became law. It might have returned in a modified form later on, but King Edward VI died on 6 July and the advent of the Catholic Queen Mary I ensured that it disappeared into oblivion. When Mary was succeeded by her half-sister Elizabeth I the legislation of Edward VI was revived, but although that included the Book of Common Prayer and the Articles of Religion, the canon law revision was ignored, presumably because it had never become law.

That did not mean that it was forgotten, however. When Elizabeth I ascended the throne, the reform of the Church's discipline was as urgent as ever. Its great champion was none other than John Foxe, whose fame rests on his history of the Reformation martyrs. Foxe retrieved a now lost manuscript of the canon law revision and printed it in 1571, giving it the title *Reformatio legum ecclesiasticarum*, or 'Reformation of the ecclesiastical laws', the name by which it is known today. It was Foxe's hope that the 1571 parliament would enact it, along with the final version of the Thirty-nine Articles of Religion, but that did not happen. Instead the Church issued a collection of stop-gap canons, the first of a series that would appear at intervals during Elizabeth's reign but that parliament would never ratify. Even the queen refused her assent until 1597, when she at last gave in. After her death in 1603 there was another attempt to produce a collection of canons, which by default were destined not to be replaced until 1969, but which never received either parliamentary or royal sanction. As a result, the Church of England, which began its independent existence as an exercise in canon law revision, is now the only church in Christendom that still recognises the ongoing validity of the medieval canon law, which even Rome abrogated in 1917. It is further proof, if any were needed, that there is nothing so permanent as a temporary expedient.

Once it was printed, the *Reformatio* did not disappear, and it was frequently cited as authoritative in later centuries. In 1713 Bishop Edmund Gibson included substantial extracts from it in his *Codex* of English canon law, after which it took on a life of its own. It was not until 1912 that Sir Lewis Dibdin (1852-1938), dean of the arches (the Church of England's leading law officer) and a prominent evangelical layman, finally laid it to rest, by pointing out that it had never had the force of law and therefore lacked all authority. To be fair, everyone (including Gibson) had known that all along, but most people believed that although the *Reformatio* was never ratified, it was an accurate representation of how the canon law had been understood (and more importantly, how it had been applied) in Elizabeth I's reign. According to this view, it had unfortunately been overthrown by the judgments of some reactionary high churchmen in the early seventeenth century. The general assumption was that if the *Reformatio* had become law, Puritanism would not have arisen and the Church of England would now be more unified and more Protestant than it is. It is therefore somewhat ironic that it was a strong evangelical churchman who disproved this thesis, but perhaps there is more substance to it than the official history might suggest. Let us examine its structure and contents before passing judgment on this, and try to understand what Cranmer and his companions were trying to do.

The Anatomy of the *Reformatio*

The *Reformatio* consists of fifty-five titles, grouped together in nine distinct sections, of which six (containing thirty-three titles) constitute the first part of the text and three (containing the remaining twenty-two titles) the second. The first part covers the doctrine, organisation and discipline of the Church, and the second outlines the structure of the ecclesiastical courts and their procedures. In general terms it can be said that most of what the *Reformatio* contains reflects the canon law tradition going back several centuries. This is especially true of the second part, which is little more than a summary of the established court structures and their procedures. What is different from anything that went before it is the order in which the material is presented, and the significance which that may have for the overall understanding of what a reformed Church ought to look like.

The first part of the *Reformatio* is broken down into sections on the doctrine of God (1-4), the sacraments (5-10), benefices (11-13; 15-18), worship (19), ministry (20-27) and clerical discipline (14; 28-33). Title 14 was misplaced in the final edit, but once that error is corrected the rest makes perfect sense. The first title, on the Trinity and the Catholic faith, was common to most canonical collections, but in medieval times it was usually restricted to the list of heresies catalogued by Isidore of Seville in the early seventh century, and not much else. On this subject the *Reformatio* is much fuller, and it is of particular interest to us because it was composed at the same time, and by the same people, as the Forty-two Articles of Religion. In other words, the *Reformatio* can legitimately be used as a commentary and a supplement to the Articles, explaining in greater detail what they mean. The seventeen paragraphs of the first title begin with general principles and go on from there to specific details. The title begins with a very clear assertion: 'Since the power to rule and the right to administer laws has come to us from God, we ought to learn about him first.' There was no doubt in the minds of the authors that this meant studying the Christian religion, the true self-revelation of God, and that those who denied that were guilty of ungodliness. Such people were to be shown no mercy. As the *Reformatio* puts it: 'all goods, and finally even life itself shall be confiscated from those who have involved themselves in that enormous crime of ungodliness' (1.1).

Having laid that principle down in no uncertain terms, the title goes on to expound the Trinity and then the person and work of Christ as set out in the three Creeds. After that comes an extensive section on Scripture, which lists the canonical books of both Testaments as well as the so-called Apocryphal books. The Old Testament and Apocryphal lists were later incorporated into the Thirty-nine Articles but as they were not in the original Forty-two, the *Reformatio* can claim to be the earliest Anglican statement on this subject, and one that was accepted without question when the Articles were revised. More importantly perhaps, there is an extended explanation of what the supreme authority of Scripture means for the life of the Church. Not only can the Church not decree anything not contained in Scripture as necessary for salvation, but it must limit itself to what Scripture says. If there is any doubt about what that is, the original manuscripts in Hebrew and Greek (and not the Latin Vulgate) are to be consulted in order to determine the correct meaning. Furthermore, although the authority of Church councils and of the ancient Fathers is recognised up to a point, it is clearly stated that 'we do not allow that the meaning of Holy Writ can be determined by their opinion' (1.15).

None of this comes as any great surprise to us today, but it is important to realise that it represented a new departure at the time. The Articles of Religion are generally less detailed than the *Reformatio* but much of what the latter expounds at some length was later to be incorporated into the Westminster Confession of Faith. It is therefore incorrect to suggest, as some have done, that the Westminster Confession represents a later theological development that was foreign to the Articles. To a considerable degree the Westminster doctrine was already present in the *Reformatio*, and must therefore be regarded as part of the legacy of the first generation of Reformers and not as a later Puritan invention.

The second title deals with heresy, always a touchy subject and especially so when the Reformers were being accused of it by their Catholic opponents. The *Reformatio* defines heretics as those who deliberately persist in error, not those who fall into it unwittingly. The latter will accept correction when their mistake is pointed out, and so should not be counted as heretics – a distinction that in the sixteenth century could mean the difference between life and death. The *Reformatio* also makes a clear distinction between schism, which is a division in the Church, and heresy, which is false teaching, though it observes that all too often one leads to the other, because to separate oneself from the Church is to remove oneself from its teaching authority, with the risk that falling into error is probably only a matter of time.

As for the heresies themselves, the *Reformatio* does not mechanically repeat the list of ancient errors given by Isidore of Seville but takes a more fundamental approach, by insisting that the root of heresy is the rejection of the authority of Holy Scripture. All true doctrine is derived from the Bible, and claims to some special knowledge or revelation apart from that must be rejected. In addition, the Scriptures must be interpreted in the right way, especially where the Old Testament is concerned. Some people ignore it altogether while others insist that it must be kept to the letter. Both these extremes must be avoided. From there, the *Reformatio* goes on to stress the need to affirm the two natures of the incarnate Christ, the divinity of the Holy Spirit, the reality of original sin, the illusion of free will in fallen human beings and justification by faith alone. After that comes the rejection of belief in the possibility of spiritual perfection in this life, the need for meritorious works and the existence of purgatory as a second chance for those who have not quite made it before dying. There is then a denunciation of universalism and of the idea of so-called 'soul sleep' after death, a controversy that was especially intense in the sixteenth century.

About half the title on heresy is given over to a condemnation of the Anabaptists, who were regarded as a major menace at the time, even though there were few who were then active in England. The Anabaptists were considered to be dangerous because they rejected the ministry of the Church on the ground that too many of its ministers were unworthy of their calling, and of course they refused to baptise infants. What the *Reformatio* has to say on that subject is particularly interesting:

> ...the children of Christians do not belong any less to God and the Church than the children of the Hebrews once did, and since circumcision was given to them in infancy so also baptism ought to be imparted to our children, since they are participants in the same divine promise and covenant... (2.18).

Once more we see how a theme generally attributed to later Puritanism crops up in the *Reformatio*, and there is even a reference to covenant theology, some decades before that would come into vogue.

The title also contains an important definition of a sacrament, making a clear distinction between the internal witness of the Holy Spirit and the external signs which speak about it. The *Reformatio* actually says that:

> ...by the Word of God which intervenes, and by the nature of the symbols presented, believers are instructed about the price of our salvation bought by Christ, the Holy Spirit and grace are instilled more deeply in the minds of believers, for then the covenant which has been made by Christ between God and us is reaffirmed, that God is nearer to us, that we are his peculiar people, and that we are dedicating ourselves to the abolition of sins and to adopting integrity of life. If these things are rightly considered, the calumny of those who want to leave the nature of the sacraments worthless and bare will necessarily be silenced (2.17).

After dealing with the Anabaptists, the *Reformatio* moves on to the papists, whose heresies included transubstantiation, the abuse of the Eucharist, the imposition of compulsory clerical celibacy and the power of the pope. Perhaps the most interesting paragraph of all is the next to last one, which condemns those who use the doctrine of predestination as an excuse to avoid any amendment of life, on the ground that God has already decided who will and who will not be saved. Not only does this paragraph affirm reprobation, or predestination to eternal damnation, but it defends predestination with even greater clarity than Article 17, pointing out, for example, that it 'reduces our arrogance, lest we believe that we are ruled by our own strength' (2.22). No Puritan would have wanted any more than that.

The third and fourth titles deal with the punishment of heretics and of blasphemers, taking care to define these terms precisely and to ensure that those accused should get a fair hearing. The content of these titles is more or less what one would expect, but there is an interesting observation on the status of repentant ministers. The *Reformatio* accepts that some clergy will fall into error and then repent of it, but what should be done about them after that? The answer was that 'they shall not return to their former position in the Church, since ministers of the Church must be of blameless reputation...' (3.11). However, the same paragraph admits that the ideal cannot always be achieved and that a shortage of ministers may force the Church to allow some former heretics back into the ministry. But such people ought not to be promoted to higher office, 'unless the greatest necessity requires it and no other solution is possible' (3.11). Modern minds will sense prevarication here and detect an ever-widening loophole through which the undeserving could gain promotion, but we should not disparage the intentions of the Reformers on that account. As all of us must in one way or another, they were trying to match principle with practice, and recognised that simple answers cannot always be given to complex problems.

The second section in the first part of the *Reformatio* is dedicated to the sacraments, starting as usual with general principles and moving from there to specific details. The section concentrates on baptism and the Lord's Supper, but the tradition of seven sacraments could not be easily abandoned and reference is made to some of the other five as well, though there is no compromise on doctrinal principle. As the second paragraph of title five puts it, a sacrament must have an obvious and appropriate sign in which the promise of God is represented to us. There must also be a direct command from God to perform the rite in question. As the *Reformatio* concludes: 'Since these three things occur with the authority of the Scriptures only in baptism and the Eucharist, we accept only these two as true and proper sacraments of the New Testament' (5.2).

The fifth title details what baptism and the Lord's Supper are, and makes it clear that although infants are to be baptised, 'we do not want anyone to be admitted to the Lord's table until he has professed his faith in church' (5.5). Infant communion was not on the cards. The title goes on to make brief references to ordination, matrimony, confirmation and extreme unction, re-titled here as the visitation of the sick, but there is no mention of penance, which was by far the most important rite after baptism and the Lord's Supper, and initially retained by Martin Luther as a sacrament in its own right. Neither it, nor any of the abuses that had grown up around it, were to have a place in the reformed Christian community.

The sixth title is given over to the condemnation of idolatry and magic, which may seem like an odd subject to include with the sacraments, but both are concerned with the way the spiritual intersects with the material, and many people had turned the sacraments into a form of magic or even idolatry as they adored the consecrated host – or stole it for occult purposes. Nowadays we would probably leave this title out on the ground that superstition is nonsense, but perhaps we should be more careful about this. Nature abhors a vacuum, and when right doctrine is absent false teaching will creep in, as the prevalence of so-called 'new age' phenomena reminds us. On this subject, the *Reformatio* is not as alien to our times as we might be tempted to believe.

Titles seven to ten deal with the two traditional sacraments that were regarded as mutually exclusive – holy orders and holy matrimony – but they do so in an entirely new way. First comes the *Reformatio*'s take on the ordained ministry, which is clearly defined – the ordained minister is called above all to be a preacher. Preaching as a category of ministry had never before figured in the canon law, though there had been stipulations that those who were authorised to preach would need a license to do so. The traditional hierarchy of bishops, priests and deacons had never singled out preachers and it was not clear to whom that task belonged, or whether it was even necessary. The *Reformatio* changed all that. As it says:

> In this task of preaching the archbishops must take precedence. Then follow the bishops, deans and those who have been appointed to dignities (as they are called). Nor must they be the only ones engaged in this most holy occupation, but the same power must be granted to pastors and incumbents among their flocks, unless there are valid reasons why their bishops have ordered them to keep silent (7.4).

In other words, everyone in ordained ministry is expected to be a preacher, and the sermon was to be the main activity of Sunday worship. As the *Reformatio* clearly states: 'Since the main Sunday worship consists in receiving the knowledge of the Holy Scriptures...those who do not want to attend sermons, or who fail to do so, shall be punished...' This is a far cry from the pre-Reformation Church, where it was attendance at the Eucharist that really mattered, and everything else was secondary to it.

Title eight is devoted to holy matrimony in general terms, and contains little that had not been present in the medieval canon law. There are however, some innovations that deserve our attention. One is that marriage without the consent of the parents would be declared invalid (8.4). This was to some extent a return to an earlier state of affairs. The medieval Church had insisted that a marriage was valid only with the consent of the parties, in an attempt to get rid of forced unions engineered by parents who saw them as business opportunities more than anything else. Here however, it was probably another kind of abuse that was in view. There was always the possibility that a wealthy heiress might be seduced by a charming but penniless rogue – the nightmare of every parent then and now. In order to minimise, if not entirely prevent this danger, parental consent was made compulsory.

The other novelty in this title was that matrimony in the reformed Church would be allowed for everyone, and not just for lay people. This was to give canonical effect to the Marriage of the Clergy Act of 1549, which had legalised clerical marriage for the first time in England. But this liberal attitude must not be taken too far. The canon actually states:

> Since matrimony is a lawful and devout custom, and prevents the evil of many shameful things, it is our will for it to be repeated as many times as necessary, as long as it is done properly. We do not bar anyone from marriage on grounds of social standing, rank or age, but we advise those Christian women who are aged and very much advanced in years, and also strongly encourage them, not to want to marry young men, both because they cannot have children from them, and because there may be great and many different kinds of perversity in such wantonness (8.9).

A further innovation, and a curiosity to modern minds, is the insistence that mothers must breast-feed their babies themselves and not hand them over to a wet nurse. This stipulation was introduced because it was believed that breast-feeding created a bond between mother and child that would be weakened if it were not practised. The idea that how a mother feeds her baby is nobody else's business was unheard of at that time, and one can only imagine what might have happened had anyone been hauled before an ecclesiastical court for failing to comply with this regulation. It is when reading provisions like these that we realise the distance that separates us from the sixteenth century and in this respect at least, we can be grateful that the *Reformatio* failed to become law.

The next title deals with the rules of consanguinity and affinity that prohibited the marriage of people who were too closely related. In the middle ages the lines had been drawn so broadly that almost everyone in a given village could have had their marriage annulled on these grounds, but the Reformers were determined to tighten up the rules. They relied on Leviticus 18, the same chapter to which Henry VIII had appealed when seeking the annulment of his marriage to Catharine of Aragón. This narrowed the degrees of consanguinity that could prevent a marriage, and the rules of affinity were largely scrapped. In pre-Reformation times it had been unlawful to marry a godchild on the ground of 'affinity', but as this has no biological – or Scriptural – basis, it was done away with (9.7). These rules were written into the *Book of Common Prayer* and became law with no further modification until the twentieth century, when some of the more distant relations were exempted.

It is title ten, dealing with adultery and divorce, that has provoked the greatest comment through the ages because it is here, more than anywhere else, that the medieval canon law was overturned. In the pre-Reformation Church there was no divorce, only annulment and what was called 'separation from bed and board', a situation in which the couple remained married but were either dispensed or prevented from living together. The Reformers knew at first hand what a mess these rules had created and were determined to do something about them. In the first place, they retained their condemnation of adultery. A crime that the Bible punished by stoning the guilty party could not be excused by the Church, even if so barbaric a punishment was to be avoided. Clergymen guilty of adultery – a non-existent category in pre-Reformation times – were to be punished more severely than laymen, by losing all their property and by being banished or imprisoned for life. It is true that laymen would also be banished or imprisoned for life, but they would lose only half their property, which they would have to hand over to their injured spouse. But adulterous wives of both clergy and laymen would be punished equally, by losing their dowries and by perpetual banishment or imprisonment. How practical this would have been is hard to say. It does not seem to have occurred to anyone that imprisoned men might form liaisons with imprisoned women and create a whole new underclass of adulterers, but something like that might well have happened if this law had ever been enforced.

Divorce and remarriage would be allowed to the innocent party, and this privilege was extended to spouses who had been deserted – in almost all cases, to women whose husbands had left them. Desertion was not to be considered lightly however, and it would first be necessary to mount a three-year search for the offending party and try to persuade him (or her) to return to the marriage. Failing that, the usual penalties would be applied and the innocent party would be free to marry again. But if the deserter were to reappear after the three-year limit was up and attempt to reclaim his or her spouse, he or she would be imprisoned for life and the second marriage would be entirely legal. However, there was one important exception to this rule – the prolonged absence of the husband on business or military service. It might well happen that a man was imprisoned in some foreign country for a long period of time and nobody at home would know where he was. In such circumstances, the abandoned wife could remarry after the prescribed delay, but if the husband were to return later she would have to go back to him, because his absence would not have constituted desertion. Once again, we are in difficult territory here, and it is easy to see why many felt that such a policy would prove to be unworkable.

Cruelty was also ground for divorce, as were irreconcilable differences, though what those were was not specified. The title goes on to deal with all sorts of possible circumstances that might arise in a divorce suit, doing its best to make sure that punishment fell most severely on the guilty party, even though both would inevitably suffer to some degree. In particular, if the suit dragged on, the husband would be responsible for the upkeep of his wife, 'account being taken of her rank and social standing'. That could have become very expensive!

Reading over the title on divorce today most people will probably think that its provisions are fairly reasonable, but this is not how the matter was viewed at the time. In the sixteenth century, and for a long time afterwards, divorce was practically unobtainable other than by a special act of parliament, which was difficult and expensive to get. The Church of England, which some would say emerged out of an attempt to end a marriage, thus found itself with some of the strictest rules on the subject in all of Christendom. Only very recently has this begun to change, though resistance remains strong, particularly in the case of remarriage after divorce, which is still frowned upon and may be regarded as grounds for putting an ordained person out of the ministry.

The next seven titles, skipping number fourteen which is out of place, deal with the question of ecclesiastical benefices. The benefice system of appointing clergy to particular posts was established by the Fourth Lateran Council in 1215 and is still in force in the Church of England today, so these titles still retain some interest. Put simply, a benefice, or a living, to use the English word for it, is a package designed to provide sufficient income for a clergyman in a particular post. The vast majority of such posts are parishes, but the term can also cover cathedral canonries, chaplaincies in the universities or at court, and so on. In the absence of any fixed form of ministerial training at the time of the Reformation, it was necessary for the Church to examine all candidates for benefices, to make sure that they were qualified to hold them. In addition, various forms of chicanery had to be avoided, like the tendency to guarantee the succession to a benefice by a procedure known as 'resignation in favour', by which the incumbent would sign the benefice over to someone else, who would then pay him a pension for life out of the income. This had been a problem before the Reformation, but afterwards it became even worse, because a married man could deed his benefice to his son and create a clerical dynasty, which actually happened in some instances. In the parish of Hildersham, for example, just outside of Cambridge, the incumbent from 19 December 1629 to 25 March 1736 – a period of more than 106 years – was a man called Henry Smith. They were three generations of clergymen, all of whom had exactly the same name and who kept the living in the family. The *Reformatio* tried to contain this tendency by demanding that an incumbent should resign in person, not by proxy (12.5), but this failed and the abuses continued despite widespread criticism.

Because of the nature of the situation, candidates for benefices were to be examined in the way that candidates for ordination are now. Furthermore, care was to be taken to ensure that a minister could hold only one benefice at a time and that he was to reside in the place where it was situated. Absenteeism and pluralism were both ruled out – at least in principle. When we remember that the young John Calvin paid for his university education in Orléans from the revenues of two benefices that he held in the cathedral of his home town of Noyon, we can grasp what a problem that was. Unfortunately, as the example of Calvin illustrates, too many people benefitted from the system for it to be easily dismantled, and it was to remain a problem until 1838, when the Pluralities Act put a stop to the abuses that had accumulated over time. Even then, the act was not retroactive, so that it was not until the last pluralists and absentees died out in the late nineteenth century that the vision of the *Reformatio* can truly be said to have been realised.

Other abuses that were tackled by the *Reformatio* included the unauthorised exchange of benefices, which was often used by bankrupt clergymen who needed to pay off debts, or the failure to keep buildings like clergy houses in good repair – or even to provide them at all. The buying and selling of benefices, a practice known as simony, was rife, and elections to cathedral offices were a farce. Simony was finally dealt with in 1925 when the sale of benefices was stopped, but in England at least, elections are still what they always were – a pantomime in which the electors go through the motions of electing a bishop or dean, but have only one candidate they can choose from. The *Reformatio* was not only ahead of *its* time; in some respects, it is still ahead of *ours*.

Title nineteen is the only one devoted to worship, much of which was regulated by the second Edwardian *Book of Common Prayer*, which appeared at the same time. The main concern of the *Reformatio* was with public worship in cathedrals and colleges, where it was to be held on a daily basis, with communion reserved for Sundays and feast days. Interestingly, there was to be no sermon in a cathedral or college on Sunday morning, but in the afternoon instead. The hope was that people would attend the sermon in their parish church in the morning and then, if they lived near a cathedral or college, go there for another sermon in the afternoon. Meanwhile, the parish minister was instructed to use the time after morning service for catechising his parishioners – the first mention we have of Sunday school, and something that was to be a constant Puritan demand in the following decades.

Private communions were forbidden, except in special cases where it was necessary to make accommodation for the sick and for some high-ranking noblemen whose business kept them away from church on Sundays. But even in those exceptional circumstances, the *Reformatio* specified that 'no one shall conduct worship in a way which is contrary to the patterns and forms of that book of ours which is written in the common tongue.' This insistence on the Prayer Book bothered John Foxe, who drew attention to it in the introduction to his edition and suggested that the requirement needed to be relaxed, a clear indication of where the Puritans would come to diverge from the *Reformatio* as well as from the canons of the Church.

The next eight titles cover the Church's ministry and need not detain us long. The most interesting thing about them is that they invert the traditional hierarchy and start from the bottom up. Title twenty kicks off with parish clerks and churchwardens before going on to deacons, presbyters, archdeacons, deans and finally, in paragraph 10, to bishops. Archbishops do not appear until paragraph 17, which is an introduction to the rules governing diocesan synods, which occupy the rest of the title.

After that, the following titles deal respectively with churchwardens, parish boundaries, parish schools and their schoolmasters and finally universities and colleges – once again in ascending order of dignity. Title twenty-five covers tithes, twenty-six outlines how parish visitations are to be conducted, and twenty-seven, which was inserted by a practising lawyer, with last wills and testaments, which formed an important part of the business of the ecclesiastical courts. These matters were covered in considerable detail, but for the most part they introduced nothing new and merely codified existing practice.

The final section of the first part tackles church discipline. It is here that title fourteen ought to have been placed, followed by the next five which deal with ecclesiastical punishments in general before going on to outline the rules governing suspension, sequestration, deprivation and excommunication, the order being determined by increasing degree of gravity. Most remarkable is title thirty-three, which concludes the first part. It is not a condemnation, but a formula for reconciling an excommunicate person. This was something entirely new in a book of canon law and demonstrates the pastoral concern that the authors of the *Reformatio* had for the Church. Discipline and punishment might be necessary, but reconciliation was always to be desired and a way to achieve it was set out in the hope that it would be.

The misplaced title fourteen is an oddity that needs some explanation. It deals with the punishment, not of the guilty but of the innocent. This is a strange concept to us, but it was based on the belief, enshrined in classical Roman law, that where there is smoke there is fire, and anyone who appeared before a court must therefore give account of himself before being set free. This was to be done by a procedure known as 'purgation'. It was achieved by the defendant when he could produce six, and in serious cases as many as ten, witnesses, known as 'compurgators', who would swear to his good character and protest his innocence. Purgation of this kind was actually fairly common in the sixteenth century and almost always succeeded, as long as there was a sufficient number of compurgators. As far as we can tell, it was only those who did not have six friends willing to testify on their behalf who ended up being punished, and those who were acquitted by this means seldom if ever faced any further objections from other interested parties. Peculiar as it seems to us, it was a way of maintaining social harmony, and not least an incentive to make friends and to keep them in case of need.

The last twenty-two titles of the *Reformatio*, which together make up the second part of the text, need not concern us now. Almost all of them deal with the ecclesiastical courts and their procedures, the three exceptions coming towards the end and dealing with odds and ends that do not fit readily elsewhere. Title forty-eight, for example, covers violence done to the clergy. It was put there by Archbishop Cranmer because he knew it had to go somewhere but did not want to draw too much attention to it. The reason for this was not that he was indifferent to the matter, but that the general public resented what was called 'benefit of clergy', the special treatment that men in holy orders received from the law courts. Similarly, title fifty covers defamation of character, a subject that had traditionally been within the purview of the ecclesiastical courts on the ground that defamation was an offence against the soul, but it was passing into the secular jurisdiction in the sixteenth century. The reason for that, apparently, is that some people were claiming that being accused of a crime in a secular court was itself an act of defamation, and that such cases ought to be heard by the Church rather than by the state. Given that the Church courts had no power to execute anyone and were generally thought to be more lenient, it is easy to see why such a loophole was unpopular. But neither Cranmer nor his colleagues wanted to surrender defamation altogether, and ecclesiastical jurisdiction over it, though already moribund, was not officially abolished until 1855.

Finally, title fifty-five contains a list of legal maxims inherited from Roman law that were meant to guide judges as they sought to weigh the merits of individual cases. Most of these are just common sense principles, and are worded in ways that favour the defendant. For example, if the principal accusation made against someone is not valid, then any other accusations tied to it must be dismissed (55.15). Considerable latitude is shown towards those who commit crimes in ignorance, even if they are supposed to know what the law says on any given subject (55.32, 48). On the whole, the maxims demonstrate a spirit of humanity that was meant to underpin the operation of the courts and that, in many cases, would have operated to mitigate the severity of what might at first sight appear to be extreme punishments.

Conclusion

And so to conclude. As we have already stated, the *Reformatio* never became law and so cannot legitimately be appealed to in the absence of confirmatory evidence supporting what it says in canons or statutes that have legal force. Yet if it cannot be used in that way, it has another value that we ought to recognise. The *Reformatio* was composed at the same time and by the same people as the Forty-two Articles of Religion and the Second Edwardian Prayer Book. It can therefore be read as a commentary on them, and as a supplement to their teaching when it is abbreviated or passed over in silence. In particular, it helps us to understand what the Reformers intended when they affirmed that Holy Scripture was the supreme authority for the life of the Church. It confirms our belief that for them, preaching was meant to be the main activity of the clergy, that there were only two sacraments, and that catechising the laity was a priority. It offers proof that many of the themes associated with Puritanism were present in the minds of the Reformers – Archbishop Cranmer would not have recoiled at what his grandchildren would be advocating, but would have supported most of their demands, and indeed was the source for many of them. In this respect, the *Reformatio* is an invaluable bridge between the early English Reformation and what some have called the Puritan revolution of the seventeenth century, and the activities of men like Archbishop William Laud are revealed as the aberrations that they were. The *Reformatio* is a genuine commentary on the theology of the English Reformers. It is a witness that can and ought to be appealed to in the face of later attempts to make them say what they did not mean, and to reintroduce unreformed beliefs and practices into the Anglican Communion. It should therefore be read for what it is and valued as a witness to what the Church of England, and the wider Anglican Communion, could have become and in some respects might still aim to be.

BISHOP JOHN HOOPER: MAVERICK OR MAGISTERIAL REFORMER?

Stephen Tong

Introduction

Towards the end of 1550, John Hooper wrote a tract entitled *A Godly Confession and protestation of the Christian faith*.[142] It was intended to be a summation of the basic tenets of the Christian faith. Right at the start of this work, Hooper wrote the following:

> I believe all the people of the world to be either the people of God, [or] either the people of the Devil. The people of God be those that with heart and mind know, worship, honour, praise, and laud God, after the doctrine of the prophets and Apostles.
>
> The people of the Devil be those that think they worship, honour, reverence, fear, laud, or praise God any other way, besides, or contrary to the doctrine of the prophets and Apostles.
>
> I believe that this people of God, which be the very true church of God, to have a certain doctrine that never was, is, or hereafter shall be violated by time, or any man's authority. This doctrine only and solely is comprehended in the sacred and holy Bible.[143]

This is just one example of how Hooper saw the world in black and white. Either you belonged to God and worshipped him, or you belonged to the devil, and worshipped in a false manner. Such a stark

---

[142] John Hooper, *A Godly Confession and protestacion of the Christian faith* (1550), in *Later Writings of John Hooper* (Cambridge: Cambridge University Press, 1852), 64-92. For context on this document, see Don S. Ross, 'Hooper's Alleged Authorship of "A Brief and Clear Confession of the Christian Faith"', *Church History* 39:1 (1970), 20.
[143] Hooper, *Later Writings*, 71.

assessment of the world's population certainly fit the times, for the Reformation was an age of polemics, and Hooper was no stranger to polemical language. What we have here, though, is not barbed rhetoric against those who might be considered opponents of evangelical reform: Roman Catholics or Anabaptists. Indeed, Hooper was well versed in the art of provoking Roman Catholic ire as well as preaching against Anabaptist doctrine and practice.[144] Rather, Hooper wrote this tract as a defence against the treatment he was receiving from his fellow evangelical allies in England.

By the time *A Godly Confession* was published in December 1550, Hooper had been under house arrest for a couple of months. He had been placed there by the direct order of Archbishop Cranmer. The issue was at the same time simple and complex, and the episode is now well known as 'The Vestments Controversy'.[145] It began at the start of 1550, during Lent, when Hooper delivered a series of sermons before the court of Edward VI. The evangelical elite were so impressed with the preacher that they offered him the See of Gloucester. John Ponet had also given a set of Lenten sermons and was similarly offered the See of Rochester. However, the ordinal, which had been recently revised by Cranmer and was appended to the 1549 *Book of Common Prayer* (*BCP*), stipulated that candidates for ordination or consecration wear clerical garb in keeping with their ecclesiastical status. This was the sticking point. Hooper repudiated clerical vestments on the grounds that they, along with candles, crosses, and altars, were trappings of Roman Catholicism; unhelpful tradition at best, heretical gimmicks at worst.[146] Such accoutrements of Roman Catholic worship were seen as 'contrary to the doctrine of the prophets and apostles' – products of a false church.

---

[144] See Hooper, *Answer to the Bishop of Winchester's Book*, in *Early Writings of John Hooper* (Cambridge: Cambridge University Press, 1843), 97-248; *A Lesson on the Incarnation of Christ*, in *Later Writings*, 1-18.

[145] For a full account see John Primus, *The Vestments Controversy: An Historical Study of the Earliest Tensions within the Church of England in the Reigns of Edward VI and Elizabeth* (Kampen: J. H. Kok, 1960).

[146] John Hooper, *An Oversight and Deliberation upon the holy Prophet Jonas* in *Early Writings*, 534.

Hooper therefore refused to wear clerical vestments at his consecration service. In contrast, Ponet was happy to oblige and was duly consecrated Bishop of Rochester. Hooper's refusal was rewarded with house arrest, before being imprisoned in the Fleet Prison until February 1551. He then returned to the public eye repentant – yet resplendent – in episcopal attire the following month at his own consecration service, where he swore an oath to 'promise all due reverence and obedience to you, T[homas] Archbishop and to the metropolitical Church of Canterbury and to your successors'.[147]

Was this utterance an act of one who belonged to God or one who belonged to the Devil, as per Hooper's definition set out in *A Godly Confession*? How was it that someone who had taken such a principled stance against aspects of a foundational document of the Church of England now submitted to them as though they embodied 'the doctrine of the sacred and Holy Bible'? This essay makes an initial attempt to answer such questions by bringing some clarity to Hooper's place within Anglican history. The following discussion will focus in and around 1550 before turning to consider Hooper's legacy for both the Tudor Church and modern Anglicanism. In doing so, a chief aim is to re-establish Hooper as a magisterial reformer; a reformer who was willing to use the ecclesiastical structures of his day to forward the kingdom work of proclaiming the Gospel of Jesus Christ – and one who modern Anglicans can learn from.

Hooper in History

The events, decisions, and personalities surrounding the vestments controversy have allowed historians to depict Hooper as a born-again radical reformer. Such a characterisation was popularised in the mid-1950s by W.M.S. West, who wrote a series of articles entitled 'John Hooper and the Origins of Puritanism'.[148] West was a Baptist minister and an active Reformation scholar throughout his life. He completed his doctoral studies on Hooper, which formed the basis of his articles on the same subject. These articles provide excellent insights into

---

[147] Lambeth Palace Library, Cranmer's Register, fol. 333.
[148] W.M.S. West, 'John Hooper and the Origins of Puritanism', *Baptist Quarterly* xv (1954), 346-68; xvi (1955), 22-46, 67-88.

Hooper's theological framework, but one wonders about the degree to which West shoehorned Hooper onto a procrustean bed.

To reduce West's thesis to its bare essentials, it is enough to quote his concluding remark: 'Hooper was the chief influence leading towards Puritanism in England under Edward VI'.[149] Many have since followed West's assertion that Hooper was the 'Father of Nonconformity'.[150] Most recently, Karl Gunther suggested that Hooper was the instigator of nonconformity, the germ of English Presbyterianism. According to such an argument, the ecclesiastical troubles that plagued English Protestantism from Elizabeth's reign to the Glorious Revolution of William III in 1688 can, and should, therefore, be traced directly to one man: John Hooper.[151]

A key component of this argument is that Hooper undermined the structure of episcopacy to the point that he outwardly challenged it and sought to overturn it. In addition, Hooper's refusal to wear clerical garb has often been viewed as a symbolic rejection of the entire ecclesiastical structure that the Church of England had inherited from the medieval Roman Catholic Church. Indeed, the retention of the threefold structure of bishop, priest, and deacon puzzled many sixteenth- and seventeenth-century churchmen. Although Hooper is relatively silent on the matter, some Elizabethan Puritans sought to devolve the national Church into a Presbyterian-style conglomerate of congregations according to the Genevan model; their nonconformist successors carried this impetus further in subsequent centuries. Hooper's positive influence on these later developments has generally

---

[149] Ibid. xvi (1955), 84.
[150] Ibid. 83-4: '...there can be little doubt that Hooper, in his call to reform the Church according to Scripture and to return it to the state of apostolic simplicity, in his theology of the covenant between God and man, in his emphasis upon the soul and salvation of the individual, in his family like, and indeed in his whole life and thought, sowed the seeds of Puritanism in the England of Edward VI. Hooper rightly bears the title of "Father of Nonconformity", or better "Father of English Puritanism"'.
[151] Karl Gunter, *Reformation Unbound* (Cambridge: Cambridge University Press, 2014).

been accepted without question.[152] Historians have pointed to Hooper's intimate links with Heinrich Bullinger in Zürich, and his principled stance against the ecclesiastical authorities during the vestments controversy to confirm this interpretation. However, Hooper's eventual acceptance of a bishopric and subsequent episcopal career raise some questions about his caricature.

Once he was installed in Gloucester, Hooper became a model reforming bishop. He used his episcopal office to promote the Gospel where he could. As bishop, Hooper provided daily hospitality for the poor in his diocese, he exacted high standards of morality and biblical knowledge from his clergy, and instituted 'superintendents' to assist him in preaching salvation by faith alone throughout Gloucestershire and Worcestershire.[153] The highly pastoral bishop also penned a sermon to be used in times of widespread plague which sought to comfort his diocese with the balm of the Gospel during times of suffering and disease.[154] It was with first-hand experience of these qualities that led John Foxe to describe Hooper as one who possessed 'all those virtues and qualities required of St Paul in a good bishop in his epistle to Timothy'. Indeed, Hooper 'behaved himself so well' that 'his enemies ... could find no fault with him'.[155] One also wonders whether it was these same qualities that saw Hooper become the first bishop, and second of 300 evangelicals, to be burnt at the stake by Queen Mary. In the light of his episcopal career, the popular image of Hooper as a maverick proto-puritan is worth revisiting.

---

[152] For example, John Primus claimed that Hooper was Thomas Cartwright *avant la lettre* in *The Vestments Controversy*, 30.
[153] The diocese of Gloucester was amalgamated with Worcester in 1552, and Hooper was given responsibility over both dioceses.
[154] John Hooper, 'An Homily to be read in a time of Pestilence', in *Later Writings*, 157-75.
[155] John Foxe, *Actes and Monuments* (1570) xi, 1714-5.

Vestments Controversy

When the vestments controversy broke out, Hooper was still a relative new comer to the evangelical milieu of the Edwardian court.[156] Having fled to Zürich after the Act of Six Articles was announced by Henry VIII in 1539, Hooper had only returned to his home county in May 1549. It was in Zürich that he became a disciple of Bullinger. He also wrote a number of tracts against Roman Catholicism from Zürich, and when he arrived to England, he was a headline act used by the establishment to combat the Anabaptist threat. A graduate of Merton College, Oxford, Hooper was no intellectual slouch, and, as we have noted, he was a powerful and persuasive preacher who was in constantly high demand.[157] It is perhaps no surprise, then, that Hooper was invited to give the 1550 Lenten sermons before the Royal Court in the lead up to Easter. In light of these circumstances, Hooper's nomination for the See of Gloucester was therefore both appropriate and significant. With the deprivation of various Roman Catholic-minded bishops, the Edwardian administration needed talented men who were theologically sound to further their goal of nationwide reformation.[158] Thus, Hooper's refusal to wear clerical vestments at his consecration had the potential to upset the apple cart in a serious way.

So then, why did Hooper refuse to wear the mandated vestments? The simple answer is that Hooper was reacting to the 1550 ordinal, which he did not believe went far enough in terms of reforming public worship. He used his Lenten sermons to voice his opposition on two major points.[159]

In the first instance, Hooper refused to be ordained according to the recently revised ordinal, which had been published in February 1550.

---

[156] For a description of this period, see Diarmaid MacCulloch, *Thomas Cranmer: a life* (New Haven: Yale University Press, 1996), 474-98.
[157] John Foxe, *Actes and Monuments* (London, 1570), xi, 1714; *Original Letters II*, 636.
[158] Barrett Beer, 'Episcopacy and Reform in Mid-Tudor England', *Albion: A Quarterly Journal Concerned with British Studies* xxiii (1991), 231-52.
[159] Hooper, *Early Writings*, 479.

The issue lay in the wording of 'The Oath of the King's Supremacy'.[160] It was not that Hooper objected to the Royal Supremacy, rather that he took offence at the inclusion of 'saints' when each ordinand was asked to invoke the help of 'God, all saints and the holy Evangelist' in their new ministries.[161] For Hooper, any hint at praying to the saints smacked of Roman Catholicism. The young king concurred, and had the offensive phrase removed days after Hooper's opinions were made public.[162] Not only does this reveal the power of the Royal Supremacy, but it also indicates something about the evangelical fervour of Edward VI.

The second aspect of the 1550 ordinal that Hooper took exception to was the demand for him to wear clerical vestments at his ordination service. He laid out his criticism in the light of the reformation principle of *sola scriptura*. Since vestments were not ordained 'in the word of God ... nor yet in the primitive and best church', wearing them 'seemeth to repugn plainly' with scripture.[163] Moreover, clerical dress reminded Hooper of 'the habit and vesture of Aaron and the gentiles, [not] of the ministers of Christ'.[164] Whatever theological feathers Hooper may have ruffled in these sermons, he was still offered the See of Gloucester.

Initially, the Privy Council was happy to allow Hooper to attend the service without the vestments. However, Cranmer and Nicholas Ridley, the Bishop of London, refused to ordain Hooper without them. Hooper stood his ground, and eventually lost this particular battle. The reasons why Hooper finally succumbed and yielded to Cranmer's episcopal

---

[160] *The First and Second Prayer Books of King Edward the Sixth*, ed. Ernest Rhys (London-Toronto: J. M. Dent, 1910, reprint 1927), 299-300. Hereafter BCP49, and BCP52.
[161] Ibid. 300.
[162] John Ab Ulmis to Henry Bullinger (22 Aug. 1550), *Original Letters Relative to the English Reformation vol. II* (Cambridge: Cambridge University Press, 1847), 416.
[163] Ibid.
[164] Ibid.

authority are not entirely clear.[165] It is worth noting, however, that this imbroglio involved many of the major Reformers of the day. Along with the English churchmen, other high-profile international Reformers such as Martin Bucer, Peter Martyr Vermigli, Henry Bullinger, and Jan Łaski all intervened at some point.

Taken at face value, Hooper's argument against the ordinal's stipulation to wear vestments is straightforward and biblical at its core. However, there was more political and theological complexity in this stance than Hooper may have first realised. Before going further, it is worth pausing to consider a short document Hooper penned for the Council in October 1550, just as the vestments controversy was turning into a serious issue. Known as Hooper's 'Notes to the King's Council', it is a document that gives us an insight into Hooper's biblical hermeneutics.

Adiaphora

The reason Hooper wrote his 'Notes' was to define his understanding of *adiaphora*, or things indifferent. The argument outlined here became Hooper's primary defence against wearing vestments at his ordination service:

> Nothing is to be used in the Church which is not expressly authorised by the Word of God, or else is a thing indifferent of itself, the doing or use of which brings no advantage, and the not doing or omission of which is not harmful.
>
> Special and distinctive vestures in the Ministry do not have the Word of God as their authority nor are they matters indifferent of themselves. Therefore they should not be used.[166]

---

[165] Stephen Tong, 'Evangelical Ecclesiology and Liturgical Reform in the Edwardian Reformation, c. 1545-1555', unpublished PhD thesis (Cambridge University, 2018), 55-9.

[166] C. Hopf, 'Bishop Hooper's 'Notes' to the King's Council, 3 October 1550', *Journal of Theological Studies* xliv (1943), 194-9. I thank Derek Scales for providing a full translation of these Latin notes. Another translation can be

The criticisms Hooper aimed at the ordinal in his Lenten sermons were repeated and refined here. Vestments fell beyond the definition of *adiaphora* because they lacked the 'primitive characteristic which is required in things indifferent'. That is to say, they did not have a definitive 'source and ground in the Word of God', nor did they have a 'positive command by which [they] are ordered'. The reformation principle of *sola scriptura* was being taken in a rather literal way. It allowed Hooper to conclude that 'we [should] exclude vestments from the number of adiaphora'. Thus, we see hints of what would later be called the regulative principle emerge in English Protestantism before the widespread influence of Calvin took root a generation later. Yet, this is not to say that Hooper wanted to break from his evangelical compatriots, rather he was urging further reform at a faster pace.

To twist the knife deeper, the practical application of Hooper's theology to public worship had ecclesiological consequences. Just as he did in his Lenten sermons, Hooper drew comparisons with the robes worn by the Old Testament priesthood of Aaron, which 'has been abolished in the priesthood of Christ'.[167] Then he suggested that the preservation of vestments in the Church of England mirrored the false worship of Roman Catholics: 'If therefore those shadows of Aaronic priesthood are not able to consist with the priesthood of Christ, much less can that papistical priesthood'.[168] This was a serious charge to level at Cranmer and the liturgical reformation he had overseen. For the Church of England to retain any form of Roman Catholic tradition or ceremony which had little to no Scriptural warrant was, for Hooper, tantamount to promoting false worship. And since vestments were neither *adiaphora* nor had a positive command in Scripture, they should be abolished altogether. Their retention was worse than unhelpful because any link to the papistical priesthood was equated with the existence of the false church. To echo *A Godly Confession*, either the liturgy of the Church of England enabled the faithful to worship God in purity according to 'the doctrine of the prophets and Apostles', or it did not. If the BCP and the ordinal were not purged of such impurities,

---

found in Iain H. Murray (ed.), *The Reformation of the Church: A Collection of Reformed and Puritan documents on Church issues* (Edinburgh: The Banner of Truth Trust, 1965, reprint 1997), 55-8.
[167] Ibid.
[168] Ibid.

then the Church of England would continue to consist of 'people of the Devil'.

Cranmer and Ridley, among others, were neither impressed nor persuaded by Hooper's argument. Ridley responded with his own set of 'Notes' to the Council in which he laid out clear theological reasoning for why he believed vestments should be considered as things indifferent, were therefore acceptable within the Church of England.[169] This swayed the Council, and thus the vestments controversy erupted when Hooper refused to accept defeat.

While we must acknowledge the theological complexities of the vestments controversy, there is another significant point worth noticing. Hooper's overriding concern was that the *form* of worship matched the *content* of worship. As much as anything else, this was a liturgical concern. For all the scholarship on deep theological questions raised during the Reformation that are fundamental to the Christian faith, we should not ignore the fact that the Reformers were also engaged in reshaping liturgy. They were highly aware of the ways in which public worship reflect the theological realities that unite congregations. This was precisely why the *BCP* underwent a significant revision in 1552, even though the 1549 edition had already signalled a significant break from the medieval past. Even here, we can detect the ramifications of Hooper's liturgical concerns.

In the first edition of the *BCP*, Cranmer included a short essay entitled 'Of Ceremonies' to explain why some ceremonies of the medieval church had been jettisoned from public worship, while others had been retained. Perhaps in reaction to the evangelically inhouse quarrel about vestments, this essay was moved from the back of the *BCP* to the front in 1552. Without highlighting specific examples, Cranmer's general principle was one of maintaining a 'decent order in the Church'.[170] Wearing clerical vestments during a period of flux can be seen as one way in which Cranmer sought to maintain a decent order. On the one hand, vestments created a visual connection to the past, but since the

---

[169] See A Townsend (ed.), *The Writings of John Bradford* (Cambridge: Cambridge University Press, 1853), 373-94.
[170] BCP49, 286.

theological foundations of public worship had been radically reordered, their use in a new context could be interpreted in a new light through an evangelical lens that saw them as *adiaphora*. Notwithstanding such ambiguity, it does appear as though Cranmer responded to Hooper's criticisms in more concrete ways. In the 1552 version of the ordinal, ordinands were no longer required to wear an alb, nor did bishops have to wear surplices or copes during their consecration. Furthermore, a priest presiding over Holy Communion did not have to wear 'the vesture appointed for that ministry', as he was instructed to do in the rubrics of the 1549 *BCP*.[171] One might deduce from these alterations that the Edwardian vestments controversy had finally found resolution.

Concluding Thoughts

Historical analysis rarely pays dividends to those who invest in counterfactual speculation. It is somewhat irresponsible, therefore, to suggest that Hooper set out to establish a nonconformist group within the Church of England by protesting the use of vestments in the ordinal. The fact is that Hooper did indeed conform, and was consecrated in vestments. Instead, as I have argued elsewhere, a better way to interpret this episode is to see it within the wider liturgical reformation that was going on at the time.[172]

It was a period in which public worship underwent a visual, oral, physical, and spiritual transformation as Archbishop Cranmer applied evangelical theology to church practice. And as we have seen, one of the questions that arose during this process of liturgical re-formation was about how stringent the principle of *sola scriptura* should be applied to the minutiae of public worship. A full-blown debate over the regulative and normative principles within English Protestantism would emerge in a later generation.[173] What is remarkable about Hooper's temporary intransigence is the apparent unity of the

---

[171] BCP49, 212.
[172] Tong, 'Evangelical Ecclesiology and Liturgical Reform', 31-83.
[173] See Primus, *Vestments Controversy*.

evangelical guard during the reign of Edward VI.[174] Considering the idiosyncratic theological differences and various personalities of the Edwardian Reformers, at base level, they all shared the primary desire to use the available resources to proclaim the Gospel. Although we do not know exactly why Hooper finally agreed to be consecrated in his robes, we do know that he did, which suggests firstly, that he came to see his consecration garments as *adiaphora,* and secondly, that he was willing to put secondary matters to one side in order to serve the greater goal of increasing God's Kingdom.

Throughout the vestments controversy, Hooper demonstrated a desire to ensure that doctrine and practice were intertwined. It was taken for granted that the theological framework of one's intellect necessarily shaped the spiritual yearnings of the heart, and in turn determined the physical behaviours of one's life. It was a theological outlook akin to that of Cranmer.[175] And for both men, of course, this had direct consequences for the shape of public worship.

This attitude was nothing new for Hooper, nor was it limited to liturgical matters. He encouraged all Christians to think about their lives as evangelistic opportunities. Writing from Zürich back in 1547, Hooper explained that

> [The Christian] must obey the law, and serve in his vocation according to the scripture, [so] that the exterior facts may bare testimony of the inward reconciliation ... the science of scripture if practive and not speculative, it requires a doer and not a speaker only.
>
> There be many that dissemble faith, and have a certain show of religion when indeed in the inward man is no faith at all: let every man therefore search his own conscience with what faith he is induced and remember that Christ said it is

---

[174] An observation that Catherine Davies makes in, *A religion of the Word: The Defense of the Reformation in the Reign of Edward VI* (Manchester-New York: Manchester University Press, 2002), 231-3.

[175] Ashley Null, *Thomas Cranmer's Doctrine of Repentance: Renewing the Power to Love* (Oxford: Oxford University Press, 2000).

a straight way and narrow that leads to life (Matt 7), and but a few that walk therein.[176]

From an early stage in his career, Hooper firmly believed that the Word of God has power not only to save, but also to transform. Although inward spiritual regeneration was the work of the Spirit, it was expected that the redeemed sinner would display a renewed life in public. Such an understanding of the restorative and sanctifying power of God's Word and the Holy Spirit remained a constant element throughout Hooper's ministry.

Rather than viewing Hooper's legacy as begetting the nonconformist strand of English Protestantism, a more accurate interpretation would be to consider his propensity to question the form and content of public worship according to the rule of Scripture as something worth emulating. In doing so, we would be keeping something of the spirit of Reformation Anglicanism.

---

[176] John Hooper, *Christ and His Office*, in *Early Writings*, 95.

Melanchthon, Oecolampadius, Cyril, and Cranmer on the Eucharist

Ashley Null

In June 1537, Thomas Cranmer wrote to Joachim Vadian, clearly rejecting his exposition of a symbolic understanding of the sacrament in his recent book on the Eucharist.

> I have seen almost every thing that has been written and published either by Œcolampadius or Zuinglius, and I have come to the conclusion that the writings of every man must be read with discrimination . . . I wish that they . . . had not . . . done violence to the authority of the ancient doctors and chief writers in the church of Christ. . . . And this error, most certainly, if error it be, has been handed down to us by the fathers themselves, and men of apostolic character, from the very beginning of the church. And what godly man could endure to hear this, much less to believe it? Not to mention in the mean time, that our gracious Lord would never have left his beloved spouse in such lamentable blindness for so long a period. Wherefore, since this catholic faith which we hold respecting the real presence has been declared to the church from the beginning by such evident and manifest passages of scripture, and the same has also been subsequently commended to the ears of the faithful with so much clearness and diligence by the first ecclesiastical writers; do not, I pray, persist in wishing any longer to carp at or subvert a doctrine so well grounded and supported.[177]

---

[177] J. E. Cox, *The Miscellaneous Writing and Letters of Thomas Cranmer* (Cambridge: Parker Society, 1846) [Henceforth, Cox II], p. 344; Diarmaid

In short, Cranmer insisted that he would have to see "stronger evidence brought forward" than that which Vadian had provided before he would agree "to be the patron" or "the approver" of reformed sacramental theology.[178]

Cranmer's immediate subsequent research on the Eucharist continued to be consistent with this approach. In his 1538 copy of the *Hierarchiae ecclesiasticae assertio*,[179] Cranmer underlined Albert Pigge's assertion that Oecolampadius and Zwingli had resurrected afresh Berengar of Tour's blasphemy that the Eucharist was only a memorial meal.[180] When Pigge then provided extensive quotations from fathers earlier than Berengar (d. 1088) to prove the opposite, Cranmer heavily annotated the text in black ink.[181] On one reading, he marked numerous passages by writing the author's name in the margin and adding a quotation mark beside each line of text he wished to highlight. On another reading, he underlined the text extensively, normally within the passages which were also highlighted with quotation marks. On a third reading, he inserted brackets around fourteen quotations

---

MacCulloch, *Thomas Cranmer: A Life*, revised edition (New Haven, CT: Yale University Press, 2016), pp. 179-81.

[178] *Ibid.*, p. 343.

[179] Albert Pigge, *Hierarchiae ecclesiasticae assertio* (Cologne: Melchior von Neuß, 1538). Cranmer's copy is now found in the British Library, Shelfmark 1142.cc.16. David Selwyn assigned this volume number 258 in his magisterial catalogue of Cranmer's library [Henceforth, "CL"]; *The Library of Thomas Cranmer* (Oxford: Oxford Bibliographical Society, 1996), p. 70.

[180] 'Berengarius . . . affirmauit: post consecrationem panis et vini in altari, aeque vt prius manere eorundem substantias. Christi vero ea carnem et sanguinem propterea vocari, quod in memoriam crucifixae carnis eius, et de latere effusi sanguinis in ecclesia celebrentur', CL 258, fol. 26r; Oecolampadius, Zvuinglius, et alij nonnulli sacramentariorum antistites, detestandi illius Berengarii, blasphemiam resuscitarunt ex integro', *ibid.*, fol. 27r.

[181] CL 258, fols 27r-36r.

within previously annotated sections of the text.[182] Here are some examples:[183]

> {Theophylact, the Bishop of the Bulgarians, comments on John: '"The bread which I will give is my flesh which I will give for the life of the world." Notice, he said that the bread which we eat in the mysteries is <u>not merely some kind of figure of the flesh of the Lord, but it is the very flesh of the Lord</u>. For he did not say, "The bread which I will give is a figure of my flesh." <u>For secret words, through mystical blessing and the coming of the Holy Spirit, transform the bread into the flesh of the Lord</u> . . . .'}[184]

---

[182] This reconstruction of Cranmer's readings is based on five observations: i) the *marginalia* of names and quotation marks were obviously made in concert and are the most extensive highlighting of the text; ii) the black ink of the underlinings is clearly a lighter shade than that used for either the *marginalia* or the brackets and, thus, must have been made during a separate reading from when the other annotations were made; iii) underlinings are normally within material marked with quotation marks, but not always (see ibid., fols 29v, 32v); iv) in all cases but one, the brackets are selected from within material highlighted by quotation marks (for the exception, where the initial bracket is placed earlier than material annotated with quotation marks, see, *ibid.,* fol. 29v); iv) the brackets were clearly written over the underlinings. Based on the probability (although not necessity) that Cranmer's annotations became more selective as he re-read the text, it would seem the *marginalia* came first, then the underlinings, and finally the brackets.

[183] Cranmer bracketed one extract from Theophylact, an extensive passage from John of Damascus, three quotations from Leo I, one from Gregory the Great, three from Augustine and five from Cyril of Alexandria; CL 258, fols 27r-32r.

[184] '{Theophylactus ille Bulgarorum episcopus, exponens illud Joannis: Panis quem ego dabo, caro mea est, quam ego dabo pro mundi vita: Attende, inquit, quod panis qui a nobis in mysteriis manducatur, <u>non est tantum figuratio quaedam carnis domini, sed ipsa caro domini</u>. Non enim dixit, panis quem ego dabo, figura est carnis. <u>Transformatur enim arcanis verbis panis ille, per mysticam benedictionem, et accessionem spiritus sancti in carnem domini</u> . . . }', with Cranmer's *marginalia*: '[T]heophilactus' and quotation marks, CL 258, fol. 27r-v. *NB*, although Theophylact was actually a younger contemporary

[John of Damascus] writes ... { ... Therefore, if you now ask, 'How does the bread become the body of Christ and the wine and water the blood of Christ?', I will answer you that the Holy Spirit overshadows them and does those things which surpass discussion and understanding ... }[185]

{... Thus [Augustine] says, 'Recognize in the bread what hung upon the cross. Recognize in the cup what flowed from Christ's side. For his death will not be life for the one who thinks Christ is a liar.}'[186]

[Cyril of Alexandria comments on John] ... {Jesus says to them ... 'Now, I say, since the time for figures has passed and truth is at the door, [my Father] gives you the bread of heaven, not as a shadow [of the thing to come like manna], nor only as another better sign, but the true bread itself.[187]

Finally, Cranmer incorporated the bracketed passages into the first and largest of two sections of patristic quotations in the *locus* on the

---

of Berengar, Pigge believed he wrote 'trecentis circiter annis ante Berengarium', *i.e.*, 'about three centuries before Berengar', *ibid.*, fol. 27v.

[185] '[Ioannes Damascenus] scribit ... { ... Itaque si et nunc interrogas, quomodo panis fit corpus Christi, et vinum et aqua sanguis Christi ? Respondeo et ego tibi: Spiritus sanctus obumbrat, et haec supra sermonem et intelligentiam operatur ... }', with Cranmer's *marginalia*: 'Damascenus' and quotations marks, CL 258, fols 27v-28v.

[186] '{ ... ita loquitur: Hoc accipite in pane quod pependit in cruce, hoc accipite in calice, quod effusum est de latere Christi. Erit enim illi mors non vita, qui mendacem putauerit Christum.}, with Cranmer's *marginalia*: 'Aug*ustinu*s' and quotations marks, CL 258, fol. 29r-v.

[187] '{Dixit ergo eis Iesus . . . Nunc, inquam, quando figurarum tempus exactum est, et veritas adest in ianuis, dat vobis panem de caelo, non vmbraticum, aut alterius melioris significationis tantum causa, sed ipsum verum.}', with Cranmer's *marginalia*: 'Cyrillus' and quotation marks, CL 258, fol. 30.

Eucharist in his 'Great Commonplaces'.[188] Since this section of 'Cranmer's Great Commonplaces' was mostly compiled *circa* 1538,[189] Cranmer must have repeatedly returned to Pigge's patristic scholarship to support his own real presence position within the first year of acquiring his copy of *Hierarchiae ecclesiasticae assertio*.

This new identification of Pigge as a major secondary source for the initial patristic quotations on the Eucharist in the 'Great Commonplaces' helps solve a conundrum first proposed by Peter Newman Brooks:

> a careful comparison of the passages in question proves beyond hesitation that the Swiss Reformer's work was one of the sources used by Cranmer in his compilation of quotations relative to the Eucharist from the writings of Gelasius, Leo, Cyprian, Irenaeus, Cyril, Hilary, Chrysostom and Jerome. This reliance on Oecolampadius is the more intriguing when, starting from the same Fathers, Cranmer is able, as the marginal notes indicate, to hold a view of the eucharistic presence that is completely contrary to the Swiss doctrine.[190]

Is Brooks' correct? It is an important question because we also have Cranmer's annotated copy of Oecolampadius' *Dialogus* which was

---

[188] The eucharistic commonplace in BL Royal MS 7.B.XI [referred to here as 'Cranmer's Great Commonplaces' and abbreviated as 'CGC I'], fols 78r-123v, has two sections of patristic quotations, CGC I, fols 79r-101v, and fols 120r-123v. *Cf.* CGC I and CL 258: Leo I, CGC I, 79v-80r, and CL 258, fol. 29r; Cyril, CGC I, fol. 84v-85r, and CL 258, fols 30r-v, 32r; Augustine, CGC I, fol. 91v, and CL 258, fol. 29v; Gregory, CGC I, fol. 94v, and CL 258, fol. 28v; Theophlyact, CGC I, fol. 99r-v, and CL 258, fol. 27r-v; and John of Damascus, CGC I, fols 100r-101v, and CL 258, fol. 28r-v.
[189] Warner and Gilson, *Royal Manuscripts*, p. 172. *NB*, however, two references to the *Antididagma* (1544) were added later to the eucharistic commonplace; CGC I, 99r.
[190] Peter Newman Brooks, *Thomas Cranmer's Doctrine of the Eucharist*, 2nd ed. (Basingstoke: Macmillan, 1992), pp. 34-5.

included in Bibliander's *Letters of Oecolampadius and Zwingli* (1536).[191] In order to date properly the annotations in Cranmer's *Dialogus* (CL 234), we will need to examine carefully Brooks' claim that Cranmer used Oecolampadius' work as a source for his patristic research *circa* 1538.

As we have seen with CL 258, it was Cranmer's common practice to bracket quotations in his books to be recorded in his 'Great Commonplaces'.[192] Hence, the first question we need to ask is whether the quotations on Brooks' list are bracketed in CL 234? The answer is negative for Gelasius,[193] Cyprian,[194] Irenaeus,[195] Cyril,[196] Hilary,[197] Chrysostom[198] and Jerome.[199] The only exceptions are two quotations from Leo.[200] Yet, even here we must exercise caution. When Cranmer's copy of Oecolampadius's *Dialogus* is compared with both his copy of Pigge's *Hierarchiae* and the 'Great Commonplaces', it is clear that the

---

[191] Theodor Bibliander, ed., *Ioannis Oecolampadii et Huldrichi Zvinglii Epistolarum Libri Quatuor* (Basel: Thomas Platter and Balthasar Lasius, 1536), Cranmer' Copy: Cambridge University Library, Shelfmark H*.8.17(c); CL 234. The *Dialogus* begins on CL 234, fol. 130r.
[192] Selwyn, *Cranmer's Library*, pp. lxxxiii-lxxxiv.
[193] *Cf.* Gelasisus: CGC I, fol. 79v, and CL 234, fol. 153v.
[194] *Cf.* Cyrpian: CGC I, fol.81r, and CL 234, fol. 138r-v.
[195] *Cf.* Irenaeus: CGC I, fol. 81r-v, and CL 234, fol. 138v.
[196] *Cf.* Cyril: CGC I, 82v-84v, and CL 234, fol. 136r-137r. *NB,* Brooks cited only the lengthy extract from Cyril on John 6 as being in both the *Dialogus* and CGC I: CL 234, fols 136r-137r, and CGC I, 82v-84r; *Cranmer's Doctrine of the Eucharist*, p. 35, footnote 1. In fact, there is a second, shorter extract from Cyril on John 15 also found in both. *Cf.* CL 234, fol. 136r, and CGC I, 84r-v.
[197] *Cf.* Hilary: CGC I, fols 85v-86r, and CL 234, fols 137v-138r.
[198] *Cf.* Chrysostom: CGC I, fol. 86r-v, and CL 234, fol. 137r-v.
[199] *Cf.* Jerome: CGC I, fol. 89v, and CL 234, fol. 148r.
[200] A comparsion of CGC I, 79r-80r, and CL 234, fol. 153r, shows two quotations from Leo are both bracketed in CL 234 and recorded in the CGC. *NB*, however, Brooks only cited one quotation in common, from Leo's *Sermon 91 on the Fast of the Seventh Month VI*, CGC I, 80r; *Cranmer's Doctrine of the Eucharist*, p. 35, footnote 1. However, a quotation from Leo's *Letter 59 to the Clergy and People of Constantinople* is also bracketed in CL 234, fol. 153r, and found in CGC I, 79r-80r.

quotations from Leo in the 'Great Commonplaces' were actually directly copied out from Pigge.

'Great Commonplaces' CGC I, fols 79v-80r	Pigge's *Hierarchiae* CL 258, fol. 29r	Oecolampadius's *Dialogus* CL 234, fol. 153r
'Leo in Epistola ad **Constantinopolitanos.** In ecclesia dei **omnium ore** ... in carnem ipsius, qui caro nostra factus est, transeamus.' (fols 79v-80r)	[Leo] '{in epistola ad **Constantinopolitanos:** In ecclesia Dei **omnium ore** ... in carnem ipsius, qui caro nostra factus est, transeamus.}'	[Leo] 'arguit, {*Constantinopolitanis* scribens. In ecclesia Dei, *in omnium ore* ... in carnem ipsius qui caro nostra factus est transeamus.}'
'Idem in sermone de Ieiunio **mensis septimi.** Hanc **(inquit)** confessionem dilectissimi ... non habebitis vitam in **vobis**, **sic** sanctae mensae communicare debetis ... quod accipitur, disputatur.'[201] (fol. 80r)	'Rursus {in sermone de ieiunio **mensis septimi:** Hanc, **inquit,** confessionem dilectissimi ... non habebitis vitam in **vobis: sic** sanctae mensae communicare debetis ... quod accipitur, disputatur.}'	'LEO IN SERMONE DE IEIVNIO *SEPTIMI MENSIS.* [ca.3] *Hanc confessionem dilectissimi ... non habebitis uitam in uobis. Sic sanctae mensae communicare debetis ... quod accipitur, disputatur*}.'
'Idem in Epistola ad Anastasium Thessalonicensem Episcopum suum per Orientem legatum: Aliter enim ... sacramentum propitiationis exequitur.' (fol. 80r)	'Item {in epistola ad Anastasium Thessalonicensem episcopum suum per Orientem legatum: Aliter enim ... sacramentum propitiationis exequitur:}'	
		[Leo, in sermone de ieiunio septimi mensis, ca. 2] '{Fides catholica quae ... qui Deus est}.'

- The CGC extract from Leo's *Letter 59 to the clergy and people of Constantinople* is addressed to '*ad Constantinoplitanos*' as

---

[201] CGC I, 80r, lacks 'Christi' in 'de veritate corpis Christi et sanguinis', due to a copyist's error, since both CL 258 and CL 234 include it.

in Pigge, but '*Constantinopolitanis*' in Oecolampadius, and both CGC and Pigge have only '*omnium ore*' whereas Oecolampadius has '*in omnium ore*'.
- Both the CGC's and Pigge's quotation from Leo's *Sermon 91 on the Fast of the Seven Month* include '*inquit*', but this insertion in the text is lacking in Oecolampadius. Both CGC and Pigge follow the same order in '*mensis septimi*', whereas Oecolampadius has '*septimi mensis*'. Both CGC and Pigge include the clause beginning with '*sic*' as part of the previous sentence. Oecolampadius has it begin the next.
- The passage ascribed to Leo's *Letter to Anastasius*[202] is found in both CGC and Pigge, but not Oecolampadius.
- Cranmer's second bracketed extract from Leo's *Sermon 91* in his copy of the *Dialogus* is not found in CGC, but it is included along with the first extract (albeit in a more polished form) in Cranmer's later Edwardian eucharistic commonplaces: 'Leo primus de ieiunio septimi mensis sermone 6 fides catholica quae . . . qui deus est. Et Mox. Hanc confessionem dilectissimi . . . quod accipitur disputatur'.[203]

In the light of all this evidence, it seems indisputable that the three quotations from Leo I found in 'Cranmer's Great Commonplaces' were copied out from Cranmer's copy of Pigge's *Hierarchiae ecclesiasticae assertio*, not his copy of Oecolampadius' *Dialogus*.

The next question we need to ask is whether there is any further overlap between Cranmer's copy of Pigge, his copy of Oecolampadius and his 'Great Commonplaces'. Of the remaining seven fathers cited by Brooks, only Cyril is found both on Brooks' list and in CL 258's bracketed material, yet here the conundrum only deepens. On the one hand, five bracketed quotations from Cyril in Pigge were indisputably recorded in 'Cranmer's Great Commonplaces'.[204] On the other hand,

---

[202] *Recte, Letter 80 to Anatolius.*
[203] Bibliothèque nationale de France Latin MS 3396, fol. 128r-v.
[204] *Cf.*, Cyrillus, 'Dixit ergo ... sed ipsum verum': CL 258, fol. 30r, and CGC I, fol. 84v; 'Mortui sunt inquit ... vivificat ista caro': CL 258, fol. 30v, and CGC I, fol. 84v; 'Itaque quae pauloante ... olio opus habet': CL 258, fol. 30v, and CGC I, fol. 85r; 'Litigabant ad haec ... impossibile apud deum': CL 258, fol. 30v, and

two further quotations from Cyril are not derived from Pigge, but are indeed found in the *Dialogus*. The first is an extended extract from Cyril's commentary on John 6, the second a shorter quotation on John 15.[205] Yet, as we noted earlier, neither are bracketed in CL 234.[206] Finally, to make matters even more interesting, the lengthy quotation from Cyril's commentary on John 6 found in both the *Dialogus* and 'Cranmer's Great Commonplaces' is also found in Pigge's more extensive extracts from Cyril, but in a different translation.

'Great Commonplaces' CGC I, fols 82v-84v	Oecolampadius's *Dialogus* CL 234, fols 136r-137r	Pigge's *Hierarchiae* CL 258, fols 30v-31v
Nam cum oporteret eos qui divinam virtutem saluatoris, ac potestatem ... gustu, tactu, et cibo ad immortalitatem reduceretur.	Nam cum oporteret eos qui diuinam virtutem Saluatoris ac potestatem ... gustu, tactu, et cibo ad immortalitatem reduceretur.	Oportuisset sane eos, qui diuinam Saluatoris virtutem ac potestatem ... gustu, tactu, et cibo ad immortalitatem reduceretur.

Finally, the bracketed quotation in Pigge beginning with '*Litigabant ad haec Iudaei*' slightly overlaps with the beginning of the extract from John 6 in the *Dialogus*, resulting in 'Cranmer's Great Commonplaces' having two different translations of the same text recorded in separate entries:

| CGC I, fol. 84v: 'Cirillus in Iohannem Ca. 6. Nam cum oporteret eos qui divinam virtutem salvatoris, ac potestatem signorum miraculo perceperunt sermonem eius libenter suscipere, et si qua difficilia videbantur, eorum solutionem quaerere, contra | CGC I, fol. 85r: '[Cirillus, li. 4, ca. 23] ... Oportuisset sane eos, qui divinam salvatoris virtutem ac potestatem, tot signorum miraculo perceperunt, eius sermoni credere et si qua difficilia videbantur, humiliter inquirere, et petere eorum elucidationem. At contra hii de deo |

CGC I, fol. 85r; 'Audientes enim: Nisi ... et commendavit) cognoverant': CL 258, fol. 32r, and CGC I, fol. 85r.
[205] *Cf.* Extract from Cyril on John 6: CL 234, fols 136r-137r, and CGC I, 82v-84r; Extract from Cryil on John 15: CL 234, fol. 136r, and CGC I, 84r-v.
[206] CL 234, fol. 136r-137r.

omnino faciunt, et quomodo potest hic carnem suam nobis dare, de deo non sine magna impietate conclamant, nec in mentem venit, nihil impossibile esse[207] apud deum.'	non sine magna impietate conclamant. Quomodo hic potest carnem suam nobis dare? nec in mentem venit nihil impossibile esse[208] apud deum.'

Clearly, Pigge was a source for the quotations from Cyril, but not the only one. Is the *Dialogus* the other source, as Brooks has suggested?

To help us answer that question, we next need to return to that third quotation from Leo I bracketed with red ink in CL 234, the second extract from Leo's *Sermon 59 on the Fast of the Seventh Month VI*. Although not found in 'Cranmer's Commonplaces', it is included in Cranmer's later Edwardian eucharistic commonplaces. That would suggest that the red ink annotations in CL 234 date from that period. An annotation beside the quotation from Irenaeus, Book 5, page 294, would seem to corroborate that view. Written in a slightly different shade of red ink, Cranmer's *marginalium* cross-references the text: 'Read the response afterwards on folio 162'.[209] This annotation draws the reader's attention to the fact that early on in the *Dialogus*, Oecolampadius quotes Philipp Melanchthon's *Sententiae veterum aliquot scriptorum de Coena Domini* in full in order to the subsequently refute its arguments.[210] Interestingly, the quotations from Leo bracketed in CL 234 come from Oecolampadius' refutation of Melanchthon. They are not found in the *Sententiae* itself.

'Cranmer's Great Commonplaces', however, do draw directly on the *Sententiae*. In the contemporary debate section of the eucharistic locus, fols 115v-117r record a lengthy extract from Melanchthon arguing for a literal interpretation of "This is my body."[211] Hence, the next question we need to consider is whether the quotations Brooks cited as coming

---

[207] CL 234: 'esse impossibile'.
[208] CL 258: 'esse impossibile'.
[209] Cranmer's *marginalium* in red ink: 'lege responsum post fo. 162'; CL 234, fol. 138v.
[210] Philipp Melanchthon, *Sentenciae Veterum aliquot scriptorum, de Coena Domini, bona fide recitatae* (Wittenberg: Joseph Klug, 1530).
[211] *Cf.* CGC I, 115v-117r, and Melanchthon, *Sententiae*, sigs C4r-[C6]r.

from the *Dialogus* were among those Oecolampadius had taken over from Melanchthon. In fact, seven quotations in 'Cranmer's Great Commonplaces' which Brooks has attributed to the *Dialogus* also exactly match Melanchthon's *Sententiae*.

'Cranmer's Great Commonplaces' I	Melanchthon's *Sententiae*
Fol. 81r: '[Ciprianus] de coena domini. Panis iste, quem dominus discipulis porrigebit . . . usque ad participationem spiritus.'	Sig. B5r-v : 'CYPRIANVS IN SERMONE DE COENA DOMINI . . . PANIS ISTE QVEM DOMINus discipulis porrigebat . . . usque ad participationem spiritus.'
Fol. 81r-v: 'Irenaeus li. 5. Contra Valentinum. pa. 29. Vani autem omni modo qui universam dispositionem Dei contemnunt . . . qui est uita aeterna, quae sanguine et corpore Christi nutritur.'	Sig. 'IRENEVS LIB. V. CONtra Valenti. Pagi. 294. Vani autem omni modo qui uniuersam dispositionem Dei contemnunt . . . qui est uita aeterna, quae sanguine et corpore Christi nutritur.'
Fols 82v-83r: 'Cirillus in Iohannem Ca. 6. Nam cum operteret eos . . . arroganita magna significatur?'	Sigs a5v-[A7]r: 'CYRILLVS IN CAP. SEXTO IOHANNIS . . . NAM CVM OPORTEret eos . . . arroganita magna significatur?'
Fols 83r-84r: 'Et Mox. Amen Amen dico vobis, nisi manducaverits . . . gustu, tactu, et cibo ad immortalitatem reduceretur.'	Sigs [A7]r-[A8]v: 'ET DEINDE. AMEN AMEN DICO uobis, nisi manducaueritis . . . gustu, tactu, et cibo ad immortalitatem reduceretur.'
Fol. 84r-v: 'Idem in Iohannem. Ca. 15. Non tamen negamus recta nos fide . . . nisi naturalis vitae corpus ei coniungeretur.'	Sig. A5r-v: 'CYRILLVS IN CAP. XV. IOHANNIS . . . 'NON TAMEN NEGAmus recta nos fide . . . nisi naturalis uitae corpus ei coniungeretur.'
Fol. 86r-v: '[Christostomus] in Iohannem Capitus 6. Homilia 45. Quando enim subit quaestio, quomodo aliquid fiat . . . Hoc enim amantium maxime est.'	Sig. B1r-v: 'CHRYSOSTOMVS IN VI. CAP. IOHAN. HOMILIA XLV. QUANDO ENIM Svbit quaestio quomodo aliquid fiat . . . Hoc enim amantium maxime est.'
Fol. 86v: 'Idem. de sacerdotum dignitate. O ingens miraculum . . . dat se volentibus circundare et complecti.'	Sig.B2v: 'CHYRSOSTOMVS DE DIGNITATE SAcerdotum . . . O ingens miraculum . . . dat se uolentibus circundare et complecti.'

A further quotation from Hilary cited by Brooks would appear to be an interesting mixture of adding a short beginning from Pigge to a long extract found in the *Dialogus* but which is also identical to Melanchthon:

'Great Commonplaces' I, fols 85r-86r	*Hierarchiae ecclesiae assertio* CL 258, fols 33v-34r	Melanchthon's *Sententiae*, sigs B3v-B5r
'Hilarius. li. 8. De trinitate *Si enim vere verbum caro factum est... Quia in Christo Pater* (fol. 86r) *et Christus in nobis, unum in hiis esse nos faciunt.* Si vere igitur carnem corporis nostri Christus assumpsit... Anne hoc veritas non est? **Contingat plane his verum non esse, qui Christum Iesum uerum esse Deum negant. Est ergo ipse in nobis per carnem, et sumus in eo, dum secum hoc quod nos sumus, in deo est.** Quod autem in eo per sacramentum... et vos in me, et ego in vobis. **Si voluntatis tantum unitatem intelligi vellet... quod autem naturaliter in nobis, haec vnitas sit** ... cum ipse viuat per patrem ? **Item. Haec autem idcirco commemorata sunt a nobis ... naturalis unitatis sit praedicandum.**'	'*Eos nunc,* inquit, qui inter patrem et filium . . . Si enim vere verbum caro factum est . . . Quia in Christo pater et Christus in nobis, unum in his esse nos faciunt.* Si vere igitur carnem corporis nostri Christus assumpsit . . . An ne hoc veritas non est? & caetera. Quod autem in eo per sacramentum . . . et vos in me, et ego in vobis, & caetera. Quod autem in nobis naturalis haec vnitas sit . . . cum ipse viuat per patrem?' [Cranmer	'HILARIVS LIBRO OCTAVO DE TRINITATE SI VERE IGITVR carnem corporis nostri Christus assumpsit . . . Anne hoc ueritas non est? **Contingat plane his uerum non esse, qui Christum Iesum uerum esse Deum negant. Est ergo in nobis ipse per carnem, et sumus in eo, dum secum hoc quod nos sumus, in Deo est.** Quod autem in eo per sacramentum . . . et uos in me, et ego in uobis, **Si voluntatis tantum unitatem intelligi uellet ... quod autem naturaliter in nobis haec unitas sit** . . . cum uiuat ipse per patrem ?

		marginalia: 'Hilarius' with quotation marks.]	Item. Haec autem idcirco commemorata sunt a nobis .. . naturalis unitatis sit praedicandum.'

One further extract from Irenaeus found in 'Cranmer's Great Commonplaces' is mostly found also in the *Sententiae* which was exactly taken over into the *Dialogus*.

'Cranmer's Great Commonplaces' I, 81v	*Sententiae*, sig. [B6]r
'[Irenaeus], li. 4, contra Valentinum, pa. 237. *Quomodo autem constabit . . . mundi filum dicant. Et Mox.* Quomodo autem rursus dicunt carnem in corruptionem devenire, et non percipere vitam, quae a corpore domini et sanguine alitur? Et paulo post. Quemadmodum enim qui est **in** terra panis percipiens vocationem dei, iam non communis panis est, sed eucharistia ex duabus rebis constans, terrena et coelestis [recte, coelesti] sic et corpora nostra percipientia eucharistiam, iam non sunt corruptibilia *spem resurrectionis habentia*.'	'Ireneus . . . lib. 4. Contra Valent. Pag. 237. Quomodo autem rursus dicunt carnem in corruptionem deuenire, et non percipere uitam, quae a corpore domini et sanguine alitur. Et paulo post Quemadmodum enim qui est *a* terra panis percipiens uocationem Dei, iam non communis panis est, sed eucharistia ex duabus rebis constans terrena et coelesti sic et corpora nostra percipiencia Eucharistiam, iam non sunt corruptibilia, etc.'[212]

Only two of the authors cited by Brooks are found in the *Dialogus* and not in the *Sententiae*, but their quotations show far less congruity to the entries in the 'Great Commonplaces' than the others. Less than a third of the passage from Gelasius in the *Dialogus* is found in the 'Great Commonplaces'. Moreover, they offer different titles, and even in this brief extract their texts clearly diverge at two points:

---

[212] *Cf.* CL 234, fol. 138v.

'Great Commonplaces', fol. 79v	CL 234, fol. 153v
'[Gelasius] adversus Eutichen et Nestorium. Certe sacramenta quae sumimus, corporis et sanguinis Christi, divina res **est**. propter quod, et per eadem, divinae efficimur consortes naturae, et tamen **esse non desunt** substantia vel natura panis et vini.'	'GELASIVS PAPA IN CONCILIO ROMANO. Certe sacramenta quae sumimus corporis et sanguinis Christi, divina res *sunt,* propter quod et per eadem, diuinae efficimur consortes naturae, et tamen *non desinit esse* substantia uel natura panis et vini.'

Similar issues are found with the last of Brooks' quotations, two entries in the 'Great Commonplaces' from Jerome's *Epistle 120 to Hebibia*. The Commonplace material is found within a twice-as-large, single block in the *Dialogus*, and both the ascription and several aspects of the text differ:

'Great Commonplaces', fol. 89v	CL 234, fol. 148r
'Hieronimi **hedibiae Quaestio 2. Quidam** mille annorum fabulam struunt . . . in quibus Christum regnaturum **corporaliter esse** contendunt, et bibiturum vinum, quod ex illo tempore usque ad consummationem mundi non biberit. Nos autem audiamus, **panem, et quem** fregit dominus deditque **discipulis suis,** esse corpus domini salvatoris, **ipso dicente ad eos. Accipite et comedite, hoc** est corpus meum, et Calicem illum esse, de quo iterum locutus est. Bibite ex hoc omnes, Hic est sanguis meus, novi testamenti qui pro multis **effundetur. Et. Mox. Si ergo** panis qui de caelo descendit, **corpus domini est**, et vinum, quod discipulis dedit, **sanguis illius est,** novi testamenti **qui pro multis effusus est** in remissionem peccatorum: Iudaicas fabulas repellamus.'	HIERONYMVS *AD HEdibiam, in dictum Domini, Non bibab amodo, etc. Ex hoc loco quidam* mille annorum fabulam struunt, in quibus Christum regnaturum *esse corporaliter* contendunt, et bibiturum uinum quod ex illo tempore usque ad consummationem mundi non biberit. Nos autem audiamus, *panem* quem fregit Dominus, deditque *discipulis,* esse corpus Domini saluatoris, *dicente ipso, Hoc* est corpus meum: et calicem illum esse, de quo iterum locutus est, Bibite ex hoc omnes. Hic est enim calix noui testamenti, qui pro multis *effundetur in remissionen peccatorum . . . Si enim* panis qui de caelo descendit *est corpus Domini,* et uinum quod discipulis dedit *sanguis est illius* noui testamenti, *qui effunditur* in remissionem peccatorum: Iudaicas fabulas

	repellamus . . . *quod est regnum patris.*

Finally, none of these texts from Gelasius and Jerome are bracketed in CL 234.²¹³ In the light of all these discrepancies, it would seems unlikely that Cranmer used the *Dialogus* as his source for these quotations.

Yet, what of the high correlation between the eight Commonplace entries found in both the *Dialogus* and the *Sententiae*? Since we know that Cranmer had a copy of Melanchthon's *Sententiae* and quoted Melanchthon's real presence argument at length in a different section of the eucharistic *locus* in the 'Great Commonplaces', it seems only logically that Cranmer would have also mined the *Sententiae* for its patristic quotations to support his own view. Presumedly, if Cranmer's copy of the *Sententiae* had survived, we would find the passages which have been recorded in the 'Great Commonplaces' bracketed in Melanchthon's text like they are in Pigge's *Hierarchiae ecclesiasticae assertio*. As Brooks admitted, it would have made much more sense for Cranmer to have drawn on Oecolampadius later, when his views on the Eucharist were shifting toward a more reformed perspective. Thus, in the late 1530s Cranmer's public position and private research both supported a real presence position.

Yet, by 1550 all scholars agree that Cranmer had reversed himself on this crucial issue. In that year he published *A Defence of the True and Catholic doctrine of the sacrament of the body and blood of our Saviour Christ, with a confutation of sundry errors concerning the same, grounded and established upon God's Holy Word, and approved by the consent of the most ancient doctors of the Church.*²¹⁴ In this book, Cranmer adopted a strongly reformed view of the sacrament and argued, as the full title makes clear, that this was the teaching of both Scripture and the early Church. Of course, such claims were the complete opposite of Cranmer's views in the 1530s. What happened?

---

²¹³ CL 234, fols 148r, 153v.
²¹⁴Thomas Cranmer, *A Defence of the True and Catholike doctrine of the sacrament of the body and bloud of our sauiour Christ* (London: Reginald Wolfe, 1550).

While Cranmer never wavered in his commitment to an effectual presence in Holy Communion, he eventually changed his understanding of its mode. This led him in the end to maintain simultaneously two positions. On the one hand, since Christ's ascension, his human body is now located in heaven and totally absent from the earth until his return. Christ is present in this world, in the sacrament, and in believers only by his divinity. To this end, Cranmer quotes in his *Defence* (1550), amongst many other fathers, Cyril of Alexandria: 'Christian people must believe, that although Christ be absent from us as concerning his body, yet by his power he governeth us and all things, and is present with all them that love him'.[215] Because God relates to his people by the Spirit, Cranmer argues that even if Christ's human body were present during Holy Communion, that would be of no supernatural benefit to believers.[216] On the other hand, those with saving faith receive in the sacrament 'Christ himself, whole body and soul, manhood and Godhead' for 'nourishment and augmentation'.[217] How did Cranmer conclude it was possible to have only a spiritual presence of Christ in Holy Communion, yet for it still to be right to teach that in the sacrament a believer was united to the whole Christ? Understandably, not a few scholars have seen in these twin tenets a fundamentally irreconcilable contradiction.[218] I would

---

[215] J. E. Cox, ed., *Writings and Disputations of Thomas Cranmer . . . relative to the Sacrament of the Lord's Supper* (Cambridge: Parker Society, 1844) [Henceforth, Cox I], p. 96.

[216] '[Christ] is in heaven only . . . although sacramentally, as in a sign and figure, he be in the bread and wine, (and so is he also in the water of baptism;) and in them that rightly receive the bread and wine he is in a much more perfection than corporally, (which shall avail them nothings.)', Cox I, p. 183; 'For unto the faithful Christ is at his own holy table present, with his mighty Spirit and grace, and is of them more fruitfully received than if corporally they should receive him bodily present:', *ibid.,* p. 219.

[217] *Ibid.*, p. 25.

[218] Cyril Richardson argued that Cranmer's insistence of Christ's body being confined to heaven (because of his very broad nominalism) conflicted with his realist language of believers' union with Christ both spiritual and corporally. See Cyril Richardson, "Cranmer and the Analysis of Eucharistic Doctrine," *The Journal of Theological Studies* N.S., 16 (1965), 421-37; *Cf.* Jeanes, *Signs of God's Promise*, pp. 6-10; Brian Douglas, *A Companion to Anglican Eucharistic Theology: Volume One, The Reformation to the 19th Century*

suggest we can begin to understand Cranmer and his theological transition by examining his red annotations in his copy of Bibliander's *Letters of Oecolampadius and Zwingli*.

On the one hand, we can now see, *circa* 1538, Cranmer culled many of his patristic quotations in support of the real presence from Pigge and Melanchthon. On the other, it would seem that the red bracketing and associated markings in Cranmer's surviving copy of the *Dialogus* were not made until later, most likely during his period of reassessment in the 1540s when he was moving towards the spiritual presence which Oecolampadius advocated. We may then examine the annotations in Cranmer's copy of Bibliander for insights into the arguments that helped persuade Cranmer to come to his mature twin tenets. Three passages marked-up in red would seem to be particularly helpful.

The first is found at the beginning of the text of Melanchthon's *Sententiae* which was embedded in the *Dialogus*: 'In my judgment, it is enormously rash to establish dogma without having consulted the ancient church.'[219] Such was the view that Cranmer himself had urged upon Vadian back in 1537, but Peters Brooks has outlined a very plausible scenerio whereby in 1546 Cranmer had decided to re-evaluate what that ancient teaching actually was.[220] The spiritual presence

---

(Leiden: Brill, 2012), pp. 87-90. But Cranmer was a Neoplatonist. Consider these words on the sacrament: 'And as in the first creation of the world all living creatures had their first life by God's only word, (for God only spake his word, and all things were created by and by accordingly,) and after their creation he spake these words, "Increase and multiply;" and by the virture of those words all things have gendered and increased ever since that thime; even so after that Christ said, "Eat, this my body;" and "Drink, this is my blood: do this hereafter in remembrance of me;" by virtue of these words, and not by virtue of any man, the bread and wine be so consecrated, that whosoever with a lively faith doth eat that bread and drink that wine, doth spiritually eat, drink, and feed upon Christ sitting in heaven with his Father. And this is the whole meaning of St. Chrysostom,' Cox II, p. 183.

[219] 'Meo quidem iudicio magna est temeritas, dogmata serere non consulta Ecclesia veteri', Cranmer annotation: red-ink underlining, CL 234, fol. 136r. [We can identify the underlining as Cranmer's because of the extensive red-ink Cranmer *marginalia* on fol. 136v.]

[220] Brooks, *Cranmer's Doctrine of the Eucharist*, pp. 38-41.

writings of Ratramnus († *c.* 868) had persuaded Nicholas Ridley to reread the early fathers in their light, after which, he adopted a spiritual understanding of the Lord's presence in the sacrament as the true teaching of the ancient church. At his trial in Oxford, Cranmer readily admitted that it was Ridley who 'by sundry persuasions and authorities of doctors drew me quite from my opinion'.[221] Thus, by his own testimony—following his own instincts, Melanchthon's advice and Ridley's *exempla*—Cranmer's *volte-face* was the result of listening to the ancient church afresh.

The second set of annotations is found in the text of a letter from Oecolampadius to Martin Bucer, dated 3 September 1530. Here the Basel reformer offered his explanation as to how it was possible to insist on a spiritual presence in the Lord's Supper and, not withstanding, also to maintain that believers still received the whole Christ, both spirit and body, in the sacrament.

> And although we may not say that [Christ's] salvific body (*panaceum*) is united with the bread or properly pressed between lips and teeth, we have never said, however, that because of this it can be separated from his divine spirit. On the contrary, we abhor that real separation as the worst plague. For Christ's body or humanity is not therefore divided from his deity, since the latter is immeasurable and everywhere, while the former is, however, circumscribed and occupying a fixed place. We say that his body and blood is nevertheless passed on and received together with the bread and the wine in a symbolic manner through faithful contemplation.[222]

---

[221] Cox II, p. 218.
[222] 'Et quamuis non dicamus corpus illud panaceum, uel pani unitum, uel labijs ac dentibus proprie premi: non tamen ipsum a spiritu diuino ipsius separari propterea unquam diximus, imo separationem illam realem uti

Cranmer responded by underlining the key sentences as shown above and writing in the margin: 'How the true body of Christ is present in the Supper'. That Cranmer used the adjective 'true' beside this description of Christ's body given in the sacrament – a word nowhere found in Oecolampadius's text – would seem to suggest Cranmer now found the Christological argument convincing.

The third significant annotated passage would appear to offer a explanation from the fathers as to why Cranmer came into agreement with Oecolampadius. This set of annotations is in a different shade of red and the script of its *marginalium* slightly smaller, suggesting that it might predate the first. It also comes from the *Dialogus* proper, at the point when the Basel reformer argued that believers were sanctified, made one with Christ and quickened to eternal life through the Holy Spirit, not by Christ's bodily presence within the elements of communion.[223] To show patristic support for his emphasis on the Spirit, Oecolampadius quoted Cyril of Alexandria's exposition of his eleventh anathema against Nestorius:

> {In church we celebrate the holy, life-giving and bloodless sacrifice, not because we believe that the offering is the body of an ordinary person like ourselves, or that the same is true of the precious blood. Rather, we understand the offering to have become the very own body and blood of the all-powerful Word. For ordinary flesh cannot give life, as our Saviour himself testifies: 'The flesh is of no use; it is the Spirit who gives life'.[224] Because the offering has became the Word's own flesh, we therefore deem it life-giving, which it is. As our Saviour himself says, 'Just as the living Father

---

summam pestem execramur. Non enim ideo separatur corpus uel humanitas Christi a deitate, quia haec ubique est ac immensa: illa uero circumscripta, et certum locum occupans. Cum pane etiam ac uino symbolikῶς (sic) nihilominus et contemplatione fidei, corpus et sanguinem tradi et accipi dicimus', CL 234, fol. 128r—Cranmer marginalium: 'Qu*omod*o in c*oe*na sit veru*m* corpus Christi'.
[223] CL 234, fol. 134v
[224] John 6:63 [Vulgate: John 6:64].

sent me and I live because of the Father, the one who feeds on me will live because of me'.²²⁵ Therefore, since Nestorius (and those who agree with him) ignorantly destroy the power of the mystery, he has rightly been anathematized.}²²⁶

Here we can clearly see Cyril's Christology at work, defending the unity of Christ's human and divine natures as one single subject, the Incarnate Word of God, against Nestorius' insistence on maintaining a strict separation between Christ's humanity and divinity when describing his activities, *e.g.*, the man Jesus wept, but God the Logos, raised Lazarus from the dead. Because the Incarnate Word could not be divided, as a single entity, when Jesus' humanity walked the earth, his divinity still filled the heavens. Likewise, as a single entity, when Jesus' humanity ascended to Heaven to be seated at the right hand of God, his divinity still filled the whole earth.²²⁷ Hence, Cyril argued in this text that Christ's flesh in the sacrament gave life because where his body was, his Spirit and its ἐνέργεια, its life-giving powers, were also. Indeed, according to modern scholarship, Cyril developed his

---

[225] John 6:57 [Vulgate: John 6:58].
[226] '{Sanctum ac uiuificum et incruentum in ecclesijs operamur sacrificium, non unius qui sicut nos, et communis hominis corpus esse credentes, quod proponitur, similiter et uenerabilem sanguinem: sed accipientes magis, ut factum proprium corpus, et etiam sanguinem etiam sanguinem omnipotentis uerbi. Communis enim caro uiuificare nequit, cuius testis est ipse Seruator dicens, Caro prodest nihil, spiritus est qui uiuificat: quoniam propria facta est uerbi. Sic igitur cogitatur, et est uiuifica, sicut dicit ipse Seruator: Et sicut misit me uiuens pater, et ego uiuo propter patrem, et qui manducat me uiuet propter me. Quoniam igitur Nestorius, et qui eadem sentient, indocte destruunt mysterij uirtutem, ob hoc et recte factus est anathematismus}', CL 234, fol. 151r—Cranmer marginalia: 'Hic locus quærendus est'; 'Nota'; NB that the black underlinings in the text are not by Cranmer.
[227] See John McGuckin, *Saint Cyril of Alexandria and the Christological Controversy* (Crestwood, N.Y.: Saint Valdimir's Seminary Press, 2004), especially pp. 175-226; Hans van Loon, *The Dyophysite Christology of Cyril of Alexandria* (Leiden: Brill, 2009).

Christology specifically to defend his understanding of Christ's life-giving corporal presence in the elements of the Sacrament.[228]

Yet, we have already seen Oecolampadius apply the principle of an undivided Christ to make the opposite argument, that where his Spirit was, a direct connection to his absent body was also; consequently, his body didn't need to be present in the elements of the sacrament for participants to be united to the spiritual energies of Christ's body. In the *Dialogus* Oecolampdius supplied his patristic confirmation for this claim. Even more important, however, Cyril's doctrine of the *communicatio idiomatum* (communication of properties) is also on display here. The Incarnate Word's union resulted in the Divine Spirit enhancing his human nature, yet without violating the basic nature of either. Hence, Christ's flesh had the power to give eternal life to the fallen flesh of other human beings precisely because it would bear the Spirit to them. Oecolampadius, however, used these very principles to come to the opposite conclusion. Christ's body could only be in heaven, lest the *communicatio idiomatum* destroyed his basic human nature, but that was no impediment to the sacrament giving deepened supernatural life to believers through a spiritual presence, nor for the spiritual presence to connect them to Christ's physical body in heaven, since Christ himself remained undivided. In Cyril's own use of John 6:63 to emphasis the Spirit as the agent of renewal in Holy Communion Oecolampadius found a key patristic source for his own understanding of an effectual presence through the Spirit.

What was Cranmer's response to Oecolampadius' use of Cyril on these key points during his patristic research in the 1540s? After all, Melanchthon had used lengthy quotes from Cyril to argue for a real presence position which Cranmer had duly recorded in his 'Great Commonplaces' during the 1530s.[229] These quotations, however, emphasized the need to avoid the 'Jewish question' of 'how', but rather to believe in God's Omnipotent power. Just as his Word spoken bore supernatural power, so the Word of God uniting to human flesh made his flesh a bearer of his supernatural power. Therefore, receiving

---

[228] See, for example, Henry Chadwick, "Eucharist and Christology in the Nestorian Controversy," *Journal of Theological Studies*, NS 2 (1951), pp. 145-64, especially pp. 153-6.
[229] CGC I, 82v-84v.

Communion is to make Christ dwell in us bodily. Both of these arguments appealed to Cranmer the affective Erasmian humanist turned solifidian. Belief united a person to God, and God worked this miracle through the supernatural power of his Word written. Oecolampadius, however, was making a very different argument based on Cyril. So ever the cautious scholar, he now bracketed the whole passage, drew a red line in the margin beside it, marked it with his symbol for 'Note!' and wrote, 'This place must be examined'. And that is precisely what he did.

Cranmer eventually commissioned a major theological research project dedicated to the Eucharist, from which would eventually emerge his book *A Defence of the True and Catholike Doctrine of the Sacrament of the Body and Bloud of our Sauiour Christ*.[230] The working papers for this project are now found in BnF Latin MS 3396. Almost three hundred folio pages of quotations on the Eucharist listed by author from over 40 major theologians from Dionysius to Innocent III. Given Cranmer's humanist preference for ancient authors, twenty-five of these authorial *loci* were from theologians who lived prior to 500 AD, and many of their works were read in course through editions of their collected works, with volume and folio number duly recorded in order of their appearance in the latest editions. In the light of all the comments about Cranmer's lack of interest in context, the length of the individual quotations from his major authors in the collection is just as important, and indeed as impressively large, as the number of them. Consider his entries from Augustine, his largest authorial commonplace. Forty-four per cent of this section consists of extracts that are at least a full folio-page long. The extracts from Chrysostom's *locus* are even longer. Seventy per cent of material from Cranmer's number-two theologian consists of quotations that are at least one-folio-page long, and forty-five per cent are at least two-folio-pages long.

And in BnF Latin MS 3396 are found twenty-seven folio pages focusing on the concept that the Spirit of the undivided Christ gives life through

---

[230] Thomas Cranmer, *A Defence of the True and Catholike Doctrine of the Sacrament of the Body and Bloud of our Sauiour Christ* (London: Reyner Wolfe, 1550).

the sacrament.²³¹ It may be worth noting that Cranmer's two extant copies of Cyril both date from 1546, suggesting, perhaps, that his questioning of the eucharistic presence in that year led him to acquire the latest editions of Cyril. What he clearly found there were not only numerous examples of Cyril's emphasis on the Spirit working immortality in the flesh of fallen human beings through Holy Communion, but also holiness through the renewing of their affections.

> Thus through many various ways the gracious mercy of God likes to draw human nature away from the desire for transitory things. <u>For although the lust of the flesh, like a great stony weight, presses down on our nature to seek what is passing away and so, as a tyrant, reduce us to its control, Christ brings us around, as if with a bridle, to the longing for better things.</u>²³²

In the light of such research into Cyril's writings, we can understand why Cranmer felt he was able to underline Oecolampadius' description of the spiritual presence and pen a positive endorsement.

The largest contributors to Cranmer's authorial commonplaces on the Eucharist were Augustine (24%), Chrysostom (19%) and Cyril (10%). Although Walsh thought the Greek East was 'all but a closed book' for Cranmer,²³³ it was in fact there that he found the patristic grounds for holding his mature, seemingly mutually exclusive, twin tenets on Holy Communion. While modern scholars are free to dispute the accuracy of Cranmer's construal of Cyril as well as the other historic theologians in his notebooks on the sacrament, it would no longer seem tenable to

---

[231] BnF Latin MS 3396, fols 65v-77v, 82. For the quotation from Cyril's explanation of the eleventh anathema Oecolampadius used in the *Dialogus*, see fol. 74v.

[232] 'Ita gratia et misericordia dei, vel a cupiditate caducarum rerum, variis multisque modis humanam solet reuocare naturam. <u>Nam quum ut, magni ponderis lapis ad haec instabilia carnis premat appetitus, et tyrannice ad imperium suum redigat, quasi freno ad desiderium rerum meliorum Christus nos circumducit</u>', *ibid.,* fol. 66r; see also fol. 70r.

[233] Walsh, 'Cranmer and the Fathers', p. 242.

claim that he had not thoroughly studied their writings in context, nor that his mature thinking was not influenced by their reasoning.[234]

---

[234] For more on how Cranmer adopted Cyril's reasoning for his description and defence of a spiritual presence, see Ashley Null, 'Thomas Cranmer', in *Christian Theologies of the Sacraments: A Comparative Introduction*, eds Justin S. Holcomb and David A. Johnson (New York, N.Y.: NYU Press, 2017), pp. 219-233.

Reformation Cathedrals: Anomalies or Opportunities?[235]

Edward Loane

In July 2019, Rochester Cathedral pioneered a new and innovative ministry in the centre of its grand medieval nave: a nine-hole mini golf course.[236] The course was designed to help visitors reflect on the engineering of nearby Rochester bridge. It was free for visitors to play golf in the cathedral and Rev. Rachel Phillips hoped that while playing, "visitors will reflect on the bridges that need to be built in their own lives and in our world today."[237] Not to be outdone, the following month Norwich Cathedral installed a helter-skelter in its nave and the bishop began giving his sermons from it.[238] These new ventures raise important questions: what is the purpose of Anglican cathedrals, and how successful have cathedrals been in achieving their purpose? These questions are not only relevant when reflecting on contemporary cathedral ministry, they have perplexed scholars of the sixteenth century English reformation. Indeed, Diarmaid MacCulloch has described cathedrals as the "anomaly" of the Reformed Protestant Church of England.[239] He claims that the English cathedrals "survived as institutions with virtually all their medieval infrastructure" which "is

---

[235] This chapter is an expanded and developed argument that was originally published in "Anglican Cathedrals and Sydney Anglicanism: The Shape of Cathedral Ministry and Mission" in Ed Loane (ed.), *Proclaiming Christ in the Heart of the City: Ministry at St Andrew's Cathedral, Sydney* (Sydney: Lulu, 2019).

[236] "Rochester Cathedral opens crazy golf course to tee-up younger generation," *Sky News*, 30 July 2019, https://news.sky.com/story/rochester-cathedral-opens-crazy-golf-course-to-tee-up-younger-generation-11773227

[237] Ibid.

[238] "Norwich Cathedral: Bishop Delivers Sermon from Helter-Skelter," *BBC News*, 18 August 2019, https://www.bbc.com/news/uk-england-norfolk-49389623

[239] Diarmaid MacCulloch, "Matters Overlooked," in *All Things Made New: Writings on the Reformation* (London: Allen Lane, 2016), 7.

a puzzle," as no other Protestant church was like this.[240] The cathedrals, he argues, "were an ideological subversion of the Church of England as re-established in 1559."[241] In fact, this interpretation is a self-acknowledged "major theme" in many of MacCulloch's writings and represents a widely accepted scholarly belief among historians of the English Reformation.[242] For example, James Saunders said "cathedrals never became much more than 'half reformed', monuments to the 'uneasy compromise' of Elizabethan religion."[243] Charles Knighton claimed that "The English cathedral service ... remains an essentially catholic form of worship, quite at odds with the intentions of sixteenth-century reformers. The consequence has been a typically English compromise, the Anglican *via media*, catholic and reformed."[244] MacCulloch, who has been one of the most vocal and successful opponents of the notion that the English Reformation was designed as a compromise, a *via media* between Rome and Geneva,[245] just finds cathedrals a conundrum. He maintains that it is not clear

---

[240] Diarmaid MacCulloch, "The Making of the Prayer Book," in *All Things Made New: Writings on the Reformation* (London: Allen Lane, 2016), 146.
[241] Ibid.
[242] Diamaid MacCulloch, *Thomas Cromwell: A Life* (London: Allen Lane, 2018), 421, fn. 70; "The Nature of Anglicanism," in *All Things Made New: Writings on the Reformation* (London: Allen Lane, 2016), 360: cf. Peter Marshall, *Reformation England: 1480–1642* (London: Bloomsbury, 2012), 143, 225.
[243] James Saunders, "The Limitations of Statutes: Elizabethan Schemes to Reform New Foundation Cathedral Statutes," *JEH* 48/3 (July 1997), 466. Saunders is quoting D. Marcombe, "Cathedrals and Protestantism: The Search for a New Identity, 1540–1660," in D. Marcombe and C.S. Knighton (eds.), *Close Encounters: English Cathedrals and Society Since 1540*, (Nottingham: University of Nottingham, 1991), 51.
[244] C.S. Knighton, "Westminster Abbey from Reformation to Revolution," in C.S. Knighton and Richard Mortimer (eds.) *Westminster Abbey Reformed, 1540–1640* (Aldershot: Ashgate, 2003), 7.
[245] E.g., Diarmaid MacCulloch, "The Myth of the English Reformation," *Journal of British Studies* 30/1 (Jan 1991):1-19.

why cathedrals were retained but posits it had "a lot to do with the personal preferences of Queen Elizabeth."[246]

My intention in this chapter is to explore the place of cathedrals in the Reformed Church of England. Rather than being institutions that maintained "virtually all of their medieval infrastructure" and were an "anomaly" in the English Reformation, we will see that cathedrals were radically reformed during the sixteenth century. Furthermore, they were deliberately retained because of the strategic gospel opportunities the cathedrals offered the cause of reform. In order to make this assessment we need to briefly give an account of the nature of cathedral ministry in the early sixteenth century.

In 1530 there were seventeen dioceses in England and four dioceses in Wales which were included in the province of Canterbury. Each diocese was governed by a bishop and the central church in which the bishop had his seat, or *cathedra*, was known as the diocesan cathedral. Each diocese had a cathedral, in fact, two English dioceses (the Diocese of Bath and Wells and the Diocese of Coventry and Lichfield) had two cathedrals.[247] These cathedrals were some of the grandest structures in the world. For example, when the towers of Lincoln Cathedral were completed in 1311 it became the tallest building in the world, surpassing the Great Pyramid in Egypt. Millions of visitors each year continue to be awestruck by the English medieval cathedrals and one can only imagine what the ordinary person of five hundred years ago must have thought about these buildings that towered over the entire built environment.

There were several aspects of late medieval cathedral ministry that are worth taking notice of. Firstly, a key feature of cathedral life was that they were centres of pilgrimage. The veneration of saints led to cathedrals accumulating large collections of relics which were purported to bring people closer to God. The people of England flocked

---

[246] Diarmaid MacCulloch, "Putting the English Reformation on the Map," in *All Things Made New: Writings on the Reformation* (London: Allen Lane, 2016), 213.
[247] Bath and Wells is still a united diocese while Coventry and Litchfield was divided into separate dioceses in 1877.

to them, from Canterbury Cathedral in the east, where Thomas Becket was martyred, to Hereford Cathedral in the west, where St Thomas Cantilupe was venerated.[248] Industries arose around this religious tourism and vast amounts of wealth accumulated.

Secondly, we should note the prevalence of monastic foundations among the cathedrals. Out of the nineteen English cathedrals, ten were monastic which were each run by the prior and the monastery supplied the large number of personnel required to keep the cathedral functioning. On the other hand, the nine secular cathedrals were each under the control of the dean who was supported by various other officials (sub-dean, chancellor, precentor etc.). The two dioceses with two cathedrals (Bath/Wells and Coventry/Litchfield) were in that position because the attempt to move the dioceses from having a secular cathedral to a monastic one failed and the compromise was to have both.

Another important theological driver of cathedral ministry was the doctrine of purgatory and the benefits that could be attained for the dead by the living. So a third aspect of the medieval cathedral ministry was the significant place given to endowed "chantries" where mass could be said for the patron. The architecture of Norman cathedrals demonstrate this theology with numerous side chapels allowing mass to be said continually. For an example of what this was like, in 1535 Lincoln Cathedral had fifty-four priests working in it.[249] These priests used no less than twenty-seven altars within the cathedral and it is estimated each altar would have been used for mass perhaps forty times every day.[250] Lincoln was a large secular cathedral but these

---

[248] Stanford Lehmberg "Reformation to Restoration, 1535-1660", in G.E. Aylmer and J.E. Tiller (eds.), *Hereford Cathedral: A History* (Hambledon Press: London, 2000), 88.
[249] A.G. Dickens, *The English Reformation* (Second ed. University Park, PA: University of Pennsylvania Press, 1989), 232.
[250] D. Lepine, *A Brotherhood of Canons Serving God: English Secular Cathedrals in the Later Middle Ages* (Woodbridge, Su.: Boydell and Brewer, 1995), 7–9. Cited in Ian Atherton, "Cathedrals," in Anthony Milton (ed.) *The Oxford History of Anglicanism Volume 1: Reformation and Identity, c 1520–1662* (Oxford, OUP, 2017), 228–242: 233.

figures give an important insight into a dominant aspect of medieval cathedral ministry just as the English reformation was taking hold.

Another driver of cathedral ministry, along with wider ministry in England was that the liturgy was said in Latin. The majority of people who came to cathedrals for spiritual nourishment, whether locals or pilgrims, would not have understood much of what was being said. This is why bells were used in the mass to indicate the point of consecration which was the most important aspect of the mass for the people to witness. So, cathedral naves were often bustling with people moving from the sound of one bell to the sound of another in order to be blessed by seeing the host. Medieval cathedral liturgy was also heavily musical and those employed by cathedrals included precentors, vicars choral and choristers who sang the Latin services.

So, we have observed a number of significant aspects of medieval cathedral ministry in England. They were pilgrimage centres usually attracting people through relic collections. Many cathedrals were monastic foundations depending on the resources of the monastery to keep the ministry functioning. Nevertheless, even secular cathedrals had very large staff teams with lots of priests saying mass multiple times per day at lots of different altars in the cathedrals and all of this in Latin. With this background in mind, how true is MacCulloch's claim that English cathedrals kept "the whole medieval shebang"?[251]

Firstly, it is worth observing the changes in cathedral ministry from 1535 until the death of Henry in 1547. Back in the 1520s Cardinal Wolsey had begun negotiating with Rome to reform English dioceses, monasteries and cathedrals. While he only saw minor outcomes from these plans, his secretary from that time, Thomas Cromwell, was able to instigate some of the most significant ecclesiastical changes through the following decade. Three significant legal innovations were to have profound effects. Firstly, 1538 was a very significant year as Cromwell issued the Second Royal Injunctions of Henry VIII. These injunctions began the movement of bringing the vernacular into church practice by declaring that by the following Easter every church was to have "one

---

[251] MacCulloch, "The Nature of Anglicanism", 360.

book of the whole Bible of the largest volume in English..."[252] Furthermore, every Sunday one sentence of the *Pater Noster*, Creed or Ten Commandments was to be plainly recited in English so the people could learn them by heart.[253] Significantly, these injunctions also backed up the 1536 injunctions in condemning images, relics and pilgrimages revering them and commanded that parishioners must be admonished "that images serve for none other purpose but as to be books of unlearned men" and they are "an occasion of so great an offence to God, and so great a danger to the souls of his loving subjects".[254] The abolition of pilgrimages and relics undermined a major aspect of medieval cathedral practice, but this was just the beginning of more far-reaching changes.

Institutionally, one of the most dramatic changes wrought in English church history was the dissolution of the monasteries. As more than half of the English cathedrals were monastic foundations the implications of this change for cathedrals was profound. Norwich was the first monastic cathedral to be refounded on 2 May 1538. The prior and twenty-one monks were dispensed from habit and rule of their order and were translated into the dean, canons and prebendaries.[255] Norwich was unique in that the other monastic cathedral foundations did not transition quite as smoothly. In the two diocese which had two cathedrals, the monastic cathedrals of Bath and Coventry simply lost their status and the dioceses were left with one cathedral. Between December 1540 and September 1542 the seven other monastic cathedrals which had been dissolved were refounded, along with the

---

[252] Walter Frere (ed.), "The Second Royal Injunctions of Henry VIII" in *Visitation Articles and Injunctions of the Period of the Reformation Vol. 2: 1536–1558* (London: Longmans, Green and Co, 1910), 35.
[253] Ibid., 36.
[254] Ibid., 38. Cf. 39. Walter Frere (ed.), "The First Royal Injunctions of Henry VIII" in *Visitation Articles and Injunctions of the Period of the Reformation Vol. 2: 1536–1558* (London: Longmans, Green and Co, 1910), 5–6.
[255] Ralph Houlbrooke "Refoundation and Reformation, 1538–1628" in *Norwich Cathedral: Church, Cathedral and Diocese, 1096–1996* (London: The Hambledon Press, 1996), 507.

elevation of six new cathedrals for new dioceses.[256] These were clearly new royal foundations and in each case there had been time elapse between the dissolution of the monastery and the establishment of the cathedral.[257] In 1547 the Norwich foundation was made to conform with the other new foundations and in 1550 the Diocese of Westminster was suppressed which meant that in twelve years England had moved from having nineteen cathedrals (ten monastic and nine secular) to having twenty two cathedrals (nine ancient foundations and thirteen new foundations). This was to remain the *status quo*, apart for the commonwealth years, for the best part of three hundred years.

The significance of Henry's reforms to most of the English cathedrals should not be underestimated. Unlike the existing secular cathedrals, the thirteen new ones were to function with a dramatically reduced staff. Prior to the Reformation the number of people associated with monastic cathedral ministry was significantly larger than in secular cathedrals.[258] Yet the largest of the former monastic cathedrals (Canterbury, Winchester, and Durham) were established with only twelve canons.[259] The others had even fewer ranging down to the miserly Carlisle Cathedral which was forced to operate with just four canons. Furthermore, the community life of each new cathedral foundation marked a decisive break with the past and a clear distinction between the chapter, who governed the cathedral, and the other minor canons emerged which had not been present in earlier monastic foundations.[260] The cathedrals of Henry's England were radically changed during the last ten years of his reign.

---

[256] These were the first new dioceses since the twelfth century. Henry's new dioceses were Bristol, Chester, Gloucester, Peterborough, Westminster and Oxford. Oxford began with Osney Abbey as its cathedral but in 1545 this was changed to the newly built Christchurch College chapel, thus being the only newly built cathedral of the period.
[257] Houlbrooke "Refoundation and Reformation", 508.
[258] Stanford E. Lehmberg, *The Reformation of Cathedrals* (Princeton: Princeton University Press, 1988), 39.
[259] For an account of the changes through this period in a particular cathedral cf. Elizabeth Biggs, "Durham Cathedral and Cuthbert Tunstall: A Cathedral and its Bishop during the Reformation, 1530–1559", *Journal of Ecclesiastical History* (2019).
[260] Houlbrooke "Refoundation and Reformation", 510.

Nevertheless, as significant as these alterations to cathedral ministry were, it should be remembered that Henry was tenaciously conservative in his understanding of the central aspect of medieval piety: the mass. As such, the main focus of cathedral ministry remained unchanged despite the break with Rome. Even though the Bible was in English, services continued to be conducted in Latin throughout Henry's reign making them incomprehensible for the general population. The most significant and enduring reformation of ministry in England took place in the reign of Henry's son, Edward VI. Under the guidance of Archbishop Cranmer, the English church experienced a theological and liturgical Reformation of greater consequence than the structural changes that Henry had overseen.

One of the first pieces of Edwardian legislation in 1547 was an Act to abolish chantries. The theological departure from what had gone before was important. Even Henry's last will and testament provided £600 to perpetually endow two priests to say mass for him for "as long as the world shall endure." Needless to say, the world endured longer than the masses. This was the beginning of the radical shift away from what, for hundreds of years, had been the heart of cathedral ministry. At York in the earlier 1540s there were forty-three chantries supporting a similar number of clergy as well as many non-ordained assistants.[261]

In Edward's abolition, vast sums of money that paid for clerics associated with cathedrals were confiscated by the crown. In this respect, it was not only the new foundations that had to adjust to dramatically reduced cathedral staff, the abolition of chantries affected cathedrals across the country. For example, Lincoln Cathedral which had fifty-four priests in 1535 had only seventeen in 1548.[262] The abolition of chantries was just the beginning of the major reform of cathedral ministry. Ornaments and fabric were removed, both officially and unofficially. In other words, sources of cathedral income dried up and the wealth of cathedrals dropped dramatically. Most importantly,

---

[261] Lehmberg, *Reformation of Cathedrals*, 23.
[262] A.G. Dickens, *The English Reformation*, 2nd ed. (University Park, PA: University of Pennsylvania Press, 1989), 232.

the Edwardian church removed the mass, which was the central rite of medieval worship. In November 1550 the privy council demanded that stone altars be removed and "honest wooden tables" orientated east-west (not north-south) which were to be placed in the main body of the church.[263] For cathedrals this meant discarding the numerous altars in side chapels as well as the high altar and providing access to the table by ordinary people, not just the priests.

Not only were the errors of the medieval cathedrals removed in the reign of Edward VI, in their place a Reformed ministry was instituted. The 1549 Prayer Book provided for church services in English and this liturgy was further modified in a revised 1552 Prayer Book. This was one of the most profound changes of the English Reformation, Latin services were replaced with ones in the language of the people. In cathedrals it became illegal to sing anthems or motets with Latin text, which presumably led to a "scramble for new liturgical music."[264] This development continued and throughout the Elizabethan period where English ecclesiastical music was composed by talented musicians, even though they did not always have the strongest reformed convictions.

We have already demonstrated that from the 1530s there was a dramatic reduction in cathedral staff, not only in the new foundations but also in the ancient secular cathedrals. But even so, there were still large numbers of clergy associated with cathedrals. Before the reformation these people could repeatedly say mass, but what were they to do once purgatory was abolished. Well, Cranmer and the other reformers saw cathedrals as providing an opportunity to be centres of learning, preaching and teaching. The 1547 Injunctions for Cathedrals required

---

[263] See Stanford E. Lehmberg, *Cathedrals Under Siege: Cathedrals in English Society, 1600–1700* (University Park: Pennsylvania State University Press, 1996), 8. While in 1550 the tables were moved to the middle of the church, in 1559 injunctions they were moved back to the east end. In the 1604 canons they were to be put back in the middle of the church. See Walter Frere (ed.), "The Royal Injunctions of Queen Elizabeth, 1559," in *Visitation Articles and Injunctions of the Period of the Reformation Vol. 3, 1559–1575* (London: Longmans, Green and Co., 1910), 27.

[264] Lehmberg and Aylmer, "Reformation to Restoration", 90.

them to build up their libraries.²⁶⁵ Through the Elizabethan period various bishops insisted that cathedrals and cathedral staff should be of a higher level of education and be involved in the equipping of ministers more widely. Take for example, Whitgift's statutes for Hereford cathedral which "provided that only holders of an MA should be appointed prebendaries or canons... that holy communion should be celebrated monthly; that a sermon lasting an hour or thereabouts should be delivered each Sunday; that there should be biblical lectures; and that the library and school be properly cared for and governed."²⁶⁶ In responding to the puritan attack on cathedrals Whitgift stated that "there was never a time wherein these churches were better furnished with wise, learned, and godly men" and they were "the chief and principal ornaments of this Realm, and next to the universities, chiefest maintainers of godliness, religion, and learning."²⁶⁷ Ian Atherton helpfully highlights the link between the universities and cathedrals in the task of equipping gospel ministers. In light of the cathedral conundrum that scholars like MacCulloch puzzle over, he maintains the survival of cathedrals has more to do with education and preaching than Elizabeth's inclination for quality music.²⁶⁸

In relation to preaching, we should be wary of asserting that preaching was a particularly Protestant distinctive. Well before the English reformation got underway the Dean of London, John Colet, was preaching against abuses in the church. In a famous 1512 sermon he preached against the clergy of whom he said, "nothing hath so disfigured the face of the church as has the fashion of secular and

---

²⁶⁵ Walter Frere (ed.), "Royal Injunctions for Cathedrals, 1547," in *Visitation Articles and Injunctions of the Period of the Reformation Vol. 2, 1536–1558* (London: Longmans and Co., 1910), 136.
²⁶⁶ These statutes basically remained in force until the nineteenth century. Lehmberg and Aylmer, "Reformation to Restoration", 94-5.
²⁶⁷ John Whitgift, "Defence of the Answer to Admonition," in *The Works of John Whitgift: The Third Portion* (Cambridge: Parker Society, 1853), 1–467: 392, 394–95.
²⁶⁸ Ian Atherton, "Cathedrals," in Anthony Milton (ed.) *The Oxford History of Anglicanism Vol. 1: Reformation and Identity, c. 1520-1662* (Oxford: Oxford University Press, 2017), 237–39.

worldly living clerks and priests".[269] He, like his close humanist friends, Erasmus, More and Fisher, believed preaching was to be championed.[270] This emphasis has often led to Colet being seen as a proto-Protestant, but this is not a valid conclusion. Rather it was the case that preaching was a shared value of both conservative humanists and evangelicals. This is illustrated by observing Cuthbert Tunstall's desires for the ministry of Durham Cathedral. Even in the Marian counter reformation in 1556, Reginald Pole and Cuthbert Tunstall created new statutes for the cathedral which emphasised intellectual leadership and preaching as cathedral ministry priorities. The cathedral's office holders were each required to preach regularly and the dean had to preach on various feasts and he was specifically commanded to preach in English rather than Latin.[271] The learned clergy of cathedrals were to provide an opportunity to educate and preach to the people of England.

One of the chief problems with the English clergy in general was their inability to preach. This is not surprising because most of them had become priests when saying mass was their chief purpose. The reformers knew that preaching was essential to the health of the church, but licensed preachers were few and far between. For example, in 1560 the diocese of Peterborough only had nine licensed preachers among the 166 clergy.[272] While official homilies were a helpful interim measure, this was not a long-term substitute for the chronic shortage of preachers. Reformed cathedrals as centres of preaching were exactly what the church needed. In the English version of John Jewel's *Apology*

---

[269] John Colet, "Sermon made to the Convocation at St Paul's 1512," in Ethan H. Shagan and Debora Shuger (eds.), *Religion in Tudor England: An Anthology of Primary Sources* (Wacc: Baylor, 2016), 27.

[270] Jonathan Arnold, "John Colet, Preaching and Reform at St Paul's Cathedral, 1505-19", *Reformation and Renaissance Review* 5/2 (2003), 204-229, 207.

[271] Biggs, "Durham Cathedral and Cuthbert Tunstall", 14.

[272] The number of licensed preachers in the diocese of Peterborough increased through Elizabeth's reign to forty preachers of 230 clergy in 1576, 60 preachers in 1586 and 144 preachers in 1603. Christopher Haigh, *English Reformations: Religion, Politics, and Society under the Tudors* (Oxford: Clarendon, 1993), 268, 272.

of the Church of England which was published in 1564 he included an appendix where he described the purpose of reformed English cathedrals. He said deans were to be "specially chosen both for their learning and godliness" and other canons were to be either preachers or scholars.²⁷³ Furthermore, in the Elizabethan period injunctions imploring cathedrals to be centres of preaching came from both the crown and the bishops.²⁷⁴ Over the reign, cathedral preaching increased in importance and frequency, with many cathedrals requiring every prebendary to exercise a preaching ministry.²⁷⁵ Durham cathedral, for example, had 170 sermons and lectures each year and the canons had to preach another 303 sermons in parish churches.²⁷⁶

So, we have been considering the question of whether the retention of cathedrals in the sixteenth century Church of England was an anomaly of the reformation? Against the charge that cathedrals were virtually unchanged from their medieval purpose we have noted the abolition of relics and pilgrimages, the dissolving and refounding of monastic cathedrals as well as new cathedral foundations, we also observed the suppression of chantries and the reformation of the mass. While the choral tradition continued, Latin ceased as the language used in cathedrals. But the reformers not only did away with errors, they also repurposed cathedral ministry. The introduction of English language for Bible reading, liturgy and preaching was a revolution. Cathedrals became centres where learned clergy could foster diocesan education, training and preaching. There was *not* a mini-golf course or helter-skelter in the reformers' plans for cathedrals!

There were many good reasons why cathedrals were retained in the Reformed Church of England. Ian Atherton, in his recent article in

---

[273] John Jewel, "An Apology of the Church of England," in *The Works of John Jewel: The Third Portion* (Cambridge: Parker Society, 1848), 52–112: 109.

[274] Walter Frere (ed.), *Visitation Articles and Injunctions of the Period of the Reformation Vol. 3: 1559–1575* (London, Longman, Green and Co, 1910) cf. Atherton, "Cathedrals," 239.

[275] Lehmberg, *Reformation of Cathedrals*, 160–63.

[276] Christopher Haigh, *Why Do We Have Cathedrals? A Historian's View* (Perth: St George's Cathedral, 1998), 9.

volume I of the *Oxford History of Anglicanism* goes so far as to claim that in the Elizabethan period the idea of Protestant cathedrals was realised.[277] Perhaps, however, he overstates this conclusion.

While I have been arguing that there were many good reasons why the Reformers retained cathedrals in the English Reformation, we should be wary of basing all our conclusions about what sixteenth century cathedrals were like on Acts of Parliament along with Royal and Episcopal Injunctions. Such documents point to the reformers' aspirations for cathedrals and reasons why they were retained, but they do not necessarily demonstrate the reality of what took place at a local level. An important aspect of our assessment can be made by a closer look at particular cathedral records. These demonstrate that in operation they were not the utopian ecclesiastical resource the reformers hoped for. For example, in 1571 at Carlisle, "six of the eight minor canons were 'suspected of papistry'."[278] Theological error was accompanied by moral failings as, for example, in 1567 at Hereford cathedral the vicars choral were sanctioned for visiting houses of ill repute and the next year the petty canons were ordered not to walk about, talk or read books during services.[279] The lists of offences and retributions at Hereford goes on and on and readers of the crimes and punishments may wonder why cathedral staff got in more trouble for "speaking contemptuous words against the dean" than for visiting brothels, but whatever the justification, there is little doubt that in practice cathedrals did not always function the way ecclesiastical superiors believed they should.[280]

There are several other infelicities involving cathedrals in the Elizabethan period. When Edward allowed the clergy to marry, a new era of cathedral community life was begun. Mary I deprived married cathedral officers of their benefices, but Elizabeth restored them and from that point on, married men were always represented on cathedral chapters. In 1561 Elizabeth did, however, introduce an order which excluded wives and children of cathedral clergy from the cathedral

---

[277] Atherton, "Cathedrals", 241.
[278] Saunders, "The Limitations of Statutes", 445.
[279] Lehmberg and Aylmer, "Reformation to Restoration", 93.
[280] Ibid.

precincts, which must have effectively added to the issue of non-residency.[281] Another puzzle is that despite a number of attempts, reforms to the cathedral statutes of new foundations were not adopted by Elizabeth. In 1562 she ordered a commission led by Parker to draft new statutes. After a great deal of toil Parker submitted his new statutes in 1572 but they never received royal subscription. Considering the fate of the first commission, it is somewhat surprising that in 1584 John Whitgift received a commission under the great seal to reform the new foundation cathedral statutes. Like his predecessor he laboured on the new statutes and submitted them for approval in 1586 only for them to never receive royal approval.[282] Then in 1589 Whitgift was asked again to draft new statutes, which he did and submitted, but like those that had gone before they failed to receive royal assent.[283] These fruitless attempts are in a number of ways mysterious, yet even though the new foundations were established under Henry VIII, before Reformed theology shaped the practice of the Church of England, cathedral staff had been getting out of the unreformed aspects of the statutes for decades by only agreeing to them unless they were contrary to what the Word of God allows.[284] While statutes may have been unreformed, the royal and episcopal injunctions were the effective law governing cathedral practice and, as we have already demonstrated, these were undoubtedly protestant.

We noted earlier how scholarly opinion often points to the operation of cathedrals as, in practice, a subversive element in Elizabeth's church. It is suggested that they were functionally ruled by deans and chapters that were "often virtually independent of the authority of the bishop."[285] The argument is that this authority was supposedly wielded in ways contrary to the Reform programme of the bishops and the cathedrals became bastions for ancient traditions merged with the new liturgy. We have already noted that cathedrals and some college chapels continued the choral tradition, using professional musicians and robed

---

[281] Houlbrooke "Refoundation and Reformation", 518.
[282] Saunders, "The Limitations of Statutes", 453.
[283] Ibid.
[284] R.B. Walker, "Lincoln Cathedral in the Reign of Queen Elizabeth I", *JEH* 11/2 (Oct 1960): 186–201, 197.
[285] Marshall, *Reformation England*, 143.

choirs.[286] Furthermore, certain vestments like copes were retained and used in cathedrals. This is some of the evidence scholars use to argue for the unreformed state of English cathedrals and they believe Elizabeth allowed these ambiguities because she personally appreciated fine music and churchier practices.[287] However, as a basis for a claim that cathedrals were essentially unreformed, the continuation of the choral tradition and the use of certain vestments pales in comparison to the radical changes in cathedral ministry that we have already noted in this chapter.

Those advocating for the cathedral conundrum also illustrate their point by using puritan complaints from the latter sixteenth century which demanded that cathedrals should be completely dissolved. For example, in the 1573 anonymous *A View of Popish Abuses*, cathedrals were said to be "very dens of thieves... dens of lazy, loitering lubbards, the very harbourers of all deceitful and timeserving hypocrites" and they were also accused of being the pope's trojan horse in England.[288] Scholars arguing for the anomaly of reformed cathedrals, however, have placed far too much weight on the arguments of an extreme puritan wing and then only in a selective fashion. Indeed, several puritans held cathedral offices and, while some did not always conform to wearing the proscribed surplice and cope, many did, and most sought to use the cathedrals to propagate Reformed theology.[289] Furthermore, while extreme puritans were known to write off cathedral clergy as "deceitful and timeserving hypocrites", this did not stop them benefitting from the income of cathedrals. A good example was Laurence Chaderton, the Puritan Master of Emmanuel College, Cambridge, who denounced cathedrals as "parts of the whore and strumpet of Rome" while at the same time enjoying his income as an absent prebendary of Lincoln Cathedral.[290]

---

[286] Even in relation to the continuation of choral liturgy there was a significant reduction in this resources over the sixteenth century. For example, in 1535 Lincoln Cathedral had 22 vicars choral but by 1580 there were only 12. Walker, "Lincoln Cathedral in the Reign of Queen Elizabeth I", 192.
[287] MacCulloch, "Putting the English Reformation on the Map", 213.
[288] Anon. *A View of Popishe Abuses* [c. 1572] cited in Cross. "'Dens of Loitering Lubbers'", 231, 2.
[289] Lehmberg, *Reformation of Cathedrals*, 154–63.
[290] Cited in Atherton, "Cathedrals", 238.

One further reason several scholars believe the sixteenth century cathedrals were anomalies of the English reformation is because of what took place in them early in the next century. Cathedrals did become something of a seedbed for the rise in high churchmanship. Leaders in this movement such as John Overall, Lancelot Andrewes, Richard Neile and William Laud were all deans before becoming bishops. These men made changes in the church which repudiated many things the reformers held dear. For example, when Laud became Dean of Gloucester in 1616 he moved the communion table from the middle of the quire to the east end of the cathedral. But rather than demonstrating that sixteenth century cathedrals were a subversion to church reform, Atherton correctly points out that the very fact that this was a *change* by Laud demonstrates that cathedrals were not relics of a pre-reformation church. It is somewhat anachronistic to read back the movement that began in cathedrals in the seventeenth century into the ethos of their ministry in the sixteenth.

The question this chapter has been seeking to answer is why cathedrals were retained in the Reformed Church of England in the sixteenth century. Diarmaid MacCulloch described them as an "anomaly" and a "puzzle". Christopher Haigh claimed that English Reformers "all agreed that cathedrals as they stood were a waste of resources, irrelevant to the proper tasks of an evangelical church."[291] And Peter Marshall has said, "Reformers sometimes demanded to know what cathedrals were for in a Protestant Church, and to this, other than the defence that they could serve as centres of preaching there was no very compelling answer."[292] Perhaps, like the boy who saw the emperor was not wearing any clothes, the most obvious answer to why cathedrals were retained in the reformation has been overlooked. Surely the most fundamental answer to this question is that the Church of England retained cathedrals because it retained episcopal government. Why do we have cathedrals? Because we have bishops and they need somewhere to sit! The Tudor church was always committed to episcopal government. The attacks on cathedrals by extreme puritans were part and parcel of broader attacks on episcopal polity and they only ever represented a minority view. The simple reality was, if bishops

---

[291] Haigh, *Why Do We Have Cathedrals?*, 2.
[292] Marshall, *Reformation England*, 143.

were to have a place in the church, cathedrals were a natural corollary. If we want to talk about the retention of cathedrals as "anomalies" and "puzzles", we would be better served turning our attention to St Giles' Cathedral in Edinburgh.

Heinrich Bullinger's Influence on Edwardian England

Joe Mock

The influence of Zürich on the English Church, particularly during the reign of Elizabeth I, is well known. By the 1570s, some fourteen years after Thomas Cranmer's martyrdom, Peter Martyr Vermigli's *Loci communes* and Heinrich Bullinger's *Decades* had become the two standard textbooks of theology in English universities.[293] Moreover, Archbishop Whitgift made *The Decades* compulsory reading for the less-educated clergy of the province of Canterbury.[294] Even though Calvin's *Institutes* (1559) were reprinted twice in England within the first one hundred years of the Reformation, Bullinger's *Decades* were reprinted in Latin as many as seventy-seven times. The work was translated into English and published as *The House Book* in 1558, which had 137 editions. Bullinger's influence on the Elizabethan Church was also directly felt during the vestments controversy, and through his defence of the papal bull that excommunicated the queen. While many historians have acknowledged these connections, this chapter examines some of the ways that Bullinger had a hand in shaping the course of the English Reformation under Henry VIII and Edward VI.[295] In particular, we will concentrate on Bullinger's relationship with Cranmer and the boy-king, Edward.

---

[293] Torrance Kirby, *The Zurich Connection and Tudor Political Theology* (Leiden: Brill, 2007), 3. See pages 4-12 for an account of what Kirby terms the "Zurich Connection" in Tudor England. See also Patrick Collinson, "England and International Calvinism 1558-1640" in Menna Prestwich (ed.), *International Calvinism 1541-1715* (Oxford: Clarendon Press, 1985), 214-215.
[294] Hirofumi Horie, 'The Origin and the Historical Context of Archbishop Whitgift's "Orders" of 1586', *Archiv für Reformationsgeschichte*, 83 (1992), 240-57.
[295] Diarmaid MacCulloch, "Heinrich Bullinger and the English-speaking world" in Emidio Campi and Peter Opitz (eds.), *Heinrich Bullinger: Life-Thought-Influence* (Zürich: Theologischer Verlag Zürich, 2007), 891-934.

Bullinger might be a surprising figure to contemplate since he never set foot on English soil, unlike other continental reformers such as Vermigli, Martin Bucer, John Łaski, and John ab Ulmis. Both Vermigli and Bucer were personally invited by Cranmer to England and it is not surprising that some scholars see both Vermigli and Bucer as having a significant influence on the archbishop.[296] However, we must also recognise that in addition to the 'direct contact hours' these scholars had with Cranmer, the archbishop's thinking was shaped by what he read, and who he corresponded with. Indeed, as Bruce Gordon reminds us, we 'must exercise a good deal of caution' in trying to distil the Swiss influence on the English Reformation.[297] In this regard, Bullinger's role must be reconsidered. It will become clear that Bullinger sought access to Cranmer's mind via his theological argument in the hope of moving 'the archbishop to the advanced doctrine of the Helvetian school', especially in the matter of the eucharist.[298] Such 'prophetical' influence on Cranmer will be seen through Bullinger's writings that were not necessarily directly addressed to Cranmer, but would have been read by him.[299]

---

[296] See, for example, the recent study of the debate between Cranmer and Gardiner in Amanda Wrenn Allen, *The Eucharistic Debate in Tudor England: Thomas Cranmer, Stephen Gardiner and the English Reformation* (Lanham, Maryland: Lexington Books, 2018).

[297] 'In attempting to distil Swiss influences in England, or in any area of the Reformation, one must exercise a good deal of caution, for in the flow of oral and written information nothing existed either in isolation from other ideas or in a pure, unadulterated form. The evangelical world in England was eclectic, and among the continental Reformed writers whose works were read a general theological consensus on most issues sat uneasily alongside serious disagreement on others.' Bruce Gordon, *The Swiss Reformation* (Manchester: Manchester University Press, 2002), 300-301.

[298] F.A. Gasquet and E. Bishop, *Edward VI and the Book of Common Prayer* (London, 1928, 3rd revised edition), 197.

[299] Kirby, *Zurich Connection*, 26.

Background to Bullinger's interaction with the Church in England

Throughout his years as *Antistes* (the head of a church in the Reformed Churches of Switzerland) in Zürich (1531-1575), Bullinger was active in promoting the reformation throughout Europe, particularly in eastern Europe. His connections with the churches in Hungary and Poland, for example, have been well examined.[300] With respect to England, Bullinger's attempts to influence the reformation there must be seen in the light of the personal connection that Cranmer enjoyed with Vermigli, Regius Professor of Theology at Oxford (1547-1553), and Bucer, was Regius Professor of Divinity at Cambridge (1549-1551). Cranmer was also in contact with Philip Melanchthon, one of Martin Luther's close associates from Wittenberg.[301] So, while these international reformers could claim a close connection with the Archbishop of Canterbury, Bullinger could not. It is therefore proposed here, that Bullinger sought to influence Cranmer indirectly through his writings which he was confident would, in fact, be read and carefully considered by Cranmer.

When dealing with fellow reformers, Bullinger's usual *modus operandi* was to point others to the Bible. In doing so, he would also cite certain church fathers, with whom he concurred with respect to their interpretation and understanding of the particular section(s) of Holy Scripture under discussion. This was both to emphasize continuity with the original catholic church and also to underscore his orthodoxy. Bullinger referred to the teaching of Rome as the 'new faith'

---

[300] Andreas Mühling, *Heinrich Bullingers europäische Kirchenpolitik* (Bern: Peter Lang, 2001); "Heinrich Bullinger as Church Politician" in Bruce Gordon and Emidio Campi (eds.), *Architect of Reformation: An Introduction to Heinrich Bullinger 1504-1575* (Grand Rapids: Baker, 2004), 243-254; Carrie Euler, *Couriers of the Gospel: England and Zurich 1531-1558* (Zürich: Theologischer Verlag Zürich, 2006).
[301] Charlotte Methuen, "The English Reformation in Wittenberg: Luther and Melanchthon's Engagement with Religious Change in England 1521-1560," *Reformation & Renaissance Review*, 20/3 (2018), 209-234. See also John Schofield, *Philip Melanchthon and the English Reformation* (Aldershot: Ashgate, 2007).

because it was based on the authority of Rome and its councils instead of on Scripture alone. On the other hand, the faith of the reformers was the 'old faith'.[302] This *modus operandi* of Bullinger can be illustrated by his *True Confession* (*Wahrhaftes Bekenntnis*, 1545) written in response to Luther's *Brief Confession concerning the Holy Sacrament* (*Kurz Bekenntnis D. Mart. Luthers, vom heiligen Sacrament*, 1544). Bullinger sent his work to Luther bound together with a copy of Luther's original text as if to challenge Luther to compare the two against the rule of scripture. The Swiss reformer undertook a similar approach to influencing Cranmer. That is to say, he sought to point Cranmer to the most apposite passages of scripture rather than through clever argumentation.

Cranmer was clearly aware of Bullinger's writings, which had been in circulation in England since the reign of Henry VIII. Commencing with the publication of his commentary on Thessalonians, which was published in English (1538), thirty-three editions (twenty-two books and treatises) of Bullinger's other works were published between 1538-1556. In an undated letter Nicolas Eliot, wearing rose-coloured glasses, wrote the following to Bullinger:

> Not only the church of Zürich, but all other churches which are in Christ, bear witness to the skill, and purity, and simplicity of faith, with which you have expounded the whole Bible, and especially the epistles of St. Paul. And how great weight all persons attribute to your commentaries, how greedily they embrace and admire them, (to pass over numerous other arguments) the booksellers are most ample witnesses, whom by the sale of your writings alone, from being more destitute than Irus and Codrus, you see suddenly becoming as rich as Croesus. May God therefore give you the disposition to publish all your writings as speedily as possible, whereby you will not only fill the coffers of the booksellers, but will

---

[302] This is clearly expressed in his *Der alte Glaube* (1537) which was translated as *The Old Faith* by Miles Coverdale (1547).

gain over very many souls to Christ, and adorn his church with more previous jewels.[303]

There is evidence to suggest that by the mid-1540s, Cranmer was happy for Bullinger's works to be read more widely when he was approached by John Łaski about publishing a tract of Bullinger's on the sacraments (*Absoluta de Christi Domini et catholicae eius ecclesiae Sacramentis tractatio* 1546).[304] According to George Ella, Cranmer told Łaski 'to go ahead, saying that he had no need to examine the work first as all Bullinger's works were the very best'.[305]

With this background in mind, the following discussion will focus on *The Authority of Scripture* (1538), the correspondence between Bullinger and Cranmer, Bullinger's dedications in *The Decades* and Bullinger's correspondence with Lady Jane Grey.

The Authority of Holy Scripture

In 1538, Bullinger dedicated *The Authority of Holy Scripture* to Henry VIII. The thrust of the work not only concerns the absolute authority of Scripture for the faith of the believer, but also provides guidelines for how sovereigns should reign in tandem with the leaders of the church.[306] The book was delivered by Nicolas Eliot and Nicolas Partridge. Copies were also given to Cranmer and Thomas Cromwell. Partridge's letter to Bullinger dated 17 September 1538 is quite revealing concerning Cranmer's reaction to the gift of this book:

> We therefore addressed first of all the archbishop of Canterbury, who most courteously received the copy sent

---

[303] Hastings Robinson (ed.), *Original Letters Relative to the English Reformation vol. 2* (Cambridge: Cambridge University Press, 1847), 620.
[304] This work was a forerunner to the *Consensus Tigurinus* (1549). It was published in English during the reign of Edward VI in 1551.
[305] George M. Ella, "Henry Bullinger's Influence on the Church of England," *Churchman*, 128 (2014), 134.
[306] Pamela Biel, *Doorkeepers at the House of Righteousness: Heinrich Bullinger and the Zurich Clergy 1535-1575* (Bern: Verlag Peter Lang, 1991), 34-39; Kirby, *Zurich Connection*, 26-29.

to himself: we offered him likewise, for civility's sake, and if it might be received more favourably, the book intended for the king: at first he refused, and thought it would be advantageous if it were placed in the hands of Lord Crumwell, that he might deliver it to the king but after supper he asked for the king's book of his own accord, and promised to deliver it to his lord, provided we were present, should the king wish to ask us any questions. He then set himself to the continued reading of the book, that he might not seem to recommend to the king any thing of which he himself had no knowledge.[307]

Eliot also reported to Bullinger that 'you must know as a most certain truth, that your books are wonderfully received, not only by our king, but equally so by the Lord Crumwell'.[308]

Throughout his works, Bullinger often referred to the Old Testament model of kingship, where the king, as civil leader, rules in tandem with God's appointed prophet and where both are guided by the word of God. In the dedicatory epistle within *The Authority of Holy Scripture* addressed to Henry VIII, Bullinger cited Deuteronomy 17:18-20 and declared: 'For first and foremost it is the responsibility of kings to be in charge of religion and faith'.[309]

Indeed, *inter alia* he cited the examples of David and Jehoshaphat as model kings. After reminding him that he had been appointed king over his people by God, a direct personal application to Henry VIII is given towards the end of the dedicatory epistle:

> You are the king, therefore you are the father of the nation. You are the head of the kingdom, therefore to you is also discernment for the kingdom. You are the soul of the body

---

[307] Robinson, *Original Letters vol. 2*, 611.
[308] Robinson, *Original Letters vol. 2*, 618.
[309] Emidio Campi (ed.), HBTS vol. 4, *De scripturae sanctae authoritate deque Episcoporum institutione et functione* (Zürich: Theologischer Verlag Zürich, 2009), 3 – *Nam primum et potissimum, quod ad regum cura pertinent, est religio ac fides.*

of England, consequently yours is given to the duties of holy life for their souls. You are the eye, the sun and light of the English church, therefore the church redeemed by the blood of Christ and itself snatched from the jaws of antichrist by illumination by the word of Christ having been turned upside down by superstition but restored by true religion.[310]

Bullinger was clearly endorsing England's break with Rome and being freed from its superstition. He was also underscoring the fact that the English Church was being reformed through the Word of God. By applying Matthew 6:22 directly to Henry VIII, Bullinger sought to impress upon him the gravity of his role and responsibility as the spiritual leader of England. Kirby referred to this as *cura religionis* and is the background to understanding why Bullinger strove to influence the monarchs of England.[311] Thus, in his peroration to this treatise on the authority of Scripture, Bullinger urged Henry VIII to follow the model of courageous, wise and holy kings who ruled their people according to the infallible word of God.

The Authority of Holy Scripture actually consists of two works in one volume. The second of these works deals with the role of bishops as ministers of the word of God.[312] This was clearly written with Cranmer and his colleagues in mind. The chapters that were most germane for Cranmer included those on prophecy, the doctors of the gospel, the function of bishops, the dignity and authority of ministers as well as a chapter warning about the corruption of bishops.

The passage at the end of the whole volume illustrates Bullinger's efforts to speak to both Henry VIII and Cranmer. This is evident by Bullinger's observation that 'today in England, your kingdom, there

---

[310] Campi, *De scripturae sanctae*, 6.
[311] Kirby, *Zurich Connection*, 26.
[312] The full title of the work is *De scripturae sanctae authoritate, certitudine, firmitate et absoluta perfectione deque episocopum, qui verbi dei ministry sunt, institutione et functione contra superstitionis tyrannidisque Romanae antistes ad serenissimum Angliae regem* Heinrychum VIII. *Heinrychi Bullingeri liber duo.*

flourishes an abundance of doctors, wise and pious men'.³¹³ This was an unmistakable reference to Cranmer and his reform-minded colleagues whom God provided for Henry so that 'through consultation with them, most Christian leader, you might discuss the common affairs of religion. Nor in such matters should you depend on others'.³¹⁴

Bullinger pointedly reminded Henry VIII that he was the Head of the Church in England and, with a clear reference to the title *defensor fidei*, 'defender of the catholic faith'. He therefore urged him to follow the example of King Josiah. He further clarified that, like the Levites in the Old Testament, the bishops are the ultimate keepers of the sacred things of God. Cranmer and his episcopal colleagues were thus reminded that their role was akin to that of the prophets of the Old Testament who advised and warned the kings.

Bullinger's correspondence with Cranmer

In March 1536, Bullinger contacted Cranmer via Grynäus' correspondence with the archbishop. He gifted Cranmer a book that MacCulloch has suggested was sent using the Swiss printer Christoff Froschouer and the English printer Reyner Wolfe as intermediaries as they would meet at the Frankfurt book fair. However, which book of Bullinger's is not known.³¹⁵ This circuitous route to make contact with Cranmer probably indicates that Bullinger did not have a relationship with the archbishop at this point in time, though it appears that this overture was well received.³¹⁶

On 22 August 1536 Bullinger wrote to Vadian asking him to write to Cranmer mentioning Bullinger's and Grynäus' names and, in particular, to send Cranmer a copy of Vadian's *Aphorisms*. Bullinger's clear aim was to have Cranmer read what Vadian had cited from Ratramnus' treatise (*De corpore et sanguine domini*) concerning the

---

[313] Campi, *De scripturae sanctae*, 260.
[314] Campi, *De scripturae sanctae*, 260.
[315] Diarmaid MacCulloch, *Thomas Cranmer: A Life* (New Haven: Yale University Press, 1996), 176.
[316] Euler, *Couriers*, 58.

Eucharist. After considerable time had lapsed, Cranmer replied that he did not agree with the Swiss reformed theologians on the Eucharist.[317] In fact, Cranmer stated that 'I have seen almost everything that has been written and published either by Oecolampadius or Zuinglius and I have come to the conclusion that the writing of every man must be read with discrimination'.[318]

Bullinger himself later wrote directly to Cranmer in January 1537. This letter is not extant but Bullinger noted in his *Diarium* that his letter was warmly received.[319] On the other hand, a transcript of a summary of Cranmer's reply has survived.[320] Among other things, Cranmer referred to the Pilgrimage of Grace and the perceived similarities with the Peasants War in Germany but with the pointed difference that this rebellion was led by those fiercely opposed to the Reformation. The demands of these rebels were the reinstatement of the papacy and the false teaching of Rome and the banning of the writings of Luther, Melanchthon, Oecolampadius, and others together with the restitution of the monasteries. Cranmer indicated that he had desired more advice from Bullinger and other reformers on the continent as to how to handle the situation. That is to say, Cranmer indicated that he was open to suggestions from Bullinger and others about how to handle certain situations being faced by the English church.

The next extant communication between Cranmer and Bullinger is dated some years later during the reign of King Edward VI. Bullinger had previously advised Cranmer that England should not send any delegates to the forthcoming session of Trent in May of 1551 which would focus on the Mass and transubstantiation.[321] The second point

---

[317] MacCulloch, *Cranmer*, 179-183.
[318] John Edmund Cox (ed.), *The Works of Thomas Cranmer* (Cambridge: The Parker Society Edition, The University Press, 1846), 344.
[319] Emil Egli, *Heinrich Bullingers Diarium (Annales vitae) der Jahre 1504-1574* (Basel: Basler Buch und Antiquariatshandlung, 1904), 25 – *retulit amicissimas*.
[320] This is dated 3 April 1537 according to a transcript by Johannes Kessler (St Gallen Kantonsbibliothek (Vadiana), Ms 72, 481r-482r – Hans Ulrich Bächtold and Rainer Henrich, *Heinrich Bullinger Briefwechsel*, vol. 7, *Briefe des Jahres 1537* (Zürich: Theologischer Verlag Zürich, 1998), 129.
[321] The session ended 11 October 1551.

raised in Bullinger's letter was concerning John Hooper, Bishop of Gloucester. Pointedly, Cranmer waited until more than one calendar year had elapsed before replying. Cranmer must have been taken aback at the stance taken by Hooper as well as Bullinger's defence of Hooper. Therefore, he was probably not eager, at this juncture, to discuss Trent with Bullinger. Cranmer stated his apparent tardiness in replying as:

> you must impute partly to my want of leisure, and partly to a kind of dislike to a duty of this nature, and which I must candidly admit myself to entertain. But as it is better to perform a duty tardily than not at all, you shall now receive a reply to the whole of your letter.[322]

It is possible that Cranmer may have seen Bullinger's advice as slightly presumptuous. He indicated that the English realm did not need to be advised about Trent. On the contrary, in 1552 Cranmer wanted to indicate initiative on behalf of the English church by organising a synod at which Protestant scholars would discuss the Eucharist. He wrote to Bullinger on 20 March 1552 to indicate that he would advise Edward VI not to send any delegate to Trent but, rather, to convoke a synod in 'England or elsewhere' for 'an agreement of the sacramentarian controversy'. His letter mentioned that he had written concerning the proposed synod to both Melanchthon and Calvin.[323] The letter addressed to Calvin is also dated 20 March 1552.[324] In his reply of April 1552, Calvin warmly welcomed this initiative and suggested that Melanchthon and Bullinger also be invited.[325] Cranmer's letter to Melanchthon is dated 27 March 1552.[326] However, despite the collective goodwill, this synod never took place.

---

[322] Hastings Robinson (ed), *Original Letters Relative to the English Reformation vol. 1* (Cambridge: The Parker Society Edition, The University Press, 1846), 22-23.
[323] Robinson, *Original Letters vol. 1*, 23.
[324] Robinson, *Original Letters vol. 1*, 24-25.
[325] Jules Bonnet (ed.), Letters of John Calvin vol. 2 (Edinburgh: Thomas Constable and Co, 1857), 330-333.
[326] Robinson, *Original Letters vol. 1*, 25-26.

With respect to the matter concerning Hooper, Cranmer advised Bullinger that he was now appointed the Bishop of Gloucester and Worcester and that he 'is at this time living in my house upon the most intimate terms'.[327] How intimate Cranmer considered himself with Bullinger is another matter, however. 'Your reverence's most attached' was the style in which he signed off his letter to Bullinger. This contrasts with the manner in which Cranmer signed off his letters to Calvin and Melanchthon as he urged them to attend the proposed synod. The letter to Calvin ends with 'You very dear brother in Christ',[328] whereas he ends his letter to Melanchthon with the phrase: 'Very desirous of seeing you some time'.[329] Similarly, a letter to Bucer's widow refers to Cranmer's 'agreeable remembrance of a very dear friend'.[330] By contrast, Cranmer had a distant relationship with Bullinger. However, this should not preclude us from seeing the mutual respect that these theologians held for each other. Based on this mutual respect Bullinger sought to give input to Cranmer's mind as the reformation gradually developed in England.

Dedication of the Third Decade to Edward VI (March 1550)

Bullinger dedicated his *Third Decade* to Edward VI.[331] The young king had previously expressed the mutual warmth he felt with the church in Zürich in a letter addressed to the Senate of Zürich dated 20 October 1549.[332] When Bullinger penned his dedication to Edward VI, the Council of Trent had been in progress for some five years. Because of the constant regular contact between Cranmer and Edward VI, it is probable that Bullinger hoped that Cranmer would read his *Third Decade*. In view of the fact that the Council of Trent was still in progress, Bullinger made pointed comments about Rome and the councils of the church in this dedication:

---

[327] Robinson, *Original Letters vol. 1*, 23-24.
[328] Robinson, *Original Letters vol. 1*, 25.
[329] Robinson, *Original Letters vol. 1*, 26.
[330] Robinson, *Original Letters vol. 1*, 27.
[331] Robinson, *Original Letters vol. 1*, 82.
[332] Robinson, *Original Letters vol. 1*, 1.

> Even the wisest men do very often deceive us with their counsels, and greatly endamage the followers thereof; but God, which is the Light and eternal Wisdom cannot any time either err, or conceive any false opinions or repugning counsels; much less teach others anything but truth, or seduce any man out of the right way.[333]

Bullinger thus sought to encourage the young king whom he knew to be competent in the scriptures:

> All the wise men of the world have been of the opinion, that kings and kingdoms should be most happy, if the king of the country be a wise man; if he have many wise, aged, faithful, and skillful counsellors; if his captains be valiant, warlike, and fortunate in battle; if he abound with substance; if his kingdom be on every side surely fortified; and lastly, if his people be of one mind and obedient.[334]

> I therefore, having good affiance in your Majesty's good and godly disposition, do verily hope, that this short discourse of mine touching the true causes of the felicity and calamities of kings and kingdoms shall have a profiting place with you. Even I, which twelve years since did dedicate unto the father of famous history, Henry Eighth, a book touching the authority and the institution and function of bishops against the pontifical chuffs of the Romish superstition and tyranny and now by experience know that that labour of mine brought forth no small fruit within the realm of England; am no so bold again as to dedicate these my sermons unto your royal Majesty.[335]

It is clear that Bullinger saw an opportunity to further his influence in England, and his confidence has firm foundations. Indeed, Edward VI had previously sent a letter to the church at Zürich which invited intimacy between them:

---

[333] Harding, *Decades* (The Second Tome), 3, 4.
[334] Harding, *Decades* (The Second Tome), 4.
[335] Harding, *Decades* (The Second Tome), 15.

> ...we have understood by the frequent letters of our faithful and beloved servant, Christopher Mont, both your favourable disposition towards us, and ready inclination to deserve well of us. In addition to which, there is also a mutual agreement between us concerning the christian religion and true godliness, which ought to render this friendship of ours, by God's blessing, yet more intimate.[336]

Even though the Duke of Somerset and the Duke of Northumberland held the reigns of the monarchy as Edward VI had not yet attained majority, Bullinger knew that the young king was competent to comprehend both the theological dynamics and the political ramifications of the English reformation. Hence, Bullinger was keen to address Edward VI directly, and did so through the continuation of dedicatory epistles in his *Decades*.

Dedication of the *Fourth Decade* to Edward VI (August 1550)

Bullinger's purpose in this dedication was abundantly clear:

> ... according to the gift that the Lord hath endued me withal may help forward and advance the state of Christian religion, now again happily springing up in the famous realm of England by your royal majesty's good beginnings and counsels of your worthy nobles.[337]

Bullinger referred to the role of the leaders of the English Church, which presumably was also aimed at Cranmer, who like Bullinger, sought to revive the ancient faith of the apostles.

> Therefore the authority of the prophets and evangelists giveth counsel, fully to absolve and perfectly to end the reformation of religion once begun with the fear of God, out of or by the word of God; and not to look for or stay

---

[336] Robinson, *Original Letters vol. 1*, 1.
[337] Harding, *Decades* (The Second Tome vol. 2), 115.

upon councils which are directed, not by the word of God, but by the affections and motions of men.[338]

As expected, the dedication concluded with a personal encouragement to Edward VI:

> Proceed, therefore, proceed, most holy King, to imitate the most godly princes, and the infallible rule of the holy scripture: proceed, I say, without staying for man's authority, by the most true and absolute instrument of truth, the book of God's most holy word, to reform the church of Christ in thy most happy England.[339]

Dedication of the *Fifth Decade* to Henry Grey (March 1551)

Bullinger's aim was not only directed at the king. He also sought to reach influential figures throughout the realm. John ab Ulmis had encouraged Bullinger to dedicate part of *The Decades* to Henry Grey, the Marquis of Devon, who was Duke of Suffolk.[340] The *Fifth Decade* dealt with the church and the sacraments and was, therefore, a key work in expressing reformation faith and practice. Because the Council of Trent was still in session, Bullinger used his dedication to Grey in order to warn him to 'look diligently and to be watchful' so that England would not adversely be affected by the decisions of Trent. Bullinger declared that Trent sought:

> ...to prop up ancient error and superstition and to overturn the reformations begun in Germany, England, Denmark and other nations of Christendom: in a word, to suppress pure or sincere evangelical truth.[341]

---

[338] Harding, *Decades* (The Second Tome vol. 2), 116.
[339] Harding, *Decades* (The Second Tome vol. 2), 122.
[340] Robinson, *Original Letters vol. 2*, 393.
[341] Harding, *Decades* (The Third Tome), 529.

Moreover, Bullinger stated that Pope Paul III

> ... accused and condemned of heresy all us who profess the gospel and demand a reformation agreeable with the word of God and teach that Jesus Christ, and not the pope,— nay, Christ Jesus alone, — is the Head, Pastor and Chief-priest of the Catholic church.[342]

Bullinger also warned that those who were still Romish traditionalists in England would seek at any opportunity to reinstate the practices and traditions of Rome.

> They will make it a tradition to pray for the dead. Another tradition shall be the wifeless state of ministers. They will make a tradition of the mass. The use of images in temples or churches must also be a tradition. To be short, whatever the old church of Rome hath hitherto agreeably kept shall be a tradition, although it be neither found, nor painted, nor written anywhere in any book canonical; yea, although it be quite contrary to scripture. And so that shall be a tradition what they list.[343]

The *Fifth Decade* with its clear warnings about Trent was dedicated to Grey who was to be created Duke of Suffolk on 10 October 1551. It illustrates Bullinger's attempt to influence key players in King Edward VI's reign.

Correspondence between Lady Jane Grey and Bullinger

Bullinger had been introduced to the Grey family and, therefore, to Lady Jane Grey, through John ab Ulmis. The close connection between them can be illustrated from a letter from Grey to Bullinger in which he thanks Bullinger for her attention and care to his daughter:

> I acknowledge myself also to be much indebted to you on my daughter's account for having always exhorted her in

---

[342] Harding, *Decades* (The Third Tome), 529.
[343] Harding, *Decades* (The Third Tome), 532-533.

> your godly letters to a true faith in Christ, the study of scriptures...and I earnestly request you to continue these exhortations as frequently as possible.[344]

Understandably, because of her martyrdom, much hagiography surrounds the life of Lady Jane Grey. For example, there is the account of her taking off her gloves at the scaffold, prior to her execution, with instructions for them to be passed on to Bullinger. David Keep has studied this carefully and concluded that these gloves were given to Bullinger's wife, Anna Adlischwyler, sometime between autumn 1552 and May 1553 which was just under two years before her martyrdom.[345] This underlines the close relationship that Lady Jane Grey had with Bullinger, and therefore the extent of his theological influence during the Edwardian Reformation.

It may well be that Bullinger was keen to correspond with Lady Jane Grey because of the possibility, at one time, of her marriage to Edward VI. It also appears that she had the capabilities and faculties, in her own right, to stand alongside the male reformers in England. Three letters from her to Bullinger are extant though none of Bullinger's letters to her are extant.[346]

In her first letter (12 July 1551) Lady Jane Grey showed her detailed knowledge of Scripture and of church history. In doing so, she was actually commenting on Bullinger's letter to her.

> For no better fortune can await me than to be thought worthy of the correspondence and most wholesome admonitions of men so renowned, whose virtues cannot be sufficiently eulogized; and to experience the same

---

[344] Robinson, *Original Letters vol. 1*, 4.
[345] David J. Keep, "Die Handschuhe der Lady Jane Grey," *Zwingliana*, vol. 11 (1963), 663-668.
[346] Rebecca A. Giselbrecht, "Religious Intent and the Art of Courteous Pleasantry: A Few Letters from Englishwomen to Heinrich Bullinger (1543-1562)" in Julie A. Chappell and Kaley A. Kramer (eds.), *Women during the English Reformations: Renegotiating Gender and Religious Identity* (New York: Macmillan, 2014), 50-53.

> happiness as was enjoyed by Blesilla, Paula, and Eustochium, to whom, as it is recorded, Saint Jerome imparted instruction, and brought them by his discourses to the knowledge of divine truths; or, the happiness of that venerable matron, to whom St John addressed an exhortatory and evangelical epistle; or that, lastly, of the mother of Severus, who profited by the counsels of Origen, and was obedient to his precepts.[347]

She also referred to 'that little volume of pure and unsophisticated religion, which you lately sent to my father and myself'.[348] In her second letter (7 July 1552) she acknowledged and appreciated Bullinger's gentle method to stretch her mind theologically.

> I seemed to have derived as much benefit from your excellence and truly divine precepts, as I have scarcely obtained from the daily perusal of the best authors. You exhort me to embrace a genuine and sincere faith in Christ my Saviour. I will endeavour to satisfy you in this respect, as far as God shall enable me to do; but as I acknowledge faith to be his gift, I ought therefore only to promise so far as he may see fit to bestow it upon me. And to this I will add, as you exhort me, and with the divine blessing such holiness of life, as my (alas!) too feeble powers may enable me to practise. Do you, meanwhile, with your wonted kindness, make daily mention of me in your prayers.[349]

This mentoring of Lady Jane Grey by Bullinger was soon curtailed because various precipitous events stook place in quick succession. Lady Jane Grey's cousin, King Edward VI, fell ill in January of 1553 and then she had been hastily married to Lord Guilford Dudley on 21 May 1553. She wrote her third letter to Bullinger before June 1553. It is tantalizing to consider if she might have been aware that Edward VI had plans for her succession to the throne of England. What the letter

---

[347] Robinson, *Original Letters vol. 1*, 5-6.
[348] Robinson, *Original Letters vol. 1*, 5. The book in question was Bullinger's treatise on Christian perfection (*Perfectio christianorum* (1551, HBBibl, no. 249)) which had been dedicated to King Henry II of France.
[349] Robinson, *Original Letters vol. 1*, 8.

does display is her humanistic training as can be seen by the insertion of some Greek phrases in the midst of the Latin text as well as references to Cicero. She acknowledged the pivotal role that Bullinger was playing for the reformation in several countries and prayed for Bullinger's 'long continuance in this life'.

Conclusion

This essay has sought to uncover Bullinger's attempts to influence Cranmer either directly or indirectly through key figures of the Edwardian court. Although the documentary evidence may be somewhat scant, there can be no doubt about Bullinger's intended influence on the Edwardian Church.

Throughout the period of the Edwardian Church, Bullinger sought to provide positive input both to Edward VI and to Cranmer. Although Bullinger had made formal contact with Cranmer through his *On the Authority of Scripture* and Vadian's *Aphorisms* during the reign of Henry VIII, he sought to indirectly influence Cranmer through his writings during Edward VI's reign. This he did via the dedications in *The Decades* to Edward VI and Henry Grey. His correspondence with Lady Jane Grey must also be viewed in the context of Bullinger's aim to influence the throne of England for the ongoing cause of the reformation.

Bullinger's was not the only attempt by European reformers to shape the English movement. It is well documented that Wittenberg made attempts to influence the Reformation in England early in the reign of Henry VIII and the influence of Geneva was more pronounced during the reign of Elizabeth I.[350] But under the leadership of Zwingli and Bullinger, both civil leaders and church leaders in Zürich were accountable to the Word of God in much the way it was intended for

---

[350] Charlotte Methuen, "The English Reformation in Wittenberg: Luther and Melanchton's Engagement with Religious Change in England 1521-1560," Reformation and Renaissance Review, vol.20 (no.3 2018), 209-234. Martin Davie, "Calvin's Influence on the Theology of the English Reformation," Ecclesiology, vol.6 (no 3 2010), 315-341.

the pattern of kings and prophets/priests in their leadership of Israel in the Old Testament.[351] It is little wonder that Bullinger considered the Zürich model for reform most suitable for Edwardian England and endeavoured to encourage the English reformers in that direction.

---

[351] For a study as to how Bullinger viewed collective episcopacy for Zurich see Jon Delmas Wood, "Bullinger's Model for Collective Episcopacy: Transformational Ministry in a Society Facing Final Judgment" in Luca Baschera, Bruce Gordon and Christian Moser (eds.), *Following Zwingli: Applying the Past in Reformation Zurich* (Farnham, Surrey: Ashgate, 2014), 81-105.

IN MEMORIAM MARTINI BUCERI: THE CONTESTED AFTERLIFE OF MARTIN BUCER IN ENGLAND

N. Scott Amos[352]

For someone who spent barely 20 months in Cambridge (from July 1549 to the end of February 1551), the reaction of the University (and city) to Martin Bucer's death was remarkable. Just as, in January 1550,[353] the inauguration of his lectures as Regius Professor of Divinity appeared to generate a buzz of excitement over what the University now had – the greatest continental theologian to teach in Cambridge since Erasmus – so too (in contrast) Bucer's death on 28 February/1 March 1551 left many in Cambridge stunned at the magnitude of what they had lost. The funeral was an occasion both for an outpouring of grief and for a final opportunity to pay tribute to one who, in the eyes of his hosts, had exercised a substantial influence for the good of reform in his place of exile; even if historians have not reached a consensus as to the extent of that influence, there was no doubt about that for the mourners and those who officiated at the ceremonies.

Yet that was not the sum of how Bucer was remembered and regarded after his death. It was evident during his sojourn that not all in Cambridge shared a laudatory view of the Alsatian, and their turn to give expression to their estimation of him came within a few years. In contrast with the funeral, evidence of hostility towards Bucer and his influence became dramatically clear in early 1557 when, in conjunction

---

[352] I gratefully acknowledge support for the research towards this essay that I received in a Summer Research Grant for 2018 provided by the Faculty Development Committee, University of Lynchburg.
[353] His lectures had an immediate impact, and the hall was packed with students and senior members of the University among his auditors. For instance, there is the letter of Isaac Cellarius to Francis Dryander of 23 January 1550, quoted in A. E. Harvey, 'Martin Bucer in England' (Dissertation, Marburg, 1906), 47 (n.): 'Bucer...began on 10 January to interpret publicly in the Schools the Epistle to the Ephesians, with the great approbation of all.'

with a visitation of the University to cleanse it of corruptions of various sorts and most especially of all traces of heresy, the remains of Bucer and those of his fellow exile-in-residence, Paul Fagius (who had died in November 1549), were ordered to be dug up from their respective places of burial, subjected to a trial, and then burned at the stake following their condemnation for heresy. Bucer was clearly perceived as a significant threat, even though now dead for six years, and a person whose continuing influence must be thoroughly repudiated. Happily, for those who had a positive view of the great Alsatian, the story of reactions to Bucer did not end there, and a final episode in this contest for how he should be remembered took place in 1560, shortly after the accession of Elizabeth I to the throne, during yet another visitation of the University, which included the restoration of the good name and reputation of Bucer and Fagius in yet another ceremony.

Clearly, Bucer had more than ordinary significance for mid-Tudor Cambridge, and it has been argued recently that what these events reveal, in a particular way, is that his importance is to be found as a symbol in the context of the larger struggle in Cambridge for and against Reform, what has been called a 'contested Reformation'.[354] For one side, his appointment served to demonstrate the University's commitment to Protestantism, and his funeral is said to have been an occasion to 'consolidate Cambridge's – and England's – Reformed credentials'; for the other side, he was a symbol of heresy, and even the continued presence of his corpse was a danger, a source of contagion to be eradicated.[355]

Without denying this argument regarding the symbolic significance of Bucer, I would contend that these events also tell us something about the man himself and his personal impact upon Cantabrigians during his sojourn, and something about the ways in which his contemporaries viewed his importance and influence in substantive terms. Bucer engendered strong responses in Cambridge, either of warm affection and reverence for one learned beyond all measure, or of an intense hatred strong enough to lead to the notorious exhumation and burning of his corpse: but both sides agreed that he mattered a

---

[354] Ceri Law, *Contested Reformations in the University of Cambridge, 1535-1584* (Boydell Press, 2018).
[355] Law, *Contested Reformations*, 49.

great deal. In as much as Bucer was at the heart of this particular 'contested Reformation', and in the light of recent historiography on the English Reformation, I would argue that there is a need for a fresh examination of Bucer's part in the efforts at reform in England, at the centre of which was, perhaps more than any other aspect of involvement in that enterprise, his sojourn in Cambridge.

The honored dead

As brief as Bucer's time in Cambridge was, it was effectively made all the briefer still because he was ill for much of it. This makes what he accomplished, and the impression he left, all the more remarkable.[356] However, from January 1551, he was dangerously ill, and his death came during the night of 28 February/1 March 1551.[357] While the end could hardly have been unexpected, it appears to have come as a great shock nonetheless, and left his circle of supporters as well as the wider community deeply grieved.

The evidence of this grief is most dramatically seen in the funeral itself (held on 3 March), and which was described in letters written by John Cheke to Peter Martyr Vermigli (dated 10 March, written from Westminster), and by Nicholas Carr to John Cheke (dated 15 March, written from Trinity College, Cambridge.[358] Carr was present for the

---

[356] For a short survey of Bucer's Cambridge sojourn, see N. Scott Amos, "The Alsatian among the Athenians: Martin Bucer, Mid-Tudor Cambridge and the Edwardian Reformation," *Reformation and Renaissance Review* 4.1 (June 2002): 94-124.

[357] I use 1 January as the beginning of the year rather than Lady Day (25 March), which the English did at this time. The date of 28 February is given in the letter of Peter Martyr Vermigli to Conrad Hubert, written on 8 March (found in Hastings Robinson, ed., *Original Letters Relative to the English Reformation* [Cambridge, 1849], 2:491); and Vermigli to the College of St Thomas in Strasbourg, also 8 March (G. C. Gorham, ed., *Gleanings of a few scattered ears* [London, 1857], 237). The date of 1 March is given by Nicholas Carr to John Cheke, written on 15 March (*Martini Buceri Scripta Anglicana fere omnia* [Basel, 1577], 867); and the letter of the University of Cambridge to Edward VI, dated 4 March (CCCC MS 106, nr. 164, 461-464).

[358] This correspondence was published in *De obitu doctissimi et sanctissimi Theologi Doctoris Martini Buceri, Regii in celeberrisima Cantabrigiensi*

funeral whereas Cheke was not, but Cheke's account is the more vivid in describing the setting and the emotions of the occasion. He noted that not only were all or most members of the University part of the funeral procession, as well as the Mayor of Cambridge, but also a large number of common folk, resulting in a total of some 3000 in attendance by his reckoning.[359] Given that the population of the town was likely no more than 5000-6000,[360] this was a remarkable turnout for an émigré theologian of brief tenure. Cheke judged that this showing of "the lower orders" was testimony to Bucer's concern for them, and his zeal for true religion had won their regard. The fact of the turnout is more than rhetorical exaggeration: the press of their numbers in Great St Mary's, the University Church where the service was conducted, was such that the benches in the Church were damaged – testimony to this is found in an entry in the Great St Mary's churchwardens' accounts from 1551 detailing an expense 'for nails to mend the seats in the Church when Mr Doctor Bucerr was buried'.[361]

The general description of the services for Bucer is the same in both accounts: a Latin oration, a sermon, and (on the following day) a communion service with sermon.[362] Cheke described how Walter Haddon – in his capacity as University Orator, but also as a close friend of Bucer – held forth in a moving Latin oration, the force of which was all the more striking on account of his own illness at the time (he was described by Cheke as 'a dying man ... discoursing on death').[363] The impact of the oration was such 'that tears gushed from every eye' and

---

Academia apud Anglos publice sacrarum literarum praelectoris Epistolae duae. (London, 1551). These texts, and more, were incorporated into *Historia vera: de vita, obitu, sepultura, accusatione, condemnatione, exhumatione, combustione, honorificaque tandem restitutione beatorum atque doctiss. Theologorum D. Martini Buceri & Pauli Fagii* (Strasbourg, 1562), to which I make reference in this essay. In *Historia vera*, Cheke's letter is on B^r-B.vi^r; Carr's letter is on B.vi^v-F.ii^r.

[359] Gorham, *Gleanings*, 238-239; *Historia vera*, B.iiii^r.
[360] Law, *Contested Reformations*, 8, notes that in 1587 (36 years later), the population was only 6500.
[361] J. E. Foster, ed., *Churchwardens' Accounts of St. Mary the Great Cambridge from 1504 to 1635* (Cambridge, 1905), 123.
[362] *Historia vera*, B.iii^v-B.v^v (Cheke), D.vi^v-F.ii^r (Carr).
[363] Gorham, *Gleanings*, 239; *Historia vera*, B.iiii^r.

'trickled down every cheek', not least Haddon's own, as he was overcome by emotion.[364] Haddon was then followed by Matthew Parker, Master of Corpus Christi College and sometime Vice-Chancellor of the University (and another close friend of Bucer), who preached – in English – a sermon on a Deutero-Canonical book, The Wisdom of Solomon, chapter 4:7, 10, and 14-19, and the sermon was followed by what was in effect a eulogy.[365] Bucer's body was interred in the choir, near the high altar, with all honours. On the following day, a communion service was held, again in Great St Mary's. After the celebration of the sacrament (of which 400 partook), John Redman, Master of Trinity, preached a sermon on the subject of death, and how it is to be taken,[366] and asked, 'what was laudable and worthy of imitation in the life of Bucer? What was memorable and glorious in his death?'[367] Finally, Cheke described how an abundance of epitaphs in either Greek or Latin were placed on his grave among the wreaths and garlands, some of them composed by students out of a zeal to show their regard for Bucer, but others composed by the leading lights of mid-Tudor humanism.[368]

---

[364] Gorham, *Gleanings*, 239. *Historia vera*, B.iiii^v.
[365] Gorham, *Gleanings*, 239-240; *Historia vera*, B.iiii^v-B.v^r. Parker's sermon in Latin translation is found in *Historia vera*, H.v^r-K^v; its English original will be considered in greater detail below.
[366] This perhaps echoes the title of the published form of Parker's sermon from the day before, *Howe we ought to take the death of the Godly*.
[367] Gorham, *Gleanings*, 240; *Historia vera*, B.v^{r-v}. Here, Carr's account of what Redman said is fuller. Given the tense relationship of Bucer to the fellows of Trinity College (to which I will return), of which Redman was Master, it is striking to find that while he is frank about his own differences with Bucer, he then goes on to compare Bucer to Augustine as a father of the Church. Carr reported that Redman also made reference to Bucer's commentaries on Romans and on Psalms, with words of praise for their lucidity and richness. See *Historia vera*, E.v^r-E.viii^r.
[368] Gorham, *Gleanings*, 240; *Historia vera*, B.v^v. These appear in the *Historia vera*, K.vi^v-N.iii^r. An examination of these epitaphs is found in John F. McDiarmid, "Classical Epitaphs for Heroes of Faith: Mid-Tudor Neo-Latin Memorial Volumes and Their Protestant Humanist Context," *International Journal of the Classical Tradition* 3/1 (Summer 1996):23-47.

Yet we are not left with only summary accounts of what was said on this occasion from which to infer the importance of Bucer to Cambridge. Carr's letter includes the actual text of one of the two addresses given that day, the Latin oration by Walter Haddon.[369] As Haddon presented him, Bucer stood in exalted company: he had the profound insight of Augustine; he was the master of languages like unto Jerome; he embodied doctrine and discipline as did Cyprian; he had the *scientia* of Origen; he possessed the authority of Ambrose; his preaching was the equal of Chrysostom's for its clarity (a point on which anyone familiar with Bucer's turgid verbosity would smile at); and he ranked with Bernard of Clairvaux for integrity of life. Indeed, Haddon placed Bucer among the prophets and the apostles and, because of his sufferings, with the martyrs.

In addition to the text of Haddon's oration, we also have to hand the sermon preached by Matthew Parker and his eulogy for Bucer which together paint an even more detailed picture of what Bucer meant to his fellow Reformers in Cambridge in terms of both personality and active participation in Cambridge.[370] Like others at the time, Parker

---

[369] *Historia vera*, D.viii^r-E.iii^r. He states he had a copy of this directly from Haddon a few days after its delivery, and so he inserts it in his report in lieu of his own summary. This was later published as "Gualteri Haddoni oratio, de obitu Martini Buceri," in Walter Haddon, *G. Haddoni Legum Doctoris, s. Reginae Elisabethae à supplicum libellis, lucubrationes passim collectae, & editae. Studio & labore Thomae Hatcheri Cantabrigiensis* (London, apud William Seres, 1567), 83-89.

[370] *Howe we ought to take the death of the Godly* (London, 1551). The sermon is A.ii^r-C.iii^r; the eulogy is C.iii^v-F.vi^v. Parker's sermon is not unknown, but in modern scholarship most references to it are to the 1587 printing (*A funerall sermon, both godlye, learned and comfortable, preached at S. Maries in Cambridge, Anno 1551. at the buriall of the reuerend doctor, and faithfull pastor of the Churche of Christe, Martin Bucer* [Thomas Purfoote, 1587]), produced more than a decade after the death of Matthew Parker, and which was a translation of a Latin version found in both the *Historia vera* and in the *Scripta Anglicana*, a Latin text which was itself is a translation of the English original. What is frequently missed is that Parker's sermon was first printed in English in 1551, and that this printing includes much more than what is found in the 1587 printing – as noted above, it includes the sermon, but also the eulogy which followed Parker's sermon and the prayers at its end. It is

gave voice to the grief and shock felt by many. However, much of his eulogy was concerned with Bucer's tenure as a Professor and his participation in the academic life of the University, which Bucer is said to have performed with zeal and diligence.[371] Parker was struck by how Bucer was constantly teaching or writing, taking great care in handling all subjects, showing forth a profound depth of learning in the Scriptures and the Fathers.[372] His piety was obvious to all: in his teaching he had a zeal for godly living;[373] he began and ended his lectures with prayer, and always incorporated the Psalms in his prayers.[374] He had a supremely even and peaceable temperament,[375] a disposition which manifested itself as well in his conduct of disputations; his moderation of them kept the focus on the issue at hand, not the persons disputing; he would not let pass the errors of his friends, and in his own participation in disputations he was not desirous for glory in defeating his opponents; he sought only to vindicate the truth.[376]

Bucer's zeal was not only for the teaching of scholars; he was as concerned that the unlearned grow in the knowledge of true religion as much as the learned. Parker marvelled at Bucer's commitment to reaching all levels of his audience, the 'best learned' as well as the

---

also worth noting that the *Historia vera* incorrectly identifies the Latin translation of Parker's eulogy as Haddon's oration. I am at work on an essay exploring this problem, provisionally entitled, "The curious case of Matthew Parker's sermon at Bucer's Funeral."

[371] In this respect his speech is a resource not fully exploited by historians (most of whom seem unaware of it).

[372] *Howe we ought to take the death of the Godly*, D.v^v, D.vii^v, E.viii^r. In the latter, Parker gives a concise outline of what Bucer taught in his Regius lectures on Ephesians. Carr also discussed Bucer's teaching in similar terms: *Historia vera*, C.ii^v, C.vi^r.

[373] *Howe we ought to take the death of the Godly*, D.vi^r.

[374] *Howe we ought to take the death of the Godly*, D.vi^v. He also preached at the University Church, St Mary's, whenever there was no one available to fill the pulpit, and that that his preaching influenced all those who learned from him (E.ii^v).

[375] *Howe we ought to take the death of the Godly*, C.v^r.

[376] *Howe we ought to take the death of the Godly*, D.vii^v-D.viiir.

'meanest part'.³⁷⁷ At the same time, Bucer was also declared to have had a deep commitment to charity for the poor and needy (a general awareness of which may account in part for the large turnout at his funeral), and Parker explicitly turned to the 'lower orders' attending the funeral as he spoke of Bucer's concern for the general populace.³⁷⁸ Bucer had a zeal for the 'body of the town' that they should be as well provided with preaching as the University,³⁷⁹ but his charity extended as well to 'relieving the necessity of the people as his ability would give him leave'.³⁸⁰ This social concern was of a piece with his zeal for the health and well-being of the commonwealth.³⁸¹

In addition to all that was positive about Bucer's sojourn, Parker also described the sufferings of Bucer throughout his last years. As we have already observed, Bucer was plagued by ill-health throughout his time in Cambridge.³⁸² Parker lamented that his friend pushed himself beyond what his failing physical strength permitted. He came with the first, and tarried with the last, not sparing himself in the service the gospel; Parker believed that had Bucer driven himself less relentlessly, he might still be alive at that moment to profit the Church.³⁸³ In this connection, Parker grieved that Bucer's death came just as he was taking up the matter of the Lord's Supper: 'Howe necessary had it bene

---

³⁷⁷ *Howe we ought to take the death of the Godly*, D.v^r.
³⁷⁸ *Howe we ought to take the death of the Godly*, E^v.
³⁷⁹ *Howe we ought to take the death of the Godly*, E.ii^v-E.iii^r.
³⁸⁰ *Howe we ought to take the death of the Godly*, F.iii^v.
³⁸¹ *Howe we ought to take the death of the Godly*, E.iii^r. Parker notes: "In which policie he was so notably expert to the devise therfore, that other whiles, I was in doubt wether I might judge hym to have bene befortyme more occupied in the studye of learnyng, or exercysed in the affayres of governaunce the common wealthe." Parker may be alluding to Bucer's work in composing *De regno Christi*, which would have involved consultations with other Cantabrigians concerned with the same things. Carr commented on Bucer's work in composing *De regno Christi*. *Historia vera*, D.ii^v.
³⁸² *Howe we ought to take the death of the Godly*, D.ii^v. See Carr on this: *Historia vera*, C^v, C.v^r.
³⁸³ *Howe we ought to take the death of the Godly*, D.vii^r. Parker recounts the punishing tasks to which Bucer set himself, going far beyond what would have been expected of him: D.viii^v-E^r.

to have had this learned man so long at the lest way with us, till he had debated this great controversy to an end'.[384]

His sufferings were also at the hands of those who were bitterly opposed to him. In the sermon, Parker compared Bucer to Moses in respect of the ingratitude shown to a faithful servant of God.[385] And just as God punished Israel by taking Moses from them as they were poised to enter the Promised Land, so too Bucer was taken from Cambridge in the midst of evangelical advance.[386] This theme of suffering for the sake of the God's truth is found in the eulogy as well. In his comments on Bucer's mild disposition, he referred to the 'venom' of Bucer's opponents, and their 'malicious and disdainful envy [as they] laboureth to deface his commendation'.[387] The slanders against Bucer were of a piece with the slanders against the prophets.[388] Parker also compared Bucer's persecution with that directed against Origen, in particular how Origen's enemies sought to defame him and distort his writings.[389] He says much the same of Augustine in his struggles with the Donatists,[390] of Athanasius against the Arians,[391] of

---

[384] *Howe we ought to take the death of the Godly*, E viii^v-F^r (here at F^r). Perhaps Parker is referring to the work later printed as *Exomologesis sive Confessio de S. Eucharistia aphoristice Scripta* in *SA*, 538-545. Bucer was at work on another piece on the subject of the Supper when he died. This piece appears in CCCC, MS 113, nr. 48. It is barely legible, and at one point Bucer apologized for the feebleness of his hand. Matthew Parker wrote below the text, "the last of M. Bucer's studies to be written" (*studiorum postremum scriptum M. Buceri*). This lament of Parker brings into view Bucer's fraught relationship with the Zurich theologians and their English followers, but that is a subject for another time. See Amos, "Alsatian among the Athenians," 101, 105-109.
[385] *Howe we ought to take the death of the Godly*, B.ii^v-B.iii^v.
[386] *Howe we ought to take the death of the Godly*, B.iiii^v-B.v^r; on B.v^v he further alludes to opposition to Bucer in Cambridge.
[387] *Howe we ought to take the death of the Godly*, C.v^v. At D.i^v-D.ii^r, he has more to say about the envy of Bucer's opponents.
[388] *Howe we ought to take the death of the Godly*, C.vii^r.
[389] *Howe we ought to take the death of the Godly*, C.vii^v-C.viii^r.
[390] *Howe we ought to take the death of the Godly*, C.viii^v.
[391] *Howe we ought to take the death of the Godly*, C.viii^v.

Chrysostom against his opponents,³⁹² all of whom suffered as did Bucer. Bucer was in exalted company.

Bucer's critics notwithstanding, Parker's summary judgment of Bucer is a clear demonstration of the high esteem he, and by extension others at Cambridge, had for Bucer, and the value they set on his participation in reform. His most learned days were among the English.³⁹³ He was a true catholic in the fullest sense of the term.³⁹⁴ He was a repository of wisdom,³⁹⁵ and he ranked with Augustine, Athanasius, and Jerome – indeed, he was a 'universal Epiphanius in that knowledge, expert in the controversies of all times, or rather a boke of common places drawn by long study and excellent memory out of the store of them all'.³⁹⁶ Yet Parker, for all that he had to say, felt he never fully plumbed the depth of Bucer:

> I perceived that I could not say as yet I ever knew Bucer. He was not known by a day or two, as most part of men may soon be. There was much more in him than either his books, his readings [i.e., lectures] or disputations singularly considered was able to express him. Verily he was at one word, a singular gift of God, a treasure hidden, an incomparable ornament.³⁹⁷

Lest anyone think that he was engaging in conventional rhetorical hyperbole, Parker went on to declare that what he said on this occasion was more than ceremonial: 'I speak not this of partial affection (good audience) God is record to my conscience; I speak it not of office as to satisfy the room wherein I am ...; I speak it in the testimony and duty

---

³⁹² *Howe we ought to take the death of the Godly*, Dʳ.
³⁹³ *Howe we ought to take the death of the Godly*, Bʳ.
³⁹⁴ *Howe we ought to take the death of the Godly*, C.iiʳ, E.ivᵛ, E.viiʳ.
³⁹⁵ *Howe we ought to take the death of the Godly*, E.viiʳ.
³⁹⁶ *Howe we ought to take the death of the Godly*, E.viiᵛ. Epiphanius of Salamis (ca. 316-403) was bishop of Salamis and noted for his comprehensive knowledge and refutation of heresies and his stout defense of Nicene orthodoxy.
³⁹⁷ *Howe we ought to take the death of the Godly*, E.iiiᵛ.

of my heavy conscience'.[398] He called on his auditors 'to ponder what a treasure we had, what a loss we have'.[399]

Convention had its part to play in the oratory at Bucer's funeral, but there was more than convention in what was said. There was at Bucer's funeral a heartfelt sense of loss expressed by figures of weight: Cheke, Carr, Haddon, Redman, and above all Parker. Bucer clearly meant a tremendous amount to them personally and, in their view, to the advance of reform more generally, and his death was perceived to have left a void at a critical time. There was less 'a display of Protestant piety and celebration'[400] here than there was grief at what the University had lost.

A blot to be expunged

Yet Bucer was not without his enemies in Cambridge, most notably within Trinity College, to which he was attached by virtue of his appointment as Regius Professor.[401] True, John Redman, then Master of Trinity, spoke highly of Bucer at the Communion service celebrated in honour of Bucer the day after the funeral, but he was the exception to the rule. Those most opposed to him included John Young and Thomas Sedgewick of Trinity, and Andrew Perne of Peterhouse. The nature of the opposition Bucer faced within Trinity is most clearly seen in the events of the Summer of 1550, when Bucer was challenged to a disputation by Sedgwick, Young, and Perne, and they clashed over a number of doctrinal issues generated by his lectures on Ephesians.[402] Later in the Summer, Young began a series of lectures on I Timothy,

---

[398] *Howe we ought to take the death of the Godly*, E.iii^v-E.iiii^r, here at E.iiii^r.
[399] *Howe we ought to take the death of the Godly*, E.iiii^r.
[400] Law, *Contested Reformations*, 1.
[401] For more on this, see Amos, "Alsatian among the Athenians," 110-113.
[402] Material from this dispute is printed in *Scripta Anglicana*, 711-784. The propositions as printed in the *SA* (712): "Primum. Canonici libri docent soli abunde renatos, quae sint saluti, omnia. Secundum. Nulla est in terris Ecclesia, quae non erret, tam in fide, quam in moribus. Tertium. Ita gratis iustificamur a Deo, ut ante iustificationem revera peccatum sit, iramque Dei in nos provocet, quicquid boni operis facere videamur. Iustificari autem bona opera facimus necessario." See Amos, "Alsatian among the Athenians," 113-115.

focusing in particular on the issue of justification and attacking both Bucer's position in the earlier disputation, and Bucer personally.[403] Young began to work behind the scenes, seeking to undermine Bucer's standing in the university.[404] Bucer took the threat very seriously, and a flurry of letters was the result.[405] Parker was well aware that Young was a thorn in Bucer's side,[406] and when speaking in his eulogy of the opposition Bucer encountered, Parker alluded to Young twice, in unflattering terms – an indication of the antagonism the latter had for the great Alsatian (and of the contempt Parker had for Young).[407] In light of this, it is not hard to conceive that Young (and Perne), painfully aware of all that was said in praise of Bucer at his funeral and of his interment in a place of high honor, may have been biding their time, waiting for an opportunity to have the last word about their enemy.

That opportunity came with the 1557 Visitation of the University ordered by Cardinal Pole.[408] The evidence for this phase of Bucer's

---

[403] Herbert Vogt, "Martin Bucer und die Kirche von England" (Dissertation, Münster, 1968), 52. See Bucer to Cheke, 29 August 1550, in Harvey, "Bucer in England," 127-130 (CCCC MS 113, nr. 39).

[404] These details are found in Bucer's letter to Grindal 31 August 1550, in Gorham, *Gleanings*, 163-167 (*Scripta Anglicana*, 803). Note "a" to this letter provides a concise overview of the affair.

[405] Bucer to the university of Cambridge, 24 August, 1550 (*Scripta Anglicana*, 797-807); Bucer to Cheke, 29 August 1550 (CCCC MS 113, nr. 39), in Harvey, "Bucer in England", 127-130; Bucer to Grindal, 31 August 1550 (Gorham, *Gleanings*, 163-167); Bucer to Peter Martyr, 31 August 1550 (Gorham, *Gleanings*, 163-168).

[406] Something Carr noted as well: *Historia vera*, C.ii^r-C.viii^v.

[407] "But with quiet spirite he would rather teache the truthe, than to contend with yong devines in vanities of words." *Howe we ought to take the death of the Godly*, D.viii^r. In the copy of *Howe we ought to take the death of the Godly* found in the Parker Library (SP 36), the words "yong devines" is underscored in red crayon, which is characteristic of the markings Parker himself made in his books, and in addition is a marginal note which reads "alludit ad D Younge." On D.viii^{r-v}, Parker went on to say, "And though he perceived howe easily he myghte have driven ther gayest argumentes which they most set by, to ther rebuke to winne a laude, which yong and not mortified men desier in al ther doing...."

[408] An excellent discussion of the Visitation is found in Ceri Law, "The 1557 Visitation of the University of Cambridge," in *Catholic Renewal and*

afterlife is found in two sources, this time written from two perspectives: the *Historia de 173ight173itio ... atque 173ight173itio excellentissimorum Theologorum D. Martini Buceri & Paul Fagii*;[409] and a manuscript record of the Visitation produced by John Mere, the Registrary of the University.[410] It is interesting to note that among those involved in the Visitation, in particular with reference to Bucer, were the three opponents just named, especially Perne and Young, and that much of the activity in this connection was conducted at Trinity College.[411] Admittedly, Perne was Vice Chancellor, and was of necessity involved in the Visitation by virtue of his office; Young was Regius Professor of Divinity, and would also have been normally involved in such matters; but there is no doubting their zeal to pursue their old enemy, even to the extent of an assault on his mortal remains. The Visitation provided a major opportunity for Bucer's old foes to

---

Protestant Resistance in Marian England, edited by Elizabeth Evenden and Vivienne Westbrook, 65-91 (Farnham: Surry, Ashgate, 2015). See also Law, *Contested Reformations*, 74-83.

[409] Found in *Historia vera*, Q^r -V.6^r, dated 1562. This was translated into English by Arthur Golding as *A briefe treatise....* almost immediately in the same year. Golding's work also appears in John Foxe, *Acts and Monuments*, all editions, though with some deletions from the 1570 edition onwards. At the same time, additional material was introduced in 1570 that appears to have been supplied to Foxe by Matthew Parker. When I provide cross-references to Foxe, it is generally to the 1563 edition, though on occasion I also make reference to material found in the 1570 edition. In all instances, I rely on John Foxe, *The Unabridged Acts and Monuments Online* or *TAMO* (1563 and 1570 editions) (The Digital Humanities Institute, Sheffield, 2011). Available from: http//www.dhi.ac.uk/foxe. Cross-references will be in the following format: Foxe (1563) or Foxe (1570), followed by book and page numbers. My source for the information above about the material supplied by Parker is the textual commentary in *TAMO* (1570), Bk 12, 2182 [2142].

[410] "Queen Mary=s Visitation." A printed copy of this is found in John Lamb, ed., *A Collection of Letters, Statutes and other Documents from the MS. Library of Corpus Christi College Illustrative of the History of the University of Cambridge, during the Period of the Reformation, from AD MD to AD MDLXXII* (London: John W. Parker, 1838), 184-236, to which I will refer below as Lamb. The original manuscript is CCCC MS 106.

[411] Bucer's opponents are mentioned numerous times Mere's account, as well as in *A briefe treatise*, and so Foxe. The same is true of references to Trinity College.

denounce decisively the influence of Bucer and remove from the University the stain of its association with him. Yet, in a way, their efforts and the work of the Visitation provide further evidence of the impact Bucer had upon Cambridge – the perception of his continuing influence, even after death, being sufficiently strong so as to require the rather macabre action to which we will now turn.

While much of the work of the Visitation as described by Mere involved the usual sort of investigation into the colleges of the University and the rooting out of moral and administrative corruption, the chief objective, or at least the first order of business, seems to have been the decisive repudiation of Martin Bucer. He was the source of continuing contagion in the view of more than a few in the hierarchy 'who saw so many so sore corrupted and spotted with this infection [the doctrine Bucer taught], that ... it were not possible by all likelihood to quench it many years after'.[412] It required direct, drastic action.

The Visitors arrived in Cambridge on 10 January 1557, and among their first acts was to place Great St Mary's and St Michael's under interdict because each held within the mortal remains (respectively) of Bucer and Paul Fagius, a move which reinforces the focus of the Visitation on Bucer.[413] The proceedings of the Visitation proper began on 11 January with an oration by John Stokes, University Orator, in praise of the University and of Pole and the Visitors, to which Cuthbert Scott, bishop of Chester and Master of Christ's College made response as a member of the Commission. This was followed by a sermon *ad clerum* by Thomas Peacock (of Trinity) denouncing heresies and heretics, chiefly Bilney, Latimer, Cranmer, and Ridley.[414] On 12 January, meeting in the Schools, the officers of the University took the decision to call on the Visitors to proceed on the matter of Bucer and Fagius:

---

[412] *A Briefe Treatise*, A.5^{r-v}; Foxe (1563), bk. 5, 1619 [1538].

[413] *A Briefe treatise*, A.7^v; Foxe (1563), bk. 5, 1619 [1538]. The interdict did not affect public assembly and even preaching in St Mary's, and in fact much of the public activity of the Visitation took place in the Church.

[414] *A Briefe treatise*, B^r-C.1^v (Oration by Stokes), C.1^v-C.4^v (response by Scott), and C.5^r (Peacocke's sermon, which is only mentioned here); for all this, see Foxe (1563), bk. 5, 1620 [1539]-1621 [1540]. The Latin text of Stokes's oration is found in Foxe (1570), bk. 12, 2183 [2143]-2184 [2144].

> The Vice-chancellor and the masters of the Colleges assembled at the common schools, where every man gave his verdict on what he thought meet to be done. After much debating they agreed al together in this determination. That for as much as Martin Bucer, while he lived had not only sowed pernicious & erroneous doctrine among them but also had himself been a sectary and famous heretic, erring from the Catholic church, and giving others occasion to fall from the same likewise: a supplication should be made to the L. Commissioners in the name of the whole University, that his dead carcass might forth with be digged up, (for so it was needfull to be done) to the intent that inquisition might be made as touching his doctrine, the which being brought in examination, if it were not found to be good and wholesome, the law might proceed against him: for it was against the rule of the holy Canons that his body should be buried in Christian burial.[415]

The lead in this was taken by Perne, who was appointed to the task as 'the man metest [=most fit] for the purpose'.[416] The proceedings were quite deliberate in the intent to reverse Bucer's funeral and what it said: as Scott was reported to have declared at a later point, 'now forasmuch as he was buried with great pomp & solemnity, we think it necessary that his burning be executed with no less solemnity'.[417] And over the next several weeks, the process went forward. On 13 January, Perne went to Trinity College and collected the formal sentence of condemnation, and on the 14 January the instrument of condemnation was sealed by Perne and Young, among several others, and taken to the Visitors, who then required that it be revised in light of certain points

---

[415] *A Briefe treatise*, D.2ᵛ-D.3ᵛ; Foxe (1563), bk. 5, 1622 [1541]. Lamb, 201-202 records of this: "The heddes met in the scholes where and by whom it was concluded that for as myche as Bucer had byn an arche heretycke teachynge by his life tyme many detestable heresies and errors, sute should be made unto the Visitors by thuniversity that he myght be taken upp and ordered according to the law & lykewyes P. Fagius."
[416] *A Briefe treatise*, D.4ʳ; Foxe (1563), bk. 5, 1622 [1541].
[417] *A Briefe treatise*, D.8ʳ; Foxe (1563), bk. 5, 1623 [1542].

which they changed in the original.[418] On 15 January, the revisions were made, and the business of the Visitors moved to Great St Mary's, where a new commission from the Lord Cardinal came and was read, namely '*De 176ight176ition heretic. Punitat*'.[419] At this point, Perne 'required citation of the said Bucer and Fagius to be made and further process to be made on Monday next',[420] and on the next day citations were posted at St Mary's and at the Schools.[421] There were several other legal manoeuvres that followed, including summoning witness to swear to the heresies of Bucer and Fagius (including Young and Sedgwick),[422] and on 20 January Perne called at the Mayor's 'to know if he with his company 176ight be ready on Tuesday next [26 January] to be at St Mary's for the condemnation of Bucer'.[423]

When the day of condemnation arrived, the Vice Chancellor, the Mayor, and the Visitors assembled at St Mary's, and Scott as a Visitor declared that in response to the request made of the Visitors by the University, and after due process had been followed, the moment had come for the condemnation of Bucer and Fagius as heretics, and he

---

[418] Lamb, 202-203; compare with Foxe (1563), bk. 5, 1622 [1541]; *A briefe treatise*, D.4^v.

[419] Lamb, 203-204; compare with Foxe (1563), bk. 5, 1623 [1542]; *A briefe treatise*, E.3^{r-v}.

[420] Lamb, 204; compare with *A briefe treatise*, E.3^v-E.4^r; Foxe (1563), bk. 5, 1624 [1543], both of which phrase the citation to be a call on Bucer, or someone in his stead, to answer the charges. This citation was repeated on 16 January, and again on 18 January, and at no time did anyone appear; Foxe (1563), bk. 5, 1626 [1545]).

[421] Lamb, 204.

[422] Lamb, 205-206; *A briefe treatise*, E.5^r, and Foxe (1563), bk. 5, 1625[1544]; both report that Nicholas Carr was among them, though this has been disputed (see Law, *Contested Reformations*, 77, who refers to Michael H. Crawford, "Carr, Nicholas [1522/3-1568]" *Oxford Dictionary of National Biography*). Crawford notes there was also a Richard Carr at the University at this time, with whom Nicholas Carr is often confused. However, note that also listed among the witnesses were a certain Parker and a Redman, both of whom are explicitly said not to have been those who "preached honorablye" of Bucer. This is not said here of Carr.

[423] Lamb, 207.

read out the sentence of condemnation.[424] This was then followed by a sermon preached by Perne that lasted several hours, taking as his text Psalm 132 (in the Vulgate), 'Behold how good and pleasant it is when brothers dwell in unity' (one wonders if the irony of this choice of text occurred to anyone), in which among other things he attacked Bucer's doctrine for creating divisions in the commonwealth,[425] and claimed that he taught that God was the source of both good and evil.[426] During the sermon, verses in Latin and Greek denouncing Bucer and Fagius were posted on the Church doors by students, in clear imitation of what had been done at Bucer's funeral six years earlier.[427] On the next day, the sentence of condemnation was sealed and sent by the Visitors to London for authorization for the next step – the exhumation and the burning of the corpses.[428] On 1 February, the writ *De comburendo haeretico* was received from London and delivered to the Mayor, and 6 February was set for the execution of the decree (a day so chosen because it was a market day and the greatest number of people would be present who, it was hoped, would be suitably impressed).[429] When the day came, the bodies were exhumed and burned in the marketplace, along with cartloads of books. While the bodies were 'a-roasting in the fire', Thomas Watson, one of the Visitors and bishop-elect of Lincoln,[430] preached a sermon of nearly three hours 'setting forth Bucer's wickedness and heretical doctrine'.[431] The following day, the process of restoration was complete, when both St Michael's and St Mary's were re-consecrated once the interdict was lifted.[432]

However, though the claim was that the University demanded this, not everyone in Marian Cambridge was supportive of these actions. It is

---

[424] *A briefe treatise*, F.6ᵛ-G.2r ; Foxe (1563), bk. 5, 1627 [1546]-1628 [1547]. Foxe (1570), bk. 12 2188[2148]-2189 [2149] provides the Latin text of the sentence of condemnation.
[425] *A briefe treatise*, G.3ᵛ-G.5ᵛ; Foxe (1563), bk. 5, 1628 [1547]-1629 [1548].
[426] *A briefe treatise*, G.4ᵛ; Foxe (1563), bk. 5, 1629 [1548].
[427] Lamb, 210; Foxe (1563), bk. 5, 1629 [1548]; *A briefe treatise*, G.5ᵛ-G.6ʳ.
[428] Lamb, 211; Foxe (1563), bk. 5, 1629 [1548]; *A briefe treatise*, G.6ᵛ-G.7ʳ.
[429] Lamb, 214-215; Foxe (1563), bk. 5, 1630 [1549]; *A briefe treatise*, H.1ʳ-H.2ᵛ.
[430] Foxe (1563), bk. 5, 1618 [1537]; *A briefe treatise*, A.1ᵛ.
[431] Lamb, 216-217; Foxe (1563), bk. 5, 1631 [1550]; *A briefe treatise*, H.3ʳ.
[432] Lamb, 217.

true that no one elected to speak on behalf of Bucer or Fagius when opportunity was provided at various stages of the process. But some refused to speak out against Bucer, even when called on to do so.[433] There is a lengthy passage in *A Briefe Treatise* where Scott seeks to persuade, and then oblige, an unnamed person to serve as Orator for the ceremony of condemnation, only to be met with refusal to speak against a man who, 'as he could gather by other men's talk, he was a man of such integrity & pureness of living, that not even his enemies could find any thing blame worthy in him'.[434] Also, not everyone

---

[433] *A briefe treatise*, D.6^r; Foxe (1563), bk. 5, 1623 [1542].
[434] *A briefe treatise*, D.8^r -E.3^r, here at E.1^v; Foxe (1563), bk. 5, 1623[1542]-1624 [1543]. References that follow are to *A briefe treatise*. This took place around 14 January. Scott had singled out an unnamed Cantabrigian and reminded him that the time was near when Bucer would be dealt with. "Nowe forasmuche as he was burryed with great pompe & solemnitye, we thinke it necessarye, that his burninge be executed with no less solemnitie and furniture" [D.8^r]. "When they wer buried, orations were made before the degrees of thuniversity, and sermons preached to the people: the like thinge nowe also when they shalbe burned, do we purpose to have" [D.8^v E.1^r recto]. Scott then tells this fellow that as he is known as "an expert orator", he (Scott) wants him "to do the thinge." Scott assures him he will join Nicholas Carr, a former student of Scott, with him in this [E.1^r].

The man desisted, and refused the honor, in part because he was not "able to devyse what to saye against so worthy a person ... for he knew not the mannes lyvine and conversacion. But as farre as he could gather bi other mens talke, he was a man of such integritie & purenesse of lyvyng, that not even his enemies could fynde any thyng blame worthy in him. As for his doctryne, it passed his power to iudge of it, howsoever he were deined to be of a corrupt religion, whereof he was not able to determine, considerynge it was a doubtfull Question amonge so great learned clerkes. But this was manifestlye apparante, that Bucer undoubtedly was a man of singular knowledge and dexteritye of witte: the whych for him to abase, he thought it an untolerable unshamelessnesse" [E.1^v -E.2^r].

At length, Scott became enraged, and left the man no choice but to do the opposite of what he had done at Bucer's funeral (when he was among those who lay epitaphs on Bucer's grave), and charged him in the name of the Visitors to do as he was bidden [E.2^v -E.3^r]. "After many wordes, thother answered, that no man was able to shewe anye thinge of his doing, & and if any could be brought before him, he would condiscend to satisffye their pleasure: Othewise he would not by any meanes be induced to speake against

turned in books by the two.[435] Further, Mere recorded that "a great number" of verses in *opposition* to Bucer's burning were found at St John's College.[436] And on the day of the burning, it is reported that the people abhorred what happened, and that the action was seen as cruel.[437] It seems that there were limits to what the Visitors, and Perne, could achieve, and that the over-the-top treatment of Bucer may have been counter-productive.

To be fair, this action against Bucer and Fagius was in keeping with canon law, and was not remarkably unique for the age, but the events still stand out, to say the least, as unusual. What is worth noting, though, is the prominence of Trinity College in all this, and in particular the roles played by Perne and Young. Perne is said to have had deep regrets about his involvement in this,[438] but there is no indication that the same could be said of Young. And given that Scott claimed that the Visitors undertook this action because the University demanded it, and that the will of the University was expressed by Perne, in part in consultation with fellows of Trinity, it is not too much of a stretch to suggest that this notorious action was driven by 'venomous envy and spite' (to borrow from Matthew Parker), as much as anything else. After all, it had been four years since Mary had come to the throne, and the bodies of the reformers had not caused any scandal that required something be done – until the Visitation. What is not in doubt is the passion of the occasion, this time the passion of hatred and revilement – what else could lead Perne and Watson to spend three hours apiece denouncing Bucer? And to return to a point made earlier, while we witness here the reverse image of Bucer's funeral (indeed, one could say a macabre parody of it), we also find in

---

him. At lengthe when none of his writinges could be shewed, the bishop disysted from his purpose" [E.3ʳ].
    And in the end, Scott was the one who gave the oration [which is found at F.7ᵛ-G 2ʳ; Foxe (1563), bk. 5, 1627 [546]-1628 [1547].
[435] *A briefe treatise*, F.1ʳ; Foxe 1563, bk. 5, 1626 [1545].
[436] Lamb, 215.
[437] *A briefe treatise*, H.2ᵛ -H.3ʳ; Foxe (1563), bk. 5, 1630 [1549]-1631 [1550].
[438] *A briefe treatise*, G.5ʳ⁻ᵛ; Foxe (1563), bk. 5, 1629 [1548].

this testimony of the continued relevance (even if seen negatively) of Bucer in the minds of Cantabrigians.

The restoration of honour

We come at the last to the restoration of Bucer's and Fagius's good names. In connection with the 1560 Visitation of the University, Parker, Edmund Grindal (bishop of London, pall bearer at Bucer's funeral, and a devoted friend), and Haddon saw to the restoration of the two Reformers, and thus they directed letters to the Vice Chancellor, who was still Andrew Perne, requiring him to bring this to pass.[439] Apparently Perne was reluctant to do so, but on 22 July 1560 he acted (though one doubts with alacrity and willingness), and put it to 'the degrees of the university' whether this was their will so to do, which it was.[440] This restoration could have been a simple administrative matter, but it was deemed that in light of the dignity and reputation of Bucer – and the shameful way in which his mortal remains had been treated – more was needed, and so on 30 July there was a gathering at St Mary's that formally and publicly restored what had been taken away.[441] Just as the condemnation, exhumation, and burning of Bucer was the inverse of his funeral, so too this restoration was the inverse of the events of 1557.[442]

The proceedings began with an oration by George Acworth, the University Orator.[443] His focus was chiefly on Bucer, rehearsing what he declared could be found in the writings of Cheke, Carr, and Haddon at the time of the funeral, and extolling Bucer's virtues, his daily preaching, and the impact it had upon Cambridge while he lived: 'As long as the ardent love of his religion (wherewith we were inflamed) flourished, it wrought in our hearts an incredible desire of his presence

---

[439] *A briefe treatise*, I.3ᵛ; Foxe (1563), bk. 5, 1633 [1552].
[440] *A briefe treatise*, I.3ᵛ-I.4ʳ; Foxe (1563), bk. 5, 1633 [1552].
[441] *A briefe treatise*, I.4ʳ⁻ᵛ; Foxe (1563), bk. 5, 1633 [1552].
[442] *A briefe treatise*, I.4ᵛ.
[443] The oration is in *A briefe treatise*, I.4ᵛ-L.1ᵛ; Foxe (1563), bk. 5, 1633 [1552]-1636 [1555].

among us'.[444] The time had come to make amend for the crimes against Bucer and Fagius.[445]

Acworth was followed by James Pilkington, then Regius Professor of Divinity.[446] Such was his respect for Bucer and Fagius that he avowed he was conscious of his unworthiness to praise them; but he also believed 'that he which before had done Bucer wrong, should now make him amends for the displeasure'.[447] But rather than praise Bucer at length in terms used at the latter's funeral (as Acworth did in his oration), Pilkington devoted much of what he had to say to denouncing the cruelty of so mistreating the body of dead men, linking the action to the common practice of 'papists' from early in the history of the Church, through the treatment of Wycliffe's body, to contemporary cases. Where he does pause to comment on the virtues and qualities of Bucer, it is almost incidental to his principal end in his sermon, which is to condemn the practice of contemporary Catholics. Bucer was still important, but to be frank, the ceremony of restoration was rather perfunctory and anti-climactic as regards what it reveals about Bucer in Cambridge. Of these three ceremonies, this last one fits best in the narrative of a contested Reformation in Cambridge in which Bucer served as a convenient peg on which to hang an anti-Catholic polemic; one can imagine most any martyr would have served the purpose.

Conclusion

It is generally recognized that after the 1560 Visitation, Bucer began to fade in importance for the English, and one can see this even in the last of the ceremonies we have considered. His name continued to be cited with reverence by both sides in the several internal controversies that afflicted the Elizabethan Church. Yet by then his moment had clearly passed, and other Continental theologians loomed much larger than Bucer. But for Edwardian and Marian Cambridge, Bucer was a major

---

[444] *A briefe treatise*, I.7^v; Foxe (1563), bk. 5, 1634 [1553].
[445] *A briefe treatise*, L.1^{r-v}; Foxe (1563), bk. 5, 1636 [1555].
[446] His sermon is in *A briefe treatise*, L.1^v -M.4^v; Foxe (1563), bk. 5, 1636 [1555]-1639 [1558].
[447] *A briefe treatise*, L.2^{r-v}; Foxe (1563), bk. 5, 1636 [1555]. Is this aimed at Perne, who was present now, but was also present for and active in the condemnation and burning in 1557?

figure. His sojourn was brief, and in the long term his obvious impact was equally brief, but in the view of his hosts he played an important part in the struggle for religious change during the time he spent in Cambridge, either as an ally or as an opponent. If we are to trace out his substantive influence on the wider English Reformation, we must focus on these years, and approach the question of influence bearing in mind the judgement of Matthew Parker, speaking for mid-Tudor Cambridge: '

> There was much more in him than either his books, his readings or disputations singularly considered was able to express him. Verily he was at one word, a singular gift of God, a treasure hidden, an incomparable ornament. [...] Ponder what a treasure we had, what a loss we have.[448]

---

[448] *Howe we ought to take the death of the Godly*, E.iii^v and E.iiii^r.

Appendix A: *A Fruitful Exhortation to the Reading and Knowledge of Holy Scripture*[449]

[The praise of Holy Scripture]

To a Christian man there can be nothing either more necessary or profitable, then the knowledge of Holy Scripture, forasmuch as in it is contained God's true word, setting forth his glory, and also man's duty.

[The perfection of Holy Scripture]

And there is no truth, nor doctrine, necessary for our justification and everlasting salvation, but that is (or may be) drawn out of that fountain and well of truth.

[The knowledge of Holy Scripture]

Therefore, as many as be desirous to enter into the right and perfect way unto God, must apply their minds to know Holy Scripture, without the which, they can neither sufficiently know God and his will, neither their office and duty.

[To whom the knowledge of Holy Scripture is sweet and pleasant]

And as drink is pleasant to them that be dry, and meat to them that be hungry: so is the reading, hearing, searching, and studying of Holy Scripture, to them that be desirous to know God or themselves, and to do his will.

[Who be enemies to Holy Scripture]

And their stomachs only doe loath and abhor the heavenly knowledge and food of God's word, that be so drowned in worldly vanities, that

---

[449] This modern edition of the *Homily on Scripture* is taken from the original *Certayne sermons, or homelies appcynted by the kynges Maiestie ...* (London: Richard Grafton, 1547), RSTC 13640, sigs. A.iii^v-B.iv^v. The sentences in *italics* are not headings but are printed marginal notes which serve as reading guides.

they neither favour God, nor any godliness: for that is the cause why they desire such vanities, rather than the true knowledge of God.

[An apt similitude, declaring of whom the Scripture is abhorred]

As they that are sick of an ague, whatsoever they eat and drink (though it be never so pleasant) yet it is as bitter to them as wormwood, not for the bitterness of the meat, but for the corrupt and bitter humour that is in their own tongue and mouth: even so is the sweetness of God's word bitter, not of itself, but only unto them that have their minds corrupted with long custom of sin and love of this world.

[An exhortation unto the diligent reading and searching of the holy Scripture]

Therefore, forsaking the corrupt judgement of fleshly men, which care not but for their carcass: let us reverently hear and read Holy Scriptures, which is the food of the soul (Matthew 4.4). Let us diligently search for the well of life in the books of the New and Old Testament, and not run to the stinking puddles of men's traditions (devised by men's imagination) for our justification and salvation.

[The Holy Scripture is a sufficient doctrine for our salvation]

For in Holy Scripture is fully contained what we ought to do, and what to eschew; what to believe, what to love, and what to look for at God's hands at length.

[What things we may learn in the Holy Scripture]

In these books we shall find the Father from whom, the Son by whom, and the Holy Ghost, in whom all things have their being and keeping up, and these three persons to be but one God, and one substance. In these books we may learn to know ourselves, how vile and miserable we be, and also to know God, how good he is of himself, and how he makes us and all creatures partakers of his goodness. We may learn also in these books to know God's will and pleasure, as much as (for this present time) is convenient for us to know. And (as the great clerk and godly preacher Saint John Chrysostom says) whatsoever is required to salvation of man, is fully contained in the Scripture of God. He that is ignorant, may there learn and have knowledge. He that is hard hearted, and an obstinate sinner, shall there find everlasting torments (prepared of God's justice) to make him afraid, and to mollify or soften him. He that is oppressed with misery in this world, shall there find relief in the promises of everlasting life, to his great consolation and comfort. He that is wounded by the Devil onto death, shall find there medicine whereby he may be restored again unto health. If it shall require to teach any truth, or reprove false doctrine, to rebuke any vice, to commend any virtue, to give good counsel, to comfort or to exhort, or to do any other thing requisite for our salvation, all those things (says Saint Chrysostom) we may learn plentifully of the Scripture.

[Holy Scripture ministers sufficient doctrine for all degrees and ages]

There is (says Fulgentius) abundantly enough, both for men to eat, and children to suck. There is, whatsoever is meet for all ages, and for all degrees and sorts of men. These books therefore ought to be much in our hands, in our eyes, in our ears, in our mouths, but most of all in our hearts.

[What commodities and profits the knowledge of Holy Scripture brings]

For the Scripture of God is the heavenly meat of our souls (Matthew 4.4), the hearing and keeping of it makes us blessed (Luke 11.28), sanctifies us (John 17.17), and makes us holy, it turns our souls (Psalms 19.7-10), it is a light lantern to our feet (Psalms 119.105), it is a sure, steadfast, and everlasting instrument of salvation, it gives wisdom to the humble and lowly hearts, it comforts, makes glad, cheers, and cherishes our conscience: it is a more excellent jewel or treasure, then any gold or precious stone, it is more sweet then honey, or honeycomb, it is called the best part, which Mary did choose, for it hath in it everlasting comfort (Luke 10.42). The words of holy Scripture be called words of everlasting life (John 6.68): for they be God's instrument, ordained for the same purpose. They have power to turn through God's promise, and they be effectual through God's assistance, and (being received in a faithful heart) they have ever an heavenly spiritual working in them: they are lively, quick, and mighty in operation, and sharper than any two edged sword, and enter through, even unto the dividing asunder of the soul and the spirit, of the joints and the marrow

(Hebrews 4.12). Christ calls him a wise builder, that builds upon his word, upon his sure and substantial foundation (Matthew 7.24). By this word of God, we shall be judged: for the word that I speak (says Christ) is it, that shall judge in the last day (John 12.48). He that keeps the word of Christ, is promised the love and favour of God, and that he shall be the dwelling place or temple of the blessed Trinity (John 14.23). This word, whosoever is diligent to read, and in his heart to print that he reads, the great affection to the transitory things of this world, shall be minished in him, and the great desire of heavenly things (that be therein promised of God) shall increase in him. And there is nothing that so much strengthens our faith and trust in God, that so much keeps up innocency and pureness of the heart, and also of outward godly life and conversation, as continual reading and recording of God's word. For that thing, which (by continual use of reading of holy Scripture, and diligent searching of the same) is deeply printed and graven in the heart, at length turns almost into nature. And moreover, the effect and virtue of God's word is, to illuminate the ignorant, and to give more light unto them, that faithfully and diligently read it, to comfort their hearts, and to encourage them to perform that, which of God is commanded. It teaches patience in all adversity, in prosperity, humbleness: what honour is due unto God, what, mercy and charity to our neighbour. It giveth good counsel in all doubtful things. It shows of whom we shall look for aid and help in all perils, and that God is the only giver of victory, in all battels and temptations of our enemies, bodily and ghostly. (1 Sam 14:4-23; 2 Chron 20:7, 17, 29; 1 Cor 15:57, 1 John 5:5)

[Who profit most in reading God's word]

And in reading of God's word, he most profits not always, that is most ready in turning of the book, or in saying of it without the book, but he that is most turned into it, that is most inspired with the Holy Ghost, most in his heart and life altered and changed into that thing which he reads: he that is daily less and less proud, less wrathful, less covetous, and less desirous of worldly and vain pleasures: he that daily (forsaking his old vicious life) increases in virtue more and more. And to be short, there is nothing that more maintains godliness of the mind, and drives away ungodliness, then does the continual reading or hearing of God's word, if it be joined with a godly mind, and a good affection, to know and follow God's will.

[What discommodities the ignorant of GODS word bringeth]

For without a single eye, pure intent, and good mind, nothing is allowed for good before God. And on the other side, nothing more darkens Christ, and the glory of God, nor bringeth in more blindness, and all kinds of vices, then doeth the ignorance of God's word. (Isaiah 5:13, 24; Matthew 22:29; 1 Corinthians 14:20, 37-38).

If we profess Christ, why be we not ashamed to be ignorant in his doctrine? Seeing that every man is ashamed to bee ignorant in that learning which he professes.

[God's word excels all sciences]

That man is ashamed to be called a Philosopher, which reads not the books of Philosophy, and to be called a Lawyer, and Astronomer, or Physician, that is ignorant in the books of Law, Astronomy, and Physics. Now can any man then say that he professes Christ and his religion, if he will not apply himself (as far forth as he can or may conveniently) to read and hear, and so to know the books of Christ's gospel and doctrine? Although other sciences be good, and to be learned, yet no man can deny, but this is the chief, and passes all other incomparably. What excuse shall we therefore make (at the last day before Christ) that delight to read or hear men's fantasies and inventions, more than his most holy gospel? And will find no time to do that which chiefly (above all things) we should do, and will rather read other things then that, for the which we ought rather to leave reading of all other things. Let us therefore apply ourselves, as far forth as we can have time and leisure, to know God's word, by diligent hearing and reading thereof, as many as profess God, and have faith and trust in him.

[Vain excuses dissuading from the knowledge of Christ's word]

But they that have no good affection to God's word (to colour this their fault) allege commonly two vain and feyned excuses. Some go about to excuse them by their own frailness and fearfulness, saying that they dare not read Holy Scripture, least through their ignorance, they should fall into any error. Other pretend that the difficulty to understand it, and the hardness thereof is so great, that it is meet to be read only of clerkes and learned men. As touching the first: ignorance of God's word, is the cause of all error, as Christ himself affirmed to the Sadducees, saying that they erred, because they knew not the Scripture (Matthew 22). How should they then eschew error, that will be still ignorant? And how should they come out of ignorance, that will not read nor hear that thing which should give them knowledge? He that now has most knowledge, was at the first ignorant, yet he forbear not to read, for fear he should fall into error: but he diligently read, lest he should remain in ignorance, and through ignorance in error. And if you will not know the truth of God (a thing most necessary for you) lest you fall into error, by the same reason you may then lie still, and never go, lest (if you go) you fall in the mire: nor eat any good meat, lest you take a surfeit, nor sow your corn, nor labour in your occupation, nor use your merchandise, for fear you lose your seed, your labour, your stock, and so by that reason, it should be best for you to live idly, and never to take in hand to doe any manner of good thing, lest peradventure some evil thing may chance thereof. And if you be afraid to fall into error, by reading of holy Scripture: I shall shew you how you may read it without danger of error.

[How most commodiously and without all peril the Holy Scripture is to be read]

Read it humbly with a meek and lowly heart, to the intent you may glorify God, and not yourself, with the knowledge of it: and read it not without daily praying to God, that he would direct your reading to good effect: and take upon you to expound it no further, then you can plainly understand it. For (as Saint Augustine says) the knowledge of Holy Scripture, is a great, large, and a high place, but the door is very low, so that the high & arrogant man cannot run in: but he must stoop low, and humble himself, that shall enter into it. Presumption and arrogancy is the mother of all error: and humility needs to fear no error. For humility will only search to know the truth, it will search, and will bring together one place with another, and where it cannot find out the meaning, it will pray, it will aske of other that know, and will not presumptuously and rashly define anything, which it knows not. Therefore, the humble man may search any truth boldly in the Scripture, without any danger of error. And if he be ignorant, he ought the more to read and to search Holy Scripture, to bring him out of ignorance. I say not nay, but a man may prosper with only hearing, but he may much more prosper, with both hearing and reading.

[Scripture in some places is easy, and in some places hard to be understood]

This have I said, as touching the fear to read, through ignorance of the person. And concerning the hardness of Scripture, he that is so weak that he is not able to brook strong meat, yet he may suck the sweet and tender milk, and defer the rest, until he waxes stronger, and come to more knowledge. For God receives the learned and unlearned, and casts away none, but is indifferent unto all. And the Scripture is full, as well of low valleys, plain ways, and easy for every man to use, and to walk in: as also of high hills & mountains, which few men can ascend unto.

[God leaves no man untaught, that has a good will to know his word]

And whosoever gives his mind to Holy Scriptures, with diligent study and burning desire, it cannot be (says Saint Chrysostom) that he should be destitute of help. For either God Almighty will send him some godly doctor, to instruct him, as he did to instruct Eunuchus, a noble man of Ethiopia, and treasurer to Queene Candace, who having a great affection to read the Scripture (although he understood it not) yet for the desire that he unto for God's word, God sent his Apostle Philip to declare to him the true sense of the Scripture that he read: or else, if we lack a learned man to instruct and teach us, yet God himself from above, will give light unto our minds, and teach us those things which are necessary for us, and wherein we be ignorant.

[How the knowledge of the Scripture may be attained unto]

And in another place Chrysostom says, that man's human and worldly wisdom or science, needs not to the understanding of Scripture, but the revelation of the Holy Ghost, who inspires the true meaning unto them, that with humility and diligence do search therefore. He that asks, shall have, and he that seeks shall find, and he that knocks, shall have the door open (Matthew 7:7-8).

[A good rule for the understanding of Scripture]

If we read once, twice, or thrice, and understand not, let us not cease so, but still continue reading, praying, asking of other, and so by still knocking (at the last) the door shall be opened (as Saint Augustine says). Although many things in the Scripture be spoken in obscure mysteries, yet there is nothing spoken under dark mysteries in one place, but the self-same thing in other places, is spoken more familiarly and plainly, to the capacity both of learned and unlearned.

[No man is excepted from the knowledge of Christ's will]

And those things in the Scripture that be plain to understand, and necessary for salvation, every man's duty is to learn them, to print them in memory, and effectually to exercise them. And as for the obscure mysteries, to be contented to be ignorant in them, until such time as it shall please God to open those things unto him. In the mean season, if he lacks either aptness or opportunity, God will not impute it to his folly: but yet it behoves not, that such as be apt, should set aside reading, because some other be unapt to read: nevertheless, for the difficulty of such places, the reading of the whole ought not to be set apart.

[What persons would have ignorance to continue]

And briefly to conclude, (as Saint Augustine says) by the Scripture, all men be amended, weak men be strengthened, and strong men be comforted. So that surely, none be enemies to the reading of God's word, but such as either be so ignorant, that they know not how wholesome a thing it is: or else be so sick, that they hate the most comfortable medicine that should heal them: or so ungodly, that they would wish the people still to continue in blindness and ignorance of God.

[The Holy Scripture is one of God's chief benefits]

Thus, we have briefly touched some part of the commodities of God's holy word, which is one of God's chief and principal benefits, given and declared to mankind here in earth. Let us thank God heartily, for this his great and special gift, beneficial favour, and fatherly providence.

[The right reading, use, and fruitful studying in Holy Scripture]

Let us be glad to revive this precious gift of our heavenly Father. Let us hear, read, and know, these holy rules, injunctions, and statutes of our Christian religion, and upon that we have made profession to God at our baptism. Let us with fear and reverence lay up (in the chest of our hearts) these necessary and fruitful lessons. Let us night and day muse, and have meditation and contemplation in them. Let us ruminate, and (as it were) chew the cud, that we may have the sweet juice, spiritual effect, marrow, honey, kernel, taste, comfort and consolation of them. Let us stay, quiet, and certify our consciences, with the most infallible certainty, truth, and perpetual assurance of them. Let us pray to God (the only author of these heavenly meditations) that we may speak, think, believe, live, and depart hence, according to the wholesome doctrine, and verities of them. And by that meanes, in this world we shall have God's defence, favour, and grace, with the unspeakable solace of peace, and quietness of conscience, and after this miserable life, we shall enjoy the endless bliss and glory of heaven, which he grant us all that died for us all, Jesus Christ, to whom with the Father and the Holy Ghost, be all honour and glory, both now and everlastingly. Amen.

Appendix B: *The Short Catechisme*[450]

It is the duty of those whom Christ has redeemed by his death, that they not only be servants to obey but also children to inherit, so to know what is the true trade of life and what God likes, that they may be able to answer to every demand of religion and to render account of their faith and profession.

And this is the plainest way of teaching: which not only in philosophy Socrates, but also in our religion Apollinaris has used. That both by certain questions, as it were by pointing, the ignorant might be instructed and the skilful put in remembrance, that they do not forget what they have learned, whether for having regard to the profit which we ought to seek in teaching of youth and also to shortness that in our whole schooling, there should be nothing either overflowing or wanting, have conveyed the whole sum into a dialogue, that the matter itself might be plainer to perceive and we stray less in other matters beside the purpose. Thus, they begin: the master to oppose the scholar.

Master: Since I know (dear son) that it is a great part of my duty, not only to see that you be instructed in good letters but also earnestly and diligently to examine what sort of religion you follow in your tender age, I thought it best to oppose you by certain questions to the intent that I may perfectly know, whether you have well or ill travailed therein. Now therefore, tell me (my son) what the religion is which you profess?

Scholar: That, good Master, do I profess, which is the religion of the Lord Christ, which in Acts 11 is called the Christian religion.

Master: Do you then confess yourself to be a follower of Christian godliness and religion, and a scholar of our Lord Christ?

---

[450] Transcribed and modernised from the original English edition: John Ponet, *A short catechisme, or playne instruction, conteynynge the su[m]me of Christian learning* (London: John Day, 1553), RSTC 4812. Prefatory material, printed marginal notes, and appendices such as the *Forty-two Articles of Religion* and concluding collection of prayers not included.

Scholar: That indeed I do confess, and plainly and boldly profess. Yes, therein I account the whole sum of all my glory, as in the thing which is both of more honour, than that the slenderness of my wit may attain to it; and also more approaching to God's majesty, than that I, by any feat of utterance, may easily express it.

Master: Tell me then (dear son) as exactly as you can, in what points you think that the sum of Christian religion stands?

Scholar: In two points, that is to say: true faith in God and assured persuasion conceived of all those things which are contained in the Holy Scriptures, and in charity, which belongs both to God and to our neighbour.

Master: That faith which is conceived by hearing and reading the word, what does it teach you concerning God?

Scholar: It does principally teach: that there is one certain nature, one substance, one spirit and heavenly mind, or rather an everlasting spirit, without beginning or end, which we call God: whom all the people of the world ought to worship, with sovereign honour, and the highest kind of reverence. Moreover, out of the holy words of God, which by the prophets and the beloved of almighty God are in the holy books published, to the eternal glory of his name, I learn the law and the threatening thereof; then the promises and the gospel of God. These things, first written by Moses and other men of God, have been preserved whole and uncorrupted, even to our age, and since that, the chief articles of our faith have been gathered into a short abridgement, which is commonly called the Creed, or Symbol, of the Apostles.

Master: Why is this abridgement of the faith termed with the name of a symbol?

Scholar: A symbol is as much to say, as a sign, mark, privy token, or watchword, whereby the soldiers of one camp are known from their enemies. For this reason the abridgement of the faith, whereby the Christians are known from them that are not Christians, is rightly named a Symbol.

Master: First tell me somewhat, what do you think of the law, and then afterwards of the Creed or Symbol.

Scholar: I shall do (good master) with a good will as you command me. The Lord God has charged us by Moses, that we have none other God at all, but him; that is to say, that we take him alone for our one only God, our Maker and Saviour: that we do not reverence nor worship any portraiture or any image whatsoever, whether it is painted, carved, graven, or by any other fashioning whatsoever it is, that we do not take the name of our Lord God in vain; that is, either in a matter of no weight or of no truth. Last of all, we ought to hold steadfastly and with devout conscience, that we keep holy and religiously the Sabbath Day which was appointed out from the others for rest and service of God.

Master: Very well. Now you have rehearsed to me the laws of the first table wherein is, in summary, contained the knowledge and truth service of God. Go on and tell me which are the duties of charity and our love towards mankind.

Scholar: Are you asking me (master) what I think of the other part of the law, which is commonly called the second table?

Master: That is right, my son – that is what I would like to hear about.

Scholar: I will in a few words dispatch it, as my simple wit will serve me. Moses put it together in a short summary: that is, that with all loving affection we honour and reverence our father and mother, that we kill no-one, that we commit no adultery, that we steal nothing, that we do not bear false witness against anyone, and last of all, that we covet nothing that is our neighbour's.

Master: How is that commandment, of the honouring father and mother, to be understood?

Scholar: Honour of father and mother contains love, fear, and reverence. Yes, and it also means obeying, supporting, defending, and nourishing them, if need requires. It binds us also most humbly, and with most natural affection, to obey the magistrate, to reverence the ministers of the church, our schoolmasters, with all our elders, and betters.

Master: What is contained in that commandment, do not kill?

Scholar: That we hate, or revile, no-one. Moreover, it commands us, that we love even those who oppose us, do good to those that hate us, and that we pray for all prosperity and for the good of even our worst enemies.

Master: The commandment of not committing adultery, what do you think it contains?

Scholar: Indeed, this commandment contains many things. For it forbids us from intimate conversation with another man's wife or from speaking unchastely with any other woman. But it also forbids us from toucher her, or casting a desirous eye at her, or beholding her with a lustful look, or by any ungodly way to woo her: either ourselves or others on our behalf. Finally, it forbids all kind of filthy and straying lust.

Master: What do you think of the commandment, not to steal?

Scholar: I shall show you, as briefly as I have done the rest, if it please you to hear me. It commands us, to deceive no-one, to occupy no unlawful goods, to envy nobody's wealth, and to think nothing profitable, that either is not just or differs from right and honesty. Simply, it means being willing to lose what if mine, rather than wrongfully take what is another's and then keep it myself.

Master: How may that commandment be kept, of bearing no false witness?

Scholar: If we neither ourselves speak any false or vain lie: nor allow it in others, either by speech or silence, or by our present company. But we ought always to maintain truth, as place and time serves.

Master: Now remains the last commandment, of not coveting anything that is our neighbour's. What does that mean?

Scholar: This law does generally forbid all sorts of evil lusts: and commands us to bridle and restrain all greedy insatiable desire of our will, which does not hold itself within the bounds of right and reason: and it wills that each man be content with his estate. But whosoever covets more than right, with the loss of his neighbour, and wrong to another, he breaks and bitterly loosens the bond of charity and fellowship among mankind. Yes, and upon him (unless he makes amends) the Lord God, the most stern revenger of the breaking his of law, shall execute most grievous punishment. On the other side, he that lives according to the rule of these laws shall find both praise and bliss, and will find that God is his merciful and bountiful good Lord.

Master: You have shortly set out the ten commandments. Now then tell me how all these things that you have particularly declared, Christ has in a few words contained by setting forth to us a summary of the whole substance of the law?

Scholar: Do you want me to briefly summarise in all that belongs to God and to mankind?

Master: Yes.

Scholar: Christ says: you shall love the Lord your God with all your heart, with all your soul, with all your mind, and with all your strength. This is the greatest commandment in the law. The other is like it: you shall love your neighbour as yourself. Upon these two commandments hang the whole law and the prophets.

Master: I would like you to tell me more, what law is that which you speak of, that which we call the law of nature (or similar names)?

Scholar: I remember, master, that which I learned that from you long ago. That the law was grafted into the nature of man, while nature was yet sound and uncorrupted. But after the entrance of sin, although the wise were somewhat not utterly ignorant of that light of nature; yet was it by that time so hidden from the greatest part of mankind, that they hardly perceived any shadow of it.

Master: What is the cause, that God willed it to be written out in tables, and that it should be privately appointed to one people alone?

Scholar: I will show you. By original sin and evil custom, the image of God in man, was so at the beginning darkened and the judgement of nature so corrupted, that man himself does not sufficiently understand, what difference there is between honesty and dishonesty, right and wrong. The bountiful God therefore, minding to renew that image in us first wrought this by the law written in tables, that we might know ourselves and therein, as it were in a glass, behold the filth and spots of our soul and stubborn hardness of a corrupted heart. That by this mean, yet acknowledging our sin and perceiving the weakness of our flesh and the wrath of God fiercely bent against us for sin, we might therefore fervently long for our Saviour Christ Jesus. Which, by his death and precious sprinkling of his blood, has cleansed and washed away our sins, pacified the wrath of the almighty Father, and by the holy breath of his Holy Spirit created new hearts in us and renewed our minds after the image and likeness of their creator, in true righteousness and holiness. Which thing neither the justice of the law nor any sacrifices of Moses were able to perform. And that no man is made righteous by the law it is evident, not only thereby, that the righteous live by faith, but also hereby that no mortal man is able to fulfil all that the law of both the tables command. For we have hindrances that strive against the law, as the weakness of the flesh, intractable appetites, and lust naturally engendered. As for sacrifice, cleansings, washings, and other ceremonies of the law, they were but shadows, likenesses, images, and figures of the true and everlasting sacrifice of Jesus Christ, done upon the cross. By the benefit whereof all the sins of all believers, even from the beginning of the world are pardoned by the singular mercy of God, and by no desert of our own.

Master: I do not hear yet, why almighty God's will was to declare his secret pleasure to one people alone; that is, the Israelites.

Scholar: Indeed, that I had almost forgotten. I suppose it was not done for this intent, as though the law of the ten commandments did not belong generally to all men, for the Lord our God is not only the God of the Jews but also of the Gentiles. But rather, this was thereby meant, that the true Messiah, which is our Christ, might be known at his coming into the world and must have been born of that nation, and no other, for the true performance of the promise. For this cause, God's pleasure was to appoint out for himself one certain people, holy, separated from the rest, and as it were peculiarly his own. That by this, his divine word might be continually kept holy, pure, and uncorrupted.

Master: Thus far you have well satisfied me, dear son. Now let us come to the Christian confession, which I would like you to plainly rehearse to me.

Scholar: It shall be done. I believe in God, the Father almighty, maker of heaven and earth. And in Jesus Christ, his only Son, our Lord, which was conceived by the Holy Spirit, born of the Virgin Mary, suffered under Pontius Pilate, was crucified, died, and was buried. He went down to hell, and on the third day he rose again from the dead. He went up into heaven, sits upon the right hand of God the Father almighty, and from there he shall come to judge the quick and the dead. I believe in the Holy Spirit, I believe in the holy universal church, the communion of saints, the forgiveness of sins, the rising again of the flesh, and the life everlasting.

Master: All these, my son, you have rehearsed generally and shortly. Therefore, you shall do well to set out more largely, all that you have spoken particularly that I may plainly perceive what your belief is concerning each of them. And first I would like to hear of the knowledge of God, afterward of the right serving of him.

Scholar: I will, with a good will, obey your pleasure (dear master) as far as my simply wit will suffer me. Above all things we must steadfastly believe and hold that God almighty, the Father, in the beginning and of nothing, made and fashioned this whole frame of the world, and all things whatsoever are contained therein. And that they are all made by the power of his word, that is of Jesus Christ the Son of God. Which thing is sufficiently approved by the witness of Scripture. Moreover, that when he had thus shaped all creatures, he ruled, governed, and saved them by his bounty and liberal hand. He ministered and yet also ministers greatly all that is needed, for the maintenance and preserving of our life that he should so use them, as is appropriate for mindful and godly children.

Master: Why do you call God Father?

Scholar: For two causes. The one, for that he made us of all at the beginning and gave life unto us all. The other is more weighty, for that by his Holy Spirit and by faith he has begotten us again, making us his children, giving us his kingdom and the inheritance of life everlasting, with Jesus Christ his own true and natural Son.

Master: Seeing then, that God created all other things to serve man, and made man to obey, honour, and glorify him, what can you say more of the beginning and making of man?

Scholar: Even that which Moses wrote: that God shaped the first man of clay and put into him soul and life. That he cast Adam in a dead sleep and brought forth a woman, whom he drew out of his side, to make her a companion with him of all his life and wealth. And therefore was man called Adam, because he took his beginning from the earth, and the woman called Eve, because she was appointed to be the mother of all the living.

Master: What image is that, after the likeness whereof, you say that man was made?

Scholar: That is most absolute righteousness and perfect holiness. Which most nearly belongs to the very nature of God and most clearly appeared in Christ our new Adam. Of the which in us, there are scant to be seen any sparkles.

Master: What, are there scant to be seen?

Scholar: It is indeed true, for they do not now so shine as they did in the beginning before man's fall. Forasmuch as man, by the darkness of sins and mist of errors, has corrupted the brightness of this image. In such sort has God in his wrath wreaked him upon the sinful man.

Master: But pray tell me, wherefore it came thus to pass?

Scholar: I will show you. When the Lord God had made the frame of this world, he himself planted a garden, full of delight and pleasure, in a certain place Eastward, and called it Eden. Wherein beside other passing fair trees, not far from the middle of the garden, was there one specially called the tree of life, and another called the tree of the knowledge of good and evil. Herein the Lord of his singular love placed man and committed unto him the garden to dress and look after, giving him liberty to eat of the fruits of all the trees of paradise, except the fruit of the tree of the knowledge of good and evil. The fruit of this tree, if he ever tasted it, he should without fail die for it. But Eve, deceived by the devil counterfeiting the shape of a serpent, gathered of the forbidden fruit which was, for the fairness to the eye to be desired, for the sweetness in taste to be reached at, and pleasant for the knowledge of good and evil, and she ate of it and gave it to her husband to eat of the same. For doing this they both immediately died, that is to say, that were not only subject to the death of the body but also lost the life of the soul which is righteousness. And from then the image of God was defaced in them, and the most beautiful proportion of righteousness, holiness, truth, and knowledge of God, was confounded and in a manner utterly blotted out. There remained the earthly image, joined with unrighteousness, guile, fleshly mind, and deep ignorance of godly and heavenly things. From here grew the weakness of our flesh, from here came this corruption and disorder of lusts and affections, from here came that pestilence, from here came that seed and nourishment of sins in which man is infected, and it is called original sin. Moreover, thereby nature was so corrupted and overthrown, that unless the goodness and mercy of almighty God had helped us by the medicine of grace, even as in body we are thrust down into all wretchedness of death, so must it have been, that all men of all sorts should be thrown into everlasting punishment and unquenchable fire.

Master: Oh, the unthankfulness of men! But what hope had our first parents, and from them the rest, whereby they were relieved?

Scholar: When the Lord God had both with words and deeds chastised Adam and Eve (for he thrust them both out of the garden with a most generous reproach) he then cursed the serpent, threatening him that the time should one day come, when the seed of the woman should break his head. Afterwards the Lord God established that same glorious and most bountiful promise: first with a covenant made between him and Abraham by circumcision, and in Isaac his son, then again by Moses, and last of all by the oracles of the noble prophets.

Master: What does the serpents' head mean, and what is that seed that God speaks of?

Scholar: In the serpent's head lies all his venom and the whole substance of his life and force. Therefore, I do take the serpent's head to betoken the whole power, and kingdom, or more truly the tyranny of the old serpent, the devil. The seed (as St. Paul does plainly teach) is Jesus Christ the Son of God, very God and very man, conceived by the Holy Spirit, engendered of the womb and substance of Mary, the blessed, pure, and undefiled maiden, and was so born and fostered by her as other babies be, saving that he was most far from all infection of sin.

Master: All these foundations that you have laid are most true. Now therefore let us go forward to his doings, wherein lies our salvation and conquest against the old serpent.

Scholar: It shall be done, good master. After that, Christ Jesus had delivered in charge to his Apostles, that most joyful and in all points heavenly doctrine, the gospel, which in Greek is called *Euangelion,* and in English *Good tidings*. And as by sealing, established the same with tokens, and miracles innumerable, whereof all his life was full. At length he was sorely scourged, mocked with potting, scorning, and spitting in his face. Last of all his hands and feet bored through with nails, and he was fastened to a cross. Then he truly died, and was truly buried, that by his most sweet sacrifice he might pacify the Father's wrath against mankind, and subdue him by his death, who had the authority of death, which was the devil. Forasmuch not only the living but also the dead, were they in hell or elsewhere, they all felt the power and force of this death, to whom lying in prison (as Peter says) Christ preached, though dead in body, yet relieved in spirit. After the third day he rose up again, alive in body also, and with many notable proofs during the space of forty days, he abode among his disciples, eating and drinking with them. In whose sight he was conveyed away in a cloud, up into heaven, or rather above all heavens, where he now sits at the right hand of God the Father, being made Lord of all things in heaven or in earth: king of kings, our everlasting and only High Bishop, our only attorney, only mediator, only peacemaker between God and men. Now since he has entered into his glorious majesty, by sending down his Holy Spirit to us (as he promised), he lights our dark blindness, moves, rules, teaches, cleanses, comforts, and rejoices our minds, and so will he still continually do, until the end of the world.

Master: Well, I see you have touched the chief articles of our religion, and have set out, as in a short abridgement, the Creed that you did rehearse. Now therefore, I will demand some questions on certain points.

Scholar: Do as you shall please, master. For you may more perfectly instruct me, in those things that I do not thoroughly understand. And put my in remembrance of that which I have forgotten. And print in my mind deeper, such things of which I have not taken steadfast hold.

Master: Tell me then. If by his death we get pardon of our sins, was that not enough? Why must he also rise again from the dead?

Scholar: It was not enough, with respect to either him, or to us. For unless he had risen again, he should not have been taken for the Son of God. For which cause also, while he hung upon the cross, they that say him upbraided him and said: he has saved others, but cannot saved himself. Let him now come down from the cross and we will believe him. But not rising up from the dead to everlasting continuance of life, he has showed a much greater power of his Godhead, then if coming down from the cross he had fled from the terrible pains of dead. For to die is common to all men, but to loose the bonds of death and by his own power rise again, that properly belongs to Jesus Christ the only begotten Son of God, the only author of life. Moreover, it was necessary, that he should rise again with glory, that the sayings of David and other prophets of God might be fulfilled, which were told before, that neither his body should see corruption or his soul be left in hell. As for us, we neither had been justified nor had any hope left to rise again, had he not risen again as Paul plainly shows in diverse places. For if he had remained in the prison of death, in the grave, and been held in corruption as all men beside him, how could we have hoped for safety through him who did not save himself? It was right therefore, and needful, for the part that he had in hand, and for the chief stay of our safeguard, that Christ should first deliver himself from death and afterward assure us of safety by his rising again.

Master: You have touched (my son) the chief cause of Christ's rising again. Now I would like to hear your mind about his going up into heaven. What answer do you think should be made to them who say: it would have been better for him to stay here with us, presently to rule and govern us? For beside other diverse causes, it is likely that the love of the people towards their prince, especially being good and gracious, should grow the greater by his present company.

Scholar: All these things which he could do at present, that is to say, if he were in company with us here, he does absent from us. He rules, maintains, strengthens, defends, rebukes, punishes, corrects, and performs all such things as do become such a prince, or rather God himself. All these things (I say) he does which belong either to our need or profit, honour or comfort. Besides this, Christ is not so altogether absent from the world as many suppose. For albeit the substance of his body is taken up from us, yet is his Godhead perpetually present with us, although not subject to the sight of our eyes. For things that are not bodily cannot be perceived by any bodily means. Whoever say his own soul? No man. Yet is anything more present than that? Or what is nearer to each man than his own soul? Spiritual things are not to be seen, but with the eye of the Spirit. Therefore, he who lives on earth wants to see the Godhead of Christ, let him open the eyes, not of his body, but of his mind, but of his faith. And he shall see him present, whom eye has not seen. He shall see him present, and in the midst of them wherever there are two or three gathered together in his name. He shall see him present with us, even unto the end of the world. What said I? Shall he see Christ present? Yes, he shall both see and feel him dwelling within himself in such sort as he does his own proper soul.

For he dwells and abides in the mind and heart of those who fasten all their trust in him.

Master: Very well, but our confession says that he ascended into heaven. Tell me, therefore, how that is to be understood?

Scholar: So, we commonly say of anyone that attained to any high degree or dignity, that he is ascended up or advanced into some high room, some high place or state, because that person has changed his former case and has gained more honour than the rest. In this way Christ went up as he before came down. He came down from the highest honour to deepest dishonour, even the dishonour and vile state of a servant, and of the cross. And likewise afterwards he went up, from the deepest dishonour to the highest honour, even the same honour which he had before. His going up into heaven, yes above all heavens, to the very royal throne of God, is evident by the most just reason, that his glory and majesty might in comparison agreeably answer to the proportion of his baseness and reproachful estate. This Paul teaches us, in his writing to the Philippians: he became obedient even unto death, yes the very death of the cross. Therefore, God has both advanced him to the highest state of honour, and also gave him a name above all names, that at the name of Jesus every knee should bow, from all things in heaven, earth, and hell. But although he has already gone up into heaven, nevertheless by his nature of Godhead and by his Spirit, he shall always be present in his church: even to the end of the world. Yet, this does not prove that he is present among us in his body. For his Godhead has one property, and his manhood another. His manhood was created, his Godhead uncreated. His manhood is in some one place of heaven, his Godhead is in a certain way everywhere that it fills both heaven and earth. But to make this point plainer, by a similitude or comparison: there is nothing that does more truly, like a shadow, express Christ than the sun. For it is a fitting image of the light and brightness of Christ. The sun always keeps the heavens yet we say that it is present also in the world, for without light there is nothing present, that is to say, nothing to be seen by anyone, for the sun with his light fills all things. So Christ is lifted up above all the heavens, that he may be present with all and fully furnish all things as St. Paul says.

But as touching the bodily presence of Christ here in earth (if it is lawful to place in comparison great things with small), Christ's body is present to our faith, as the sun when it is seen is present to the eye. Also Christ's body, though it does not bodily touch the eye nor is presently with it together here in earth, it still present to the sight notwithstanding so large a distance of space between. So Christ's body, which at his glorious going up with conveyed from us, which has left the world and has gone unto his Father, is a great way absent from our mouth even then when we receive with our mouth, the holy sacrament of his body and blood. Yet our faith is in heaven, and beholds that Son of righteousness, and is presently together with him in heaven in such a way that the sight is in heaven with the body of the Son, or in earth the sun with the sight. And as the sun is present to all things by his light, so is Christ also in his Godhead. Yet neither from the body can the light of the sun be separated, nor can the Godhead of Christ be separated from his immortal body. We must therefore say, that Christ's body is in some one place of heaven, and his Godhead everywhere, that we neither of his Godhead make a body, nor of his body a God.

Master: I see (my son) that you are not ignorant concerning how Christ is rightly said to be from us in body and with us in spirit. But this one thing I would like to know from you: why Christ our Lord is thus conveyed away from the sight of our eyes, and how his going up into heaven benefits us?

Scholar: The chief cause of this was to pluck out from us that false opinion, which sometimes deceived the Apostles themselves: that Christ should in earth visibly reign, as other kings and ruffling princes of the world. This error he minded to have utterly suppressed in us, so that we should think his kingdom to consist in higher things. This thing he therefore thought better, because it was more for our comfort and benefit than if some such kingdom should be set up, as if its foundations should rest upon our faith. Therefore it was necessary that he should be conveyed away from us, past the perception of all bodily senses, that this way our faith might be stirred up and exercised to consider his government and providence, which no sight of bodily eyes can behold. And forasmuch as he is not king of some one country alone, but of heaven and earth, or the quick and the dead, it was most convenient that his kingdom should be governed otherwise than that to which our senses may attain. For else he should have been constrained sometimes to be carried up to heaven and sometimes to be driven down to the earth, to remove sometimes in one country and sometimes into another, and like an earthly prince, to be carried here and there by the diverse changes and affairs driven by chance. For he could not be present with all at once, unless his body were so turned into Godhead that he might be in all or many places together, as Eutyches and other heretical opinions hold. If it was that he might be everywhere present with all at one very instant of time, then he would not be man but a ghost. Neither should he have had a true body but a fantastical one, and this would have sprung forth a thousand errors, of all which errors he has dispatched by carrying his body up whole into heaven. In the meantime he remains invisible, governs his kingdom and commonwealth, that is his church, with sovereign wisdom and power. It is for men to rule their commonwealth, by a certain civil policy of men. But for Christ and God, by an heavenly and godlike order. But all that I have said contains but a small parcel of the profit, that we take by the carrying up of Christ's body into heaven. For there are many more things that here might be rehearsed, in which a large store of fruit is to be gathered. But especially this may not be left unspoken: that the benefits are such and so great that come unto us by the death, rising again, and going up of Christ, as no tongue either of men or angels is able to express. And that you may known my mind herein, I will rehearse certain of the most chief, as it were, two principal points, from which the rest may be applied. I say therefore, that both by these and other doings of Christ, two commodities to grow unto us. The first, that all the things that he has ever done for our profit and advantage he has done them, so they are as well our own, if we will cleave unto them with steadfast and lively faith, as if we had done them ourselves. He was nailed to the cross, we were also nailed with him, and in him our sins were punished.; he died and was buried, we likewise with our sins are dead and buried; he is risen again and we are also risen with him, that is, we are made partakers of his rising again and life that from now on death has no more rule over us. For the same

Spirit is in us that raised Jesus from the dead. Finally, as he has gone up into heavenly glory, so are we lifted up with him. Albeit that these things do not now appear, yet then they shall all be brought to light, when Christ the light of the world shall show himself in glory, in whom all our bliss is laid up in store. Moreover, by his going up we are granted the gifts of the Holy Spirit, as Paul does sufficiently witness (Eph. 4). The other commodity which we take by the doings of Christ is that Christ is set for an example to us, to frame our lives thereafter. If Christ has died, if he was buried for sin, he was so only once. If he rose again, if he has done up into heaven, he has risen only once, and has only once gone up. From now on we dies not more but lives with God and reigns in everlasting continuance of glory. So, if we are dead, if we are buried to sin, how shall we now live in the same? If we are risen again with Christ, if through steadfast hope we live now in heaven with him, then we ought to set our care upon heavenly and godly things, not earthly and fail ones. And even as we have born the image of the earthly man, so from now on let us bear the image of the heavenly. As the Lord Christ never ceased to do us good, by bestowing upon us his Holy Spirit, by garnishing his church with so many notable gifts, and by perpetual praying to his father for us, the same reason ought to move us to aid our neighbour with all our endeavour, to maintain as much as lies within us the bond of charity, and to honour Christ our Lord and Saviour, not with wicked traditions and cold devices of men, but with heavenly honour and spiritual deeds most fit for us that give it, and him that shall receive it, even as he has honoured and does honour his Father. For he that honours him honours also the Father, of which he himself is a substantial witness.

Master: The end of the world Holy Scripture calls the fulfilling and performance of the kingdom and mystery of Christ, and the renewing of all things. For (says the Apostle Peter in his second epistle, the third chapter) we look for a new heaven and a new earth, according to the promise of God, wherein righteousness dwells. And after this, that corruption, unsteadfast change, and sin, wherein the whole world is subject, should at length have an end. Now by what way, and what fashion and circumstances these things come to pass, I would like to hear you say.

Scholar: I will tell you as well as I can, according to the witness of the same Apostle. The heavens shall pass away like a storm, the elements shall melt away, the earth and all the works therein shall be consumed with fire, as though he should say, as gold is to be found. So shall the whole world be purified with fire and brought to his full perfection. The lesser world, which is man following the same, shall likewise be delivered from corruption and change. And so for man this greater world (which for his sake was first created) shall at length be renewed and be clad with another hew, much more pleasant and beautiful.

Master: What then remains?

Scholar: The last and general doom. For Christ shall come, at whose voice all the dead shall rise again perfect and sound both in body and soul. The whole world shall behold him, sitting in the royal throne of his majesty, and after the examination of every man's conscience, the last sentence shall be pronounced. Then the children of God shall be in perfect possession of that kingdom of freedom from death and of everlasting life, which was prepared for them before the foundations of the world were laid. And they shall reign with Christ forever. But the ungodly that do not believe shall be thrown from there into everlasting fire appointed for the devil and his angels.

Master: You have said enough of the rising again of the dead. Now remains that you speak of the holy church, of which I would very like to hear your opinion.

Scholar: I will rehearse that in a few words shortly, which the Holy Scriptures set out at large and plentifully. Before the Lord God made the heaven and earth he determined to have for himself a most beautiful kingdom and holy commonwealth. The Apostles and the ancient fathers that wrote in Greek called it *Ecclesia*, in English, a congregation or assembly, into which he admitted an infinite number of men, that all should be subject to one king as their sovereign and only head. Him we call Christ which is as much to say anointed. For the high bishops and kings among the Jews (who in figure betokened Christ whom the Lord anointed with his Holy Spirit) were by God's appointment at their consecration, to have material oil poured on them.

To the furnishing of this commonwealth belong of them, as many as do truly fear, honour, and call upon God, wholly applying their mind to holy and godly living, and all those that putting all their hope and trust in him, do assuredly look for the bliss of everlasting life. But as many as are in this faith steadfast were forechosen, predestinate, and appointed out to everlasting life, before the world was made. The witness that they have within their hearts the Spirit of Christ the author, is the earnest and unfailable pledge of their faith. Which faith only is able to perceive the mysteries of God, only brings peace into their hearts, and only takes hold of the righteousness that is in Christ Jesus.

Master: Does then the Spirit alone, and faith (sleep we never so soundly, or stand we never so reckless and slothful) so work all things for us, as without any help of our own to carry us idly up to heaven?

Scholar: I use (master) as you have taught me, to make a difference between the cause of the effects. The first, principal, and most perfect cause of our justifying and salvation, is the goodness and love of God, whereby he chose us for himself before he made the world. After that, God granted us to be called by the preaching of the gospel of Jesus Christ, when the Spirit of the Lord is poured into us, by whose guiding and governance we are led to settle our trust in God and hope for the performance of all his promises. With this choice is joined, as a companion, the mortifying of the old man, that is our affection and lust. From the same Spirit also comes our sanctification: the love of God and of our neighbour, justice and uprightness of life, and finally to summarise, whatever is in us or may be done of us, pure, honest, true, and good, that altogether springs out of this most pleasant root, from this most plentiful foundation, the goodness, love, choice, and unchangeable purpose of God. He is the cause, the rest are the fruits and effects. Yet are also the goodness, choice, and Spirit of God and Christ himself, causes conjoined and coupled with each other, which may be reckoned among the principal causes of our salvation. As often therefore as we are used to say, that we are made righteous and saved by faith only, it is meant thereby, that faith, or rather trust alone, does lay hand upon, understand and perceive, our righteousmaking to be given of God freely. That is to say, by not deserts of our own but by the free grace of the almighty Father. Moreover, faith engenders in us the love of our neighbour and all such works with which God is pleased. For if it is a lively and true faith, quickened by the Holy Spirit, she is the mother of all good saying and doing. By this short tale it is evident, how and by what means we attain to be made righteous. For not by the worthiness of our deservings were we either chosen or long ago saved. But by the singular mercy of God and pure grace of Christ our Lord, whereby we were in him made to do those good works that God has appointed for us to walk in. And although good works cannot deserve to make us righteous before God, yet they do so cleave unto faith that neither can faith be found without them, nor good works be anywhere without faith.

Master: I like very well this short declaration of faith and works, for Paul plainly teaches the same. But can you yet further illustrate for me that congregation which you called a kingdom or commonwealth of Christians? And so set it before my eyes, that it may severally and plainly be known distinctly from every other fellowship of men?

Scholar: I will prove how well I can do it, your pleasure is (master) as I take it, that I point out for you some certain congregation that may be seen.

Master: That it is indeed, and so it shall be good for you to do.

Scholar: That congregation is nothing else but a certain multitude of men which, wherever they are, profess the pure and upright learning of Christ, and that in such a way, as it is faithfully set forth in the holy testament, by the evangelists and Apostles, which in all points are governed and ruled by the laws and statutes of their king and high bishop Christ, in the bond of charity, which use his holy mysteries that are commonly called sacraments with such pureness and simplicity (as touching their nature and substance) as the Apostles of Christ used and left behind in writing. The marks, therefore, of this church are: first, pure preaching of the gospel, then brotherly love out of which as members of all one body spring good will to each other. Thirdly, upright and uncorrupted use of the Lord's sacraments according to the ordinance of the gospel. Last of all, brotherly correction and excommunication, or banishing those out of the church who will not amend their lives. This mark the holy fathers termed discipline. That is the same church that is grounded upon the assured rock, Jesus Christ, and trust in him. This is that same church which Paul calls the pillar and upholding stay of the truth. To this church belong the keys with which heaven is locked and unlocked, for that is done by the ministration of the word, which properly appertains the power to bind and loose, to hold for guilty and forgive sins. So that whosoever believes the gospel preached in this church, he shall be saved. But whosoever does not believe, he shall be damned.

Master: Now I would like to hear your belief in the Holy Spirit.

Scholar: I confess him to be the third person of the Holy Trinity: and since he is equal with the Father and the Son, and of the very same substance, he ought equally to be worshipped with them both.

Master: What is he called holy?

Scholar: Not only for his own holiness, but because by him are made holy the chosen of God, and members of Christ. And therefore the Scriptures have termed him the Spirit of sanctification or making holy.

Master: What does this sanctification consist in?

Scholar: First, we be newly gotten by his inward motion. And therefore, said Christ, we must be new born of water and of the spirit. Then by his inspiration we are adopted, and as it were by choice, made the children of God. For this reason he is called the Spirit of adoption. By his light we are lightened to understand God's mysteries. By his judgement sins are pardoned and retained. By his power the flesh with her lusts is kept down and tamed. By his pleasure the manifold gifts are dealt among the holy. Finally by his means our mortal bodies are relived. Therefore, in the author of so great gifts, we do not without a cause believe, honour, and call upon him.

Master: Well, you have now said sufficiently of the Holy Spirit. But I would like to hear this from you: why does it immediately follow that we believe in the holy universal church and the communion of saints.

Scholar: These two things I have always thought to be most appropriately coupled together. Because the fellowships and incorporations of other men proceed and are governed by other means and policies, but the church which is an assembly of men called to everlasting salvation is both gathered together and governed by the Holy Spirit of whom we have just mentioned. Which thing, since it cannot be perceived by bodily sense or light of nature, is by right and for good reason, here reckoned among things that are known by belief. And therefore this calling together of the faithful is called universal because it is bound to no one special place. For God throughout all coasts of the world has them that worship him. Which though they are far scattered apart, by diverse distance of countries and dominions, yet they are members most nearly joined of that same body of which Christ is the head, and have one Spirit, faith, sacraments, prayers, forgiveness of sins, and heavenly bliss, common among them all, and are so knit with the bond of love that they endeavour themselves in nothing more, than each to help the other, and to build together in Christ.

Master: Seeing you have already spoken of the knowledge of God and his members, I would also like to hear what is the true service of God.

Scholar: First we must consider that the right and true knowledge of God is the principal and only foundation of God's service. The same knowledge is fostered and maintained by fear, which in the Scriptures is called the beginning of wisdom. Faith and hope are the props and stays upon which lean all the rest that I have rehearsed. Furthermore, charity which we call love, is like an everlasting bond, by the straight knot from which all other virtues are bound in one together and their force increased. These are the inward parts of God's service, that is to say, which consist in the mind.

Master: What have you to say about the Sabbath, or the holy day, which even now you made mention of, among the laws of the first table?

Scholar: Sabbath is as much to say, as rest. It was appointed for the honour and service of God alone and it is a figure of that rest and quietness which is had by those who believe in Christ. For our trust in Christ does set our minds at liberty from all slavish fear of the law, sin, death, and hell; assuring us in the mean season, that by him we please God and that he has made us his children and heirs of his kingdom; whereby there grows in our hearts peace and true quietness of mind; which is a certain foretaste of the blessed quiet which we shall have in his kingdom. As for those things that are done on the Sabbath day, as ceremonies and exercises in the service of God, they are tokens and witnesses of this assured trust. And right it is, that faithful Christians, on such days as are appointed out for holy things, should lay aside unholy works and give themselves earnestly to religion and serving God.

Master: What are the parts of that outward serving of God which you said even now, did stand in certain bodily exercises which are tokens of the inward serving him?

Scholar: First, to teach and hear the learning of the gospel, then the pure and natural use of the ceremonies and sacraments, last of all prayer made unto God by Christ, and in the name of Christ which without fail obtains the Holy Spirit, the most assured author of true serving God and upright religion.

Master: Tell me what you call sacraments?

Scholar: They are certain customable reverent doings and ceremonies ordained by Christ, that by them he might put us in remembrance of his benefits and we might declare our profession that we are of the number of them who are partakers of the same benefits, and which fasten all their pledges of allegiance in him, that we are not ashamed of the name of Christ or to be termed Christ's scholars.

Master: Tell me (my son) how these two sacraments are ministered: baptism and that which Paul calls the supper of the Lord.

Scholar: He that believes in Christ professes the articles of the Christian religion and desires to be baptised (I speak now of those who have grown to ripe years of discretion, since for the young babes, their parents' or the church's profession suffices), the minister dips in or washes with pure and clean water only, in the name of the Father, and of the Son, and of the Holy Spirit, and commends him by prayer to God into whose church he is now openly, as it were, enrolled, that it may please God to grant him his grace, whereby he may answer in belief and life agreeably to his profession.

Master: What is the use of the Lord's supper?

Scholar: Even the very same, that was ordained by the Lord himself Jesus Christ. Which (as St. Paul says) on the same night that he was betrayed, took bread, and when he had given thanks, broke it and said, 'This is my body, which is broken for you. Do this in remembrance of me.' In the like manner, when supper was ended, he gave them the cup, saying 'This cup is the new testament in my blood. Do this, as often as you shall drink of it, in the remembrance of me.' This was the manner and order of the Lord's supper which we ought to hold and keep, that the remembrance of so great a benefit, the passion and death of Christ, be always kept in mind, that after the world has ended, he may come and make us fit with him at his own board.

Master: What does baptism represent and set before our eyes?

Scholar: That we are by the Spirit of Christ new born and cleansed from sin, that we be members and parts of his church, received into the communion of saints. For water signifies the Spirit. Baptism is also a figure of our burial in Christ and that we shall be raised up again with him in a new life, and I have before declared in Christ's resurrection.

Master: What does the supper declare and betoken to us, which we solemnly use in the remembrance of the Lord?

Scholar: The Supper (as I have showed a little before) is a certain thankful remembrance of the death of Christ, forasmuch as the bread represents his body, betrayed to be crucified for us, the wine stands in the stead and place of his blood, plenteously shed for us. And even as by bread and wine, our natural bodies are sustained and nourished, so by the body that is the flesh and blood of Christ, the soul is fed through faith and quickened to the heavenly and godly life.

Master: How do these things come to pass?

Scholar: These things come to pass by a certain secret means and lively working of the Spirit, when we believe that Christ has once for all given up his body and blood for us, to make a sacrifice and most pleasant offering to his heavenly father, and also when we confess and acknowledge him as our only saviour, high Bishop, mediator, and redeemed to whom is due all honour and glory.

Master: All this you do well understand. For I think your meaning is: that faith is the mouth of the soul whereby we receive this very heavenly meat, full both of salvation and immortality, dealt among us by the means of the Holy Spirit. Now, since we have dealt with the sacraments, pass forward to the other parts of God's service.

Scholar: I will do your commandment. There remains two things, belonging to the perfection of God's service. First our Lord Jesus Christ's will was that there should be teachers and evangelists, that is to say preachers of the gospel, to this intent: that his voice might continually be heard sound in his church. He that covets (as all ought to covet) to bear the name of a Christian may have no doubt that he ought with most earnest affection and fervent desire, endeavour himself to hear and soak into his mind the word of the Lord, not like the words of any man but like (as it is indeed) the word of almighty God. Secondarily, because all that is good and that ought of a Christian to be desired, comes unto us from God and is by him granted. Therefore, of him we ought to require all things and by thanksgiving acknowledge them all received of him. Which thing he so well likes that he esteems it instead of a passing pleasant sacrifice, as it is most evident by the witness of the prophets and Apostles.

Master: Have you any certain and appointed manner of praying?

Scholar: Yes indeed, even the same that our Lord taught his disciples and in them all other Christians. Who, being required to teach them some sort of prayer, taught them this. When you pray, said he, say: Our

Father who is in heaven, hallowed by your name. Your kingdom come. Your will be done in earth as it is in heaven. Give us this day our daily bread, and forgive us our trespasses as we forgive them that trespass against us. And lead us not into temptation, but deliver us from evil. For yours is the kingdom, power, and glory forever. Amen.

Master: What do you think, is it lawful for us to use any other words of prayer?

Scholar: Although in this short abridgement are sufficiently contained all things that every Christian ought to pray for, yet Christ did not in this prayer tie us up so short as that it were not lawful for us to use other words and manner of prayer. But he did set out in this prayer certain principal points, wherein all our prayers should be referred. But let each man ask of God as his present needs require. Whatsoever you ask the Father in my name (says Christ) he shall give it to you.

Master: Forasmuch as there is in all this prayer nothing doubtful or beside the purpose, I would like to hear your mind about it.

Scholar: I do well perceive what the words do signify.

Master: Do you think then that there is in it nothing dark, nothing hidden, nothing hard to understand?

Scholar: Nothing at all. For neither was it Christ's pleasure that there should be anything in it dark or far from our capacity, especially since it belongs equally to all and is as necessary for the lewd as the learned.

Master: Therefore, declare to me in a few words, each part by itself.

Scholar: When I say our Father who is in heaven, I think this within myself: that it cannot be but that he must hear me and be pleased with my prayers. For I am his son (although unprofitable and disobedient) and he, on the other side, is my most bountiful Father, most ready to take pity and pardon me.

Master: Why do you say that he is in heaven? Is he in some one certain and limited place in heaven? What does it mean that he says of himself,

I fill both heaven and earth? Again, the heaven is my seat and the earth my footstool?

Scholar: I have spoken somewhat about this before, but I will join it with what follows. First of all, as we often as we do say 'who is in heaven', it is as much to say, as heavenly and divine. For we ought to think much higher of our heavenly Father than of our earthly. He is also said to be in heaven for this reason: that in that high and heavenly place the notable and wonderful works of God do more clearly and gloriously show themselves, and he is now declared to be in everlasting and full felicity, whereas we remain still banished – full wretchedly – in earth. Moreover, as the heaven by unmeasureable wideness of compass, contains all places, the earth and the sea, and no place is there that may be hidden from the large reach of heaven, since it is at every instant of time to everything present. So, by this, we may understand that God is likewise present to each thing in each place. He sees, hears, and governs all things: he being himself a spirit and most far from all earthly and mortal state. Witness what Jeremiah the Prophet says: Am I not (says the Lord) a God near to you? And am I a God far off? Shall any man be able to shroud himself in such a corner, that I can not see him? This is a pithy sentence to drive fear into us, that we do not offend the Lord of so large a dominion, and whereby we are also persuaded assuredly to believe that God will hear us whenever we stand in need. For he is at all times and in all places present. This foundation then laid, and so sweet and pleasant entrance prepared, there follows the first part of the Lord's prayer, wherein we require that not only we but also all others, may in holiness, honour, reverence, and worship his name.

Master: How is that to be done?

Scholar: I will show you. When we do that, when leaving all those that have the name of gods, whether in heaven or in earth or worshipped in temples in diverse shapes and images, we acknowledge him alone as our Father, pray to the true God, and Jesus Christ his only Son, whom he has sent, and by pure and genuine prayer call upon him alone, with uprightness of life and innocency.

Master: You have said very well, proceed.

Scholar: In the second part we require that his kingdom come. For we do not see all things in subjection to Christ, we do not see the stone cut off from the mountain without the work of man, which all-too bruised and brought to nothing the image which Daniel describes, that the only rock Christ may obtain and possess the dominion of the whole world, granted to him by his Father. Antichrist is not yet slain. For this reason do we long for, and pray that it may finally come to pass and be fulfilled that Christ may reign with his saints, according to God's promises, that he may live and be Lord in the world, according to the decrees of the holy gospel, not after the traditions and laws of men nor pleasure or worldly tyrants.

Master: God grant his kingdom come, and that quickly.

Scholar: Moreover, since it is the children's duty to frame their life to their father's will, and not the fathers to bow to the children's pleasure, forasmuch as our will is commonly by the tickling of the affections and stirring of lusts drawn to do those things that God is displeased with, then we hang wholly upon the command of our heavenly Father and wholly submit ourselves to his heavenly government. Thus, for this reason, we mortal men to pray that we may be obedient to his commandment as are the sun and moon and other stars in heaven, which both by ordinary courses and by lightening the earth with never-ceasing beams execute the Lord's will continually. Or that we, as the angels and other divine spirits, in all points obey him which bestow all their travail diligently to accomplish his godly commandments. Next after that he teaches us to ask of our heavenly Father, our bread. By this he means not only meat but also all other things needed for the maintenance and preserving of life, that we may learn that God alone is the author of all things, who makes the fruits of the earth to grow and increase to plenty. Therefore it is right that we call upon him alone in prayer, which (as David says) alone feeds and maintains all things.

Master: Some suppose this place to mean that bread that Christ makes mention of in the sixth chapter of John. That is, of the true knowledge and taste of Christ, that was born and died for us, wherein the faithful soul is fed. The reason that they gather this is the Greek word *epiousion* that they understand supernaturally, spiritually, heavenly, and divine. This meaning I do not refuse, for both these expositions may appropriately agree with this place. But why does it call it daily bread, which is also signified by this word *epiousion*?

Scholar: We ask daily bread that might be always present and accompany us continually, to quench and satisfy our thirsty desire, and hungry stomach, unless otherwise we should be, as Christ says, careful for tomorrow for tomorrow shall care for itself. For it shall not come without his own discommodity and care. Therefore, it is not reasonable that one day should increase the evil of another. It shall be sufficient for us to ask daily, because our most bountiful Father is ready daily to give. Now follows the fifth request, wherein we ask the Father to forgive us our trespasses and defaults that we have committed. This request is undoubtedly very necessary, since there is no man alive free from sin. Here therefore we must cast away all trust of ourselves. Here we must pluck down our courage. Here we must pray our most merciful Father, for the love of Jesus Christ his most dear and obedient son, to parden, forgive, and utterly blot out of his book, our innumerable offences. Here we ought in the meantime to be mindful of the covenant we make with God: this it may please God so to forgive us our trespasses as we ourselves forgive them that trespass against us. Therefore, it is necessary that we forgive and pardon all men all their offences, whatever sort or condition whatsoever they are. If we forgive men their faults, our heavenly Father will forgive us ours.

Master: Were these things (my son) used like this, then there should not at this day violently reign so many brawls, so many contentions, so many and so heinous disagreements, enmities, and hatreds of one man to another. But now whereas each man so stands in his own conceit that he will not lose an inch of his right, neither in honour or wealth, it happens often that they lose both their wealth, their honour, and their entire life itself. Yes they put from themselves and turn away from the favour of God and everlasting glory. But you (my son) must not be ignorant of Christ's commandment: nor of that which Paul teachers, that you do not suffer yourself so to be seduced by any other man's offence, as to repay evil for evil, but rather overcome evil with good. I mean by doing him good, he that has done the evil, by using him friendly who has showed himself the most cruel foe. Now go forward to the sixth request.

Scholar: I will, with a good will, as you command me. Forasmuch as we be feeble, weak, subject to a thousand perils and a thousand temptations, easy to be overcome, ready to yield to every light occasion, either to men fraught with malice or to our own lust and appetite, or finally to the crafty malicious serpent, the devil: therefore, we ask our Father that he brings us into no such hard escape and peril, nor leaves us in the very plunge of danger. But if it comes to that point, that he rather takes us away from the present mischief and engines of the devil, the author and principal cause of all evil, then suffer us to run headlong into destruction. Now you have, good master, in a few words, all that you have taught me unless something was slipped over in the rehearsal.

Master: Because yours is the kingdom, power, and glory forever. Amen. Why was it Christ's pleasure to knit up our prayer with this clause in the end?

Scholar: Partly, that we should declare our assured trust to obtain all things that we have before required. For there is nothing which, if it is asked with faith, he is not able or not willing to give, who rules and governs all things, who is able to do all things, who is garnished with endless glory. These things, when we say of God our Father, there remains no cause to doubt or suspect that we shall receive denial. Partly, by so saying, we teach ourselves how right it is to make our suit to God, since besides him, none glistens with so shining glory, none has dominion so large, or force so great, to be able to stop him from giving that which he has appointed according to his pleasure, or to take away, that he has already given us. And there is no evil of ours so great that may not be put away by his exceedingly great power, glory, and wisdom.

Master: I like (my son) this short declaration well, and I see nothing left out that ought to have been spoken.

Scholar: But yet this one thing I will add to it. The chief and principal thing required in prayer, is that without all doubting we steadfastly believe that God our Father will grant what we do ask, so that it is neither unprofitable for us to receive nor unfit for him to give. For he that is not assured, but doubtful, let him not think (as James says) to get anything at the hands of God.

Master: I see now (my dear son) how diligently and heedfully you have applied your mind to those things that I have taught you, how godly and upright a judgement you have of God's true service, and of the duties of neighbours one to another. This remains, that from now on you so frame your life, that this heavenly and godly knowledge does not decay in you, nor lie soulless and dead, as it were in a tomb of the flesh. But rather see that you wholly give yourself continually and earnestly to these godly studies. So shall you live, not only in this present life but also in the life to come, which is much better and more blessed than this present life. For godliness (as Paul says) has a promise, not only in this life, but in the other. It is convenient therefore, that we earnestly follow godliness, which plainly opens the way to heaven, if we seek to attain it. And the principal point of godliness is (as you have declared even now very well) to know God only, to covet him only as the chief felicity, to fear him as our Lord, to love and reverence him as our Father, with his Son our saviour Jesus Christ. This is him who has begotten and regenerated us. This is him who at the beginning gave us life and soul, who maintains, who blesses us with life of everlasting continuance. To this godliness is directly contrary godlessness. As for superstition and hypocrisy, they counterfeit and resemble it, whereas nevertheless they are most far and different from all true godliness, and therefore we ought to avoid them as a pestilence, as the venom, and most contagious enemies of our soul and salvation. The next point of godliness is to love each man as our brother. For if God did at the beginning create us all, if he does feed and govern us, finally if he is the cause and author of our dwelling in this wide frame of the world, the name of brother must most fitly agree with us, and with so much stronger bond shall we be bound together as we approach nearer to Christ who is our brother, the first begotten and eldest, whom he that does not know him, he that has no hold of him, is unrighteous indeed and has no place among the people of God. For Christ is the root and foundation of all right and justice, and he has poured into our hearts certain natural lessons, as do that (says he) to another, that you would have done unto yourself. Beware therefore, that you do nothing to anyone that you yourself would not willingly suffer. Measure always another person by your own mind and as you select in yourself. If it grieves you to suffer injury, if you think it wrong what another man does to you, judge likewise the same in the person of your neighbour that you feel in yourself, and you shall perceive that you do no less wrongfully in hurting another, than others do in hurting you. Here, if we would steadfastly fasten our foot, here if we would earnestly travail, we should attain to the very highest top of innocency. For the first degree of this is to offend no one. The next is to help all men as much as lies within us, at least to will and wish well to all. The third (which is accounted the chief and most perfect) is to do good even to our enemies that wrong us. Let us therefore know ourselves, pluck out the faults that are in us, and in their place plant virtues, like the farmer that first shrubs and roots out the thorns, brambles, and weeds, from their untilled and disregarded land, and then everywhere scatters and throws into the womb of the earth good and fruitful seeds to bring forth good fruit in their due season. Likewise, let us do that. For first let us labour to root out difficult and corrupt lusts, and afterwards plant holy and fitting conditions for Christian hearts. Which, if they are watered and fatted with the dew of God's word, and nourished with the warmth of the Holy Spirit, they shall undoubtedly bring forth the most plentiful fruit of immortality and blessed life, which God has by Christ prepared for his chosen people, before the foundations of the world were laid. To whom be all honour and glory. Amen.

Appendix C – The Forty-Five Articles of Religion (1552)

Translated by Derek Scales

I. *Of faith in the Trinity.*[1]

There is but one living and true God, and he is everlasting, without body, parts, or passions; of infinite power, wisdom, and goodness; the maker and[2] preserver of all things both[3] visible and invisible, and in unity of this Godhead there be three Persons of one substance, power, and eternity: the Father, the Son, and the Holy Ghost.

[1] XLV has *Trinitatis* (in the Trinity); XLII has *in Sacrosanctam Trinitatem* (in the Holy Trinity).
[2] XLV uses *ac* for 'and'; XLII uses *et*.
[3] XLV uses *cum ... tum* for 'both ... and'; XLII uses *tum ... tum*.

II. *That the Word of God was made a very man.*[1]

The Son, which is the Word of the Father, took man's nature in the womb of the blessed virgin[2] of her[3] substance,[4] so that two whole and perfect natures, that is to say, the Godhead and manhood, were joined together in one Person,[5] never to be divided, whereof is one Christ, very God and very man, who truly suffered, was crucified, dead, and buried, to reconcile his Father to us, and to be a sacrifice for all sin of man, both original and actual.

[1] XLV and XLII have the same Latin title (*Verbum Dei verum hominem esse factum*), but in the English version XLII adds 'or Son' after Word.
[2] XLII adds 'Mary', which is not in the Latin.
[3] XLV uses *eius* for 'her' [= of that (woman)]; XLII uses *illius*, which has the same meaning.
[4] XLV has *naturam humanam ex eius substantia* ('man's nature ... of her substance'); XLII has the two phrases reversed – *ex illius substantia naturam humanam*.
[5] Latin: *in unitate personae*; XLII has 'into one person'.

III. *Of the going down of Christ into Hell.*

As Christ died and was buried for us: so also it is to be believed, that he went down into Hell. For the body lay in the sepulchre, until the resurrection, but his Ghost departing from him,[1] was with the Ghosts that were in prison or in Hell, and did preach to the same, as the place of St. Peter doth testify. **Moreover by his going down into Hell Christ the Lord freed none from imprisonment or its pangs.**[2]

[1] XLV uses *eo* for 'him' [= (from) that (man)]; XLII uses *illo*, which has the same meaning.
[2] XLV has this last sentence indicated in bold (*At suo ad Inferos descensu nullos a carceribus aut tormentis liberauit Christus Dominus*); XLII omits it.

IV. *The resurrection of Christ.*

Christ did truly rise again from death, and took again his body with flesh, bones, and all things appertaining to the perfection of man's nature, wherewith he ascended into Heaven, and there sitteth, until he return to judge men at the last day.

V. *The doctrine of Holy Scripture is sufficient to Salvation.*

Holy Scripture containeth all things necessary to Salvation: so that whatsoever is neither[1] read therein, nor may be proved thereby, although it be sometime received of the faithful, as godly, and profitable for an order and comeliness, yet no man ought to be constrained to **teach**[2] it as an article of faith, or repute it requisite to the necessity of Salvation.

[1] XLV uses *neque* for 'neither'; XLII uses *nec*.
[2] XLV has *tradatur* ('teach', 'deliver', 'hand down'); XLII has *credatur* ('believe').

VI. *The Old Testament is not to be refused.*

The Old Testament is not to be put away as though it were contrary to the New, but to be kept still: for both in the Old and New Testaments, everlasting life is offered to mankind by Christ, who is the only Mediator between God and man, being both God and man. Wherefore they are not to be heard, which feign that the old fathers did look only for transitory promises.

No changes

VII. *The Three Creeds.*

The three Creeds, **that is**[1] [the] Nicene Creed, Athanasius' Creed, and that which is commonly called[2] the Apostles' Creed, ought thoroughly to be received: for they may be proved by most certain warrants of Scripture[3].

[1] XLV has *inquam*, which XLII omits. This is literally 'I say', being used for emphasis, particularly when repeating words. It may be used here to introduce the fuller defining of what was said briefly in 'The three creeds', and with the effect of 'that is to say'.
[2] XLV has *vocatur* for 'is ... called'; XLII has *appellatur*.
[3] XLII adds *diuinarum* – 'of *Holy* Scripture'.

VIII. *Of original or birth sin.*

Original sin standeth not in the following of Adam, as the Pelagians do vainly talk, which also the Anabaptists do nowadays renew,

XLV	XLII

but *in every person born into this world, it deserves God's wrath and damnation*, and it so mars [makes faulty] and corrupts the nature of men that it is very far gone from its first beginning.

but it is the fault and corruption of the nature of every man, that naturally is engendered of the offspring of Adam, whereby man is very far gone from his former righteousness, which he had at his creation,[1] and is of his own nature given to evil, so that the flesh desireth always contrary to the spirit, and therefore *in every person born into this world, it deserveth God's wrath and damnation*:

The desire and[2] infection of nature doth remain, yea in them that are regenerated,[3] whereby **the flesh always lusts against the spirit, and**[4] the lust[5] of the flesh called in Greek φρόνημα[6]

And this infection of nature doth remain, yea in them that are baptized,[3] whereby the lust[5] of the flesh called in Greek φρόνημα σαρκὸς

(which some do expound, the wisdom, some sensuality, some the affection,[5] some the desire of the flesh[7]) is not subject to the law of God. And although there is no condemnation **on account of Christ**[8] for them that

are regenerated[9] and believe

believe, and are baptized,[9]

yet the Apostle doth confess that concupiscence and lust[10] hath of itself the nature[11] of sin.

[1] *former ... which he had at his creation* is the translation of the Latin *originali*.
[2] *concupiscentia et*.
[3] The Latin is the same in both cases: *renatis* – 'born again, regenerate'. The translation in the XLII Articles seems to be a theological interpretation rather than a translation. The 1562 Articles translate *renatis* as 'them that are baptized'. The XXXIX Articles translate *renatis* as 'them that are regenerated', the translation supplied here for the XLV.
[4] *caro semper concupiscat adversus spiritum, et*; *concupiscat* – 'lusts'.
[5] *affectus / affectum*.
[6] XLV omits σαρκὸς [of the flesh].
[7] XLII omits *carnis*, although it understands / supplies 'of the flesh' in the English version.
[8] *propter Christum* appears in the Latin versions of XLV, XLII, 1562, and XXXIX, but is omitted in all English versions (XLII, 1562, and XXXIX).
[9] The Latin in both cases is *renatis* – 'born again, regenerate'. XLII, 1562, and at this point the XXXIX Articles translate *renatis* as them that believe and "are baptized"; the Latin word order is *renatis et credentibus*.
[10] 'concupiscence and lust' is the translation of *concupiscentiam*.
[11] XLV has *rationem in sese*; XLII has *in sese rationem*.

IX. *Of free will.*

We have no power to do good works pleasant and acceptable to God, without the grace of God by Christ, preventing us that we may have a good will, and working in us, when we have that will.

No changes

X. *Of grace.*

The grace of Christ or the Holy Ghost by him given doth take away the stony heart, and giveth an heart of flesh. And although those that have no will to good things, he maketh them to will, and those that would[1] evil things, he makes them not to will the same, yet nevertheless he enforceth not the will. And therefore no man when he sinneth can excuse himself, as[2] not worthy to be blamed or condemned, by alleging that he sinned unwillingly, or by compulsion.

[1] XLV has *volenibus*; XLII has *ex volentibus*.
[2] XLV has *ideoque* – 'and therefore'; XLII has *ut eam ob causam* – 'so that, for that reason'. The Latin order of the last two clauses ('as not worthy …', 'by alleging …') is reversed in the translation.

XI. *Of the Justification of man.*

Justification by only faith in Jesus Christ in that sense as it is declared in the homily of Justification, is a most certain and wholesome doctrine for Christian men.

No changes

XII. *Works Before Justification.*

Works done before **justification**[1] are not pleasant to God, forasmuch as they spring not of faith in Jesus Christ, neither do they make men meet to receive grace or (as the school authors say) deserve grace of congruity: but because they are not done as God hath willed and commanded them to be done, we doubt not, but they have the nature of sin.

[1] XLV has *iustificationem* – 'justification'; XLII has *gratiam Christi, et Spiritus ejus afflatum* – 'the grace of Christ and the inspiration of his Spirit'.

XIII. *Works of Supererogation.*

Voluntary works besides, over, and above God's commandments which they call works of Supererogation, cannot be taught without arrogance and iniquity. For by them men do declare that they do not only render to God, as much as they are bound to do, but that they do more for his sake,[1] than[2] of bounden duty is required: whereas Christ saith plainly, When you have done all that are commanded you, say, we be unprofitable servants.

[1] XLV has *in gratiam eius*; XLII has *in ejus gratiam*.
[2] XLII prints 'then', an older form of 'than'. The Latin text has *quam* – 'than'.

XIV. *No man is without sin, but Christ alone.*

Christ in the truth of our nature was made like unto us in all things, sin only except, from which he was clearly void both in his flesh and in his spirit. He came to be the lamb without spot, who by sacrifice of himself made once for ever, should take away the sins of the world: and sin (as Saint John saith) was not in him. But the rest, yea, although we be baptized,[1] and born again[2] in Christ, yet we all offend in many things. And if we say, we have no sin, we deceive ourselves and the truth is not in us.

No changes

[1] *baptizati.*
[2] *regenerati.*

XV. *Of sin against the Holy Ghost.*

Every deadly sin willingly committed after Baptism is not sin against the Holy Ghost, and unpardonable: wherefore the place for repentance[1] is not to be denied to such as fall into sin after baptism.

After we have received the Holy Ghost, we may depart[2] from grace given[3] and fall into sin, and by the grace of God we may rise again, and amend our lives. And therefore they are to be condemned, which say, they can no more sin as long as they live here, or deny the place for repentance[1] to such as truly repent, and amend their lives.

[1] The English text of XLII has 'penitentes' (the English noun 'penitence'); Article XVI of the XXXIX has the same Latin phrase, *locus poenitentiae*, which is rendered in the English version 'grant of repentance'.
[2] The printed text of XLV has *recidere*; but I think that the MS, which is not easy to read at this point, has *recedere*. *recedere* is the Latin in XLII and in XXXIX. There is little difference of meaning between the two verbs: *recedere* – to retire, retreat, depart (the root verb means to yield); *recidere* – to fall back, return, to relapse (the root verb means to fall).
[3] XLV has *a data gratia*; XLII has *a gratia data.*

XVI. **What** *blasphemy against the Holy Ghost* **is**[1].

Blasphemy against the Holy Ghost is, when a man of malice and stubbornness of mind, doth rail upon the truth of God's word manifestly perceived, and being enemy thereunto persecuteth the same. And because such be guilty of God's curse,

XLV	XLII
and wicked, they cannot be further restored through repentance;[2]	they entangle themselves with a most grievous and heinous crime,[3]

whereupon this kind of sin is[4] affirmed of the Lord, unpardonable.

[1] XLV has *quid sit*, which XLII omits.
[2] *et reprobi, per poenitentiam non amplius restitui possunt;*
[3] *gravissimo sese adstringunt sceleri.*
[4] XLII adds *appellatur, et* – 'called, and'.

XVII. *Of Predestination and Election.*

Predestination to life is the everlasting purpose of God, whereby (before the foundations of the world were laid) he hath constantly decreed by his own judgment secret to us, to deliver from curse and damnation those whom he hath chosen out of mankind, and to bring[1] them to everlasting salvation by Christ, as vessels made to honour: whereupon, such[2] as have so excellent a benefit of God given[3] unto them be called[4] by his spirit[5] in due season, they through grace **trust**[6] the calling, they be justified freely, they be made sons by adoption, they be made like the image of the only begotten Christ Jesus[7], they walk religiously in good works, and at length by God's mercy, they attain to everlasting felicity.

As the godly consideration of predestination and our election in Christ is full of sweet, pleasant and unspeakable comfort to godly persons, and such as feel in themselves the working of the spirit of Christ, mortifying the works of the flesh, and their earthly members, and drawing up their mind to high and heavenly[8] things, as well because it doth greatly stablish and confirm their faith of eternal salvation to be enjoyed through Christ,[9] as because it doth fervently kindle their love towards[10] God: so for curious and carnal persons lacking the Spirit of Christ to have continually before their eyes the sentence of God's predestination, is a most dangerous downfall, whereby the Devil may thrust them either into desperation, or into a wretchlessness[11] of most unclean living, no less perilous than desperation. Furthermore, although the decrees of predestination are[12] unknown unto us **(as far as men can make a judgement about men)**[13] yet we must receive God's promises **(relying on which faith renders us certain of our salvation),**[14] in such wise as they be generally set forth to us in Holy Scripture, and in our doings that will of God is to be followed, which we have expressly declared unto us in the word of God.

[1] XLV has *perducere*; XLII has *adducere*.
[2] XLII adds *illi*.
[3] XLV has *affecti*; XLII has *donati*.
[4] XLII adds *secundum propositum eius* – 'according to God's [his] purpose'.
[5] XLII adds *operante*, 'working'.
[6] XLV has *credunt* – 'trust, believe'; XLII has *parent* – 'obey'.
[7] Latin: *unigeniti Jesu Christi*, which XLII amplifies to 'of God's only begotten Son Jesus Christ'. XLV has *Christi Jesu* – 'Christ Jesus'; XLII has *Jesu Christi* –'Jesus Christ'.
[8] XLV has *superna et coelestia*; XLII reverses the Latin to *coelestia et superna* [heavenly and high].
[9] XLV has *per Christum consequenda*; XLII has *consequenda per Christum*.
[10] XLV has *erga* (towards); XLII has *in* (to).
[11] I have kept 'wretchlessness' as its use continues in the XXXIX Articles, though in modern English it would be in the form 'recklessness'. In the English text of the XLII it is spelled 'rechielisnesse'.
[12] The third edition of Hardwick's *A History of the Articles* (1876) prints *sint* (subjunctive), but the MS reading may well be *sunt*; XLII has *sunt* (indicative).
[13] XLV has *(quatenus homines de hominibus iudicare possunt)*, which XLII omits.
[14] XLV has *(quibus fides innitens certos nos reddit de nostra salute)*, which XLII omits.

XVIII. *We must trust to obtain eternal Salvation*[1] *only by the name of* **Jesus**[2] *Christ.*

They also are to be had accursed and abhorred that presume to say that every man shall be saved[3] by the law or sect which he professeth, so that[4] he hath lived without offence[5] according to that law, and the light of nature: for Holy Scripture doth set out unto us only the name of Jesu Christ, whereby men must be saved.

[1] XLV has *salus aeterna*; XLII has *aeterna salus*.
[2] XLII omits 'Jesus'.
[3] XLV has *seruandum esse*; XLII has *esse seruandum*.
[4] meaning 'provided that'.
[5] XLV has *innocenter* – innocently, without offence; XLII has *accurate* – carefully, diligently, precisely. A translation for the XLII text which followed the general character of the translation of the XLV text above might be 'so that he hath lived diligently according to that law and the light of nature', which XLII renders more fulsomely as 'so that he be diligent to frame his life according to that law and the light of nature'.

XIX. *All men are bound to keep the moral commandments of the Law.*

The Law which was given of God by Moses, although it bind not Christian men, as concerning the ceremonies and rites of the same, neither is it required that the civil precepts and orders of it should of necessity be received in any commonwealth: yet no man (be he never so perfect a Christian) is exempt and loose[1] from the obedience of those commandments, which are called moral. Wherefore they are not to be hearkened unto, who affirm that Holy Scripture is given only to the weak, and do boast themselves continually of the Spirit, of whom (they say) they have learned such things as they teach, although the same be most evidently repugnant to the Holy Scripture.

XLV has *absolutus*; XLII has *solutus*. It is translated 'exempt and loose'.

XX. *Of the Church.*

The visible Church of Christ is a congregation of faithful men, in the which the pure word of God is preached, and the sacraments be duly ministered according to Christ's ordinance, in all those things that of necessity are requisite to the same.

As the Church of Jerusalem, of Alexandria, and of Antioch hath erred: so also the Church of Rome hath erred,[1] not only in their living, but also in matters of their faith.

XLV has *errauit et*; XLII has *et erravit*.

XXI. *Of the authority of the Church.*

It is not lawful for the Church to ordain any thing[1] that is contrary to God's word written, neither may it so expound one place of Scripture, that it be repugnant to another. Wherefore although the church be a witness and a keeper of holy writ, yet as it ought not to decree any thing against the same: so besides the same ought it not to enforce any thing to be believed for necessity of Salvation.

XLV has *quippiam constituere*; XLII has *quicquam instituere*.

XXII. *Of the authority of general Councils.*

General Councils may not be gathered together without the commandment and will of Princes: and when they be gathered (forasmuch as they be an assembly of men, whereof all be not governed with the Spirit, and word[1] of God) they may err, and sometime have erred, even[2] in things pertaining unto the **substance**[3] of religious duty. Wherefore things ordained by them as necessary to Salvation have neither strength nor authority, unless it be declared,[4] that they be taken out of Holy Scripture.

When the judgement or calling of general councils is not expected, kings and godly magistrates can, in their own commonwealth, settle matters of religion according to the word of God.[5]

[1] The Latin is *verbis* (words).
[2] The Latin is *etiam* (even); XLII has 'not only in worldly matters, but also' for the same single Latin word, a filling out of the implied sense.
[3] XLV has *summam* (substance); XLII has *normam* (rule, practice). XLII's translation of *normam pietatis* (literally, 'the practice of religious duty') is [pertaining] 'unto God'.
[4] XLV has *ostenduntur* – 'be declared'; XLII has *ostendi possunt* – 'can be declared' / 'may be declared'.
[5] XLV has this last sentence (*Possunt Reges et pij Magistratus non expectata conciliorum generalium sententia aut conuocatione in Republica sua iuxta Dei verbum de rebus religionis constituere*); XLII omits it. *Respublica* is translated 'commonwealth' in Article XIX.

XXIII. *Of Purgatory.*

The doctrine of school authors concerning purgatory, **prayer for the dead**,[1] pardons,[2] worshipping and adoration as well[3] of images, as of relics,[4] and also invocation of saints, is a fond thing vainly feigned and grounded upon no warrant of Scripture, but rather repugnant to the word of God.

[1] XLV has this phrase (*de precatione pro defunctis*); XLII omits it.
[2] The third edition of Hardwick's *A History of the Articles* (1876) has a misprint, printing *derindulgentiis* for *de indulgentiis*.
[3] XLV has *cum ... tum* ('as well ... as' / 'both ... and'); XLII has *tum ... tum*.
[4] The third edition of Hardwick's *A History of the Articles* (1876) has a misprint, omitting the initial *r* of *reliquiarum*. [In seeking to correct this error the printer may have mistakenly inserted the letter *r* referred to in note 2.]

XXIV. *No man may minister in the Congregation, except he be called.*

It is not lawful for any man to take upon him the office of public preaching or ministering the sacraments in the congregation **that is well ordered**,[1] before he be lawfully called and sent to execute the same.

And those we ought to judge lawfully called and sent, which be chosen and called to this work by men who have public authority given unto them in the congregation **according to the word of God**,[2] to call and send ministers into the Lord's vineyard.

[1] XLV has this phrase – *bene constituta*; XLII omits it (and thus has 'in the congregation'). The whole phrase *in ecclesia bene constituta* might be translated 'in a church that is rightly ordered', but XLII preferred the translation 'congregation' for *ecclesia*.
[2] XLV has this phrase (*iuxta verbum Dei*); XLII omits it. It is possible that the phrase should be taken with 'into the Lord's vineyard' ('to call and send ministers into the Lord's vineyard according to the word of God').

XXV. *Men must speak in the Congregation in such tongue as the people understandeth.*

It is most seemly and most agreeable to the word of God, that in the congregation nothing be[1] read or spoken in a tongue unknown to the people, the which thing S. Paul did forbid, except some were present that should declare the same.

[1] XLII adds *publice* – 'openly'.

XXVI. *Of the Sacraments.*

Our Lord Jesus Christ hath knit together a company of new people with Sacraments, most few in number, most easy to be kept, most excellent in signification, as is Baptism, and the Lord's Supper, **which two only were ordained in the church for sacraments by Christ the Lord, and which alone have the essential nature of sacraments.**[1]

The Sacraments were not ordained by Christ to be gazed upon, or to be carried about, but that we should rightly use them. And in such only, as worthily receive the same, they have an wholesome effect and operation, and yet not that of the work wrought, as some men speak, which word, as it is strange and unknown to Holy Scripture, so it engendereth no godly, but a very superstitious sense. But they that receive the Sacraments unworthily, purchase to themselves damnation, as Saint Paul saith.

Sacraments ordained by the word of God be not only badges and tokens of profession **among Christian men**,[2] but rather they be certain sure witnesses and effectual signs of grace and God's good will toward us, by the which he doth work invisibly in us, and doth not only quicken, but also strengthen and confirm our faith in him.

[1] XLV has these clauses (*quae duo tantum in ecclesia pro Sacramentis a Christo Domino sunt instituta, et quae sola sacramentorum propriam rationem habent*); XLII omits them.
[2] XLV has *notae professionis inter Christianos* – 'tokens of profession among Christian men'; XLII has *notae professionis Christianorum* – 'tokens of Christian men's profession' ('tokens of the profession of Christian men').

XXVII. *The wickedness of the Ministers doth not take away the effectual operation of God's ordinances.*

Although in the visible Church the evil be ever mingled with the good, and sometime the evil have chief authority in the ministration of the word and sacraments: yet forasmuch as they do not the same in their own name, but do minister by Christ's commission and authority, we may use their ministry, both in hearing the word of God and in the receiving the sacraments, neither is the effect of **the Lord's**[1] ordinances taken away by their[2] wickedness, or the grace of God's gifts diminished from such as by faith and[3] rightly receive the sacraments ministered unto them, which be effectual because of Christ's institution[4] and promise, although they be ministered by evil men. Nevertheless it appertains to the discipline of the Church, that enquiry be made of such, and that they be accused[5] by those[6] that have knowledge[7] of their offences, and finally being found guilty by just judgment, be deposed.

[1] XLV has *Domini* – 'the Lord's'; XLII (and 1562) has *Christi* – 'Christ's', though it is translated as 'God's'.
[2] The third edition of Hardwick's *A History of the Articles* (1876) prints *illorum*, but the MS has *eorum*; XLII has *illorum*.
[3] XLV uses *ac* for 'and'; XLII uses *et*.
[4] XLV has *institutum*; XLII has *institutionem*.
[5] XLII adds *–que* ('and') to *accusentur* – 'and that they be accused'.
[6] XLV has *hiis* for 'those' (more strictly meaning 'these'); XLII has *iis*.
[7] XLV has *nouerunt* (indicative); XLII has *noverint* (subjunctive).

XXVIII. *Of Baptism.*

Baptism is not only a sign of profession or[1] mark of difference, whereby Christian men may be discerned from other that be not **Christians**,[3] but it is also a sign and seal of our new birth,[4] whereby, as by an instrument, we[5] that receive Baptism rightly are **visibly**[6] grafted in the Church, the promises of forgiveness of sin, and our adoption to be the sons of God, are signed[7] and sealed, faith is confirmed, and grace increase by virtue of prayer unto God.

The baptism of the infants of Christians[8] is **also**[9] to be commended, and in any wise to be retained in the Church.

[1] XLV has *aut* – 'or'; XLII has *ac* – 'and'.
[2] XLV has *discernantur* (subjunctive) – may be discerned; XLII has *discernuntur* (indicative) – are discerned
[3] The Latin is *Christianis*, the ablative of the word *Christiani* translated 'Christian men'; but XLII translates it 'Christened'.
[4] *regenerationis*.
[5] XLV has *inserimur* – 'we are grafted'; XLII has *inseruntur* – 'they are grafted'.
[6] XLV has *visibiliter* – 'visibly'; XLII omits it.
[7] XLII adds *visibiliter* – 'visibly'.
[8] The Latin is *Baptismus infantium Christianorum*, translated 'The baptism of the infants of Christians'; it might also be translated 'The baptism of Christian infants'. XLII has *Mos Ecclesiae baptizandi parvulos* – 'The custom of the Church to Christen young children' (*baptizandi* is literally 'of baptizing').
[9] The Latin text of XLV and XLII has *et* (also), which XLII omits in the English.

XXIX. *Of the Lord's Supper.*

XLV   **XLII**

The Supper of the Lord[1] is not only a sign of the love that Christians ought to have among themselves one to another, but rather it is a sacrament of our redemption by Christ's death, insomuch that to such as rightly, worthily, and with faith receive the same, the bread which we break, is a communion of the body of Christ. Likewise **also**[2] the cup of blessing is a communion of the blood of Christ.

XXX. *Of transubstantiation.*

| The transubstantiation of bread and wine **in the Lord's supper**[3] | Transubstantiation or the change of the substance of bread and wine into the substance of Christ's body and blood,[4] |

cannot be proved by holy writ, but is repugnant to the plain words of Scripture, and hath given occasion to many superstitions.

XXXI. *Of the bodily presence of Christ in the Lord's Supper.*

| Forasmuch as the truth of man's nature requireth, that | Forasmuch as the truth of man's nature requireth, that |
| it is not possible[5] to be at one time in many places, but in a fixed and certain [place]: | the body of one and the selfsame man cannot[5] be at one time in divers[6] places, but must needs be in some one certain place; |

therefore the body of Christ cannot be present at one time in many and diverse places. And because (as Holy Scripture doth teach) Christ was taken up into Heaven, and there shall continue unto the end of the world, a faithful man ought not, either to believe or openly to confess the real and bodily presence (as they term it) of Christ's flesh and blood in the Sacrament of the Lord's Supper.[7]

XXXII. *The sacrament of the Lord's Supper*[8] *ought not to be reserved.*

| The Sacrament of the Lord's supper[8] was not by Christ's ordinance to be kept, nor carried about, nor lifted up, nor worshipped. | The Sacrament of the Lord's supper[8] was not commanded[9] by Christ's ordinance to be kept, carried about, lifted up, nor worshipped. |

---

[1] XLV has the adjective *dominica* – 'the Lord's'; XLII has the genitive noun *domini* – 'of the Lord'.
[2] XLV has *et* – 'also', which XLII omits.
[3] XLII has not translated *in Eucharistia* – 'in the eucharist'; 1562 also does not translate the phrase; but XXXIX translates it 'in the Lord's Supper'.
[4] XLV, XLII, 1562, and XXXIX have the same Latin for this first section; but XLII and 1562 adds the explanatory 'or the change of the substance ... into the substance of Christ's body and blood' (for which there is no Latin), and XXXIX adds the first phrase.
[5] XLV has *possit* (present subjunctive); XLII has *posset* (imperfect subjunctive).
[6] The Latin is *multis* – 'many'.
[7] Latin *in eucharistia* – 'in the eucharist'.
[8] Latin *Eucharistiae* – 'of the eucharist'.
[9] 'commanded' is not in the Latin; it appears to be XLII's filling out of the word 'ordinance'.

XXXIII. *Of the perfect oblation of Christ made upon the cross.* [1553: XXX]

The offering of Christ made once for ever is the perfect redemption, the pacifying of God's displeasure, and satisfaction for all the sins of the whole world, both original and actual: and there is none other satisfaction for sin but that alone. Wherefore the sacrifices of masses, in the which it was commonly said, that the Priest did offer Christ for the quick and the dead,[1] were forged fables and dangerous deceits.

[1] XLII adds *in remissionem poenae aut culpae* – 'to have remission of pain or sin'.

XXXIV. *The state of single life is commanded to no man by the word of God.* [1553: XXXI]

Bishops Priests and Deacons are not commanded to vow the state of single life without marriage, neither by God's law are they compelled to abstain from matrimony, **if they do not have the gift, even though they have taken a vow, since this sort of vow is repugnant to the word of God.**[1]

[1] XLV has this last section (*si donum non habeant, tametsi vouerint, quandoquidem hoc voti genus verbo Dei repugnat*); XLII omits it.

XXXV. *Excommunicate persons are to be avoided.* [1553: XXXII]

That person which by open denunciation of the Church is **for deadly offences**[1] cut off from the unity of the Church, and excommunicate, ought to be taken of the whole multitude of the faithful as an Heathen and publican, until he be openly reconciled by penance,[2] by a Judge that hath authority thereto.

[1] XLV has *propter capitalia crimina* – 'for deadly offences'; XLII has *rite* – 'rightly'.
[2] *per poeniteniam* – by / through repentance / penance. This is referring to formal, public process. XLII adds 'and received into the Church', for which there is no Latin. This may be a considerable expansion of 'be openly reconciled' by the translator.

XXXVI. *Traditions of the Church.* [1553: XXXIII]

It is not necessary that traditions and ceremonies be in all places one or utterly like. For at all times they have been divers, and may be changed, according to the diversity of countries and men's manners, so that nothing be ordained against God's word.

Whosoever through his private judgment willingly and purposely doth openly break the traditions and ceremonies of the Church, which be not repugnant to the word of God and be ordained and approved by common authority, ought to be rebuked openly (that other may fear to do the like) as one that offendeth against the common order of the Church, and hurteth the authority of the Magistrate, and woundeth the consciences of the weak brethren.

No changes

XXXVI. *Homilies.* [1553: XXXIV]

The homilies of late given and set out by the King's authority **for the Church of England**[1] be godly and[2] wholesome, containing doctrine[3] to be received of all men, and therefore are to be read to the people diligently, distinctly, and plainly.

[1] XLV and XLII both have the words *Ecclesiae Anglicanae* ('for the Church of England'), but XLII omits them in the English version.
[2] XLV has *et*; XLII has *atque*.
[3] XLV has *atque doctrinam*; XLII has *doctrinamque*. Both mean 'and [they contain] doctrine'.

XXXVIII. *Of the book of*[1] *Ceremonies of the Church of England.* [1553: XXXV]

The Book which of very late time was given to the Church of England by the King's authority and the Parliament, containing the manner and form of praying and ministering the Sacraments in the Church of England, likewise also the book of ordering ministers of the Church, set forth by the foresaid authority, are **with respect to the truth of their doctrine**[2] godly and

XLV	XLII
with respect to the pattern of their ceremonies	
in no point repugnant to the wholesome freedom of the Gospel,	in no point repugnant to the wholesome doctrine of the Gospel,
if those ceremonies are regarded according to their own character	
but thoroughly agreeable thereunto,	but agreeable[3] thereunto,
especially furthering[4] the same in very many ways,	furthering and beautifying[5] the same not a little,

and therefore of all faithful members of the Church of England, and chiefly of the ministers of the word, they ought to be received, and allowed with all readiness of mind and thanksgiving, and to be commended[6] to the people of God.

[1] XLII adds 'Prayers and' (*Precationum et*).
[2] The Latin *quoad doctrinae veritatem* – 'with respect to the truth of [their] doctrine' – is the same in XLV and XLII, but XLII does not translate it.
[3] XLII omits 'thoroughly' (*probe* – properly, rightly, well, thoroughly).
[4] The third edition of Hardwick's *A History of the Articles* (1876) has a typographical error, inasmuch as no space was inserted between *inprimis* and *promovent*.
[5] XLII adds 'and beautifying' (*et illustrant*).
[6] XLV has *sunt commendandi*; XLII has *commendandi sunt*.

XXXIX. *Of civil magistrates.* [1553: XXXVI]

The King of England is Supreme head in earth, next under Christ, of the Church of England and Ireland, **nor does he recognize any greater than himself in the whole world, from whom his power and authority derive.**[1]

The Bishop of Rome hath no jurisdiction in this realm of England.

The civil magistrate is ordained and allowed of God: wherefore we must obey him[2] for conscience sake, **nor is it lawful to refuse tax or toll to any of those set under him, for the preservation and maintaining of the state of the kingdom or commonwealth.**[3]

The civil laws may punish Christian men with death, for heinous and grievous offences.

It is lawful for Christians, at the commandment of the magistrate, to wear weapons, and to serve lawfully[4] in wars.

[1] XLV has 'nor does he ... derive' (*neque in uniuerso orbe ullum seipso maiorem agnoscit, a quo sua potestas et autoritas pendeat*); XLII omits this.
[2] XLII adds: 'not only for fear of punishment, but also' (*non solum propter iram, sed etiam*).
[3] XLV has 'nor is it ... commonwealth' (*nec ulli ex eius subditis licet aut vectigal aut tributum negare, ad regni seu Reipublicae statum tuendum et conseruandum*); XLII omits this. *Respublica* is translated 'commonwealth' in Article XIX.
[4] *iuste bella administrare*. XLII has *justa bella administrare* – 'to serve in lawful wars'; 1562 and XXXIX translated the same Latin as 'and serve in the wars'.

XL. *Christian men's goods are not common.* [1553: XXXVII]

The riches and goods of Christians are not common as touching the right title and possession of the same (as certain Anabaptists do falsely boast); notwithstanding every man ought of such things as he possesseth, liberally to give alms to the poor, according to his ability.

No changes

XLI. *Christian men may take an Oath.* [1553: XXXVIII]

As we confess that vain and rash swearing is forbid Christian men by our Lord Jesus Christ and his Apostle James; so we judge that Christian religion doth not prohibit but that a man may swear, when the magistrate requireth in a cause of faith and charity, so it is done (according to the Prophet's teaching) in justice, judgement, and truth.

No changes

XLII. *The resurrection of the dead is not yet brought to pass.*[1]   [1553: XXXIX]

The resurrection of the dead is not as yet brought to pass, as though it only belonged to the soul, which by the grace of Christ is raised from the death of sin, but it is to be looked for **as far as all who have died**[2] at the last day: for then (as Scripture doth most manifestly testify) to those[3] that be dead[4] their own bodies, flesh and bone shall be restored, that the whole man may (according to his works) have either[5] reward or punishment, as he hath lived[6] virtuously, or wickedly.

[1] XLV has *facta est*; XLII has *est facta*.
[2] XLV has *quoad omnes qui obierunt* (perfect); XLII has *quoad omnes qui obierint* (future perfect), but does not translate the clause.
[3] XLII has 'to all that be dead', but there is no word for 'all' at this point in the Latin; perhaps XLII is here comprehending the reference to 'all' recorded in note 2 above.
[4] XLV has *vita functis*; XLII has *vita defunctis*.
[5] XLII has 'other' for 'either' (*siue*).
[6] XLV has *vixit* (perfect); XLII has *vixerit* (future perfect).

XLIII. *The souls of them that depart this life do neither die with the bodies, nor sleep idly.*   [1553: XL]

They which say that the souls of such as depart hence do sleep[1] until the day of judgement, or affirm that the souls die with the body,[2] and at the last day shall be raised up with the same,[3] do utterly dissent from the right belief declared to us in Holy Scripture.

[1] XLII adds *absque omni sensu*, which it translates fulsomely as "being without all sense, feeling, or perceiving".
[2] XLV has *corpore* – 'body'; XLII has *corporibus* – 'bodies'.
[3] XLV has *illo* – 'that' (singular; here 'the same'); XLII has *illis* – 'those' (plural; translated 'the same').

XLIV. *Heretics called Millenarii.*   [1553: XLI]

They that go about to renew the fable of heretics called Millenarii be repugnant to Holy Scripture, and cast themselves headlong into a Jewish dotage.

No changes

XLV. *All men shall not be saved at the length.*   [1553: XLII]

They also are worthy of condemnation who endeavour at this time to restore the dangerous opinion, that all men, be they never so ungodly, shall at length be saved,[1] when they have suffered[2] pains for their sins a certain time appointed by God's justice.

[1] XLV has *tandem seruandi sunt*; XLII has *seruandi sunt tandem*.
[2] XLV has *luerint* (future perfect); XLII has *luerunt* (perfect).

Translator's Notes

The MS of the XLV, the printed Latin text of the XLV (C. Hardwick, *History of the Articles of Religion*, 3rd Edn, 1876), and the printed Latin and English texts of the XLII (E. Cardwell, *Synodalia*, I, 1842) have been carefully compared. Where there is any variation, that is noted in the text when there is a change of meaning, or in footnotes if it involves no change in the translation. Possible variant readings of the Latin MS of the XLV have been noted. None of these variants is believed to alter the translation significantly.

The texts of the XLII are also in the Parker Society's *The Two Liturgies of Edward VI* (1844) and Gerald Bray's *Documents of the English Reformation* (2019): in both of these the English has been modernised.

A full, new translation of the XLV has not been made; instead, the official translation of the XLII has been used as the basis of this translation of the XLV. Where there is no difference between the Latin of the XLV and the Latin of the XLII, the translation of the XLV has been printed as the translation of the XLII, except on a few occasions where it was necessary to make the translation more faithful to the Latin. See below for details.

Because the official translation of the XLII (1553) has been used as the basis of this translation of the XLV (1552), adapting it where necessary, it can appear at first sight as though the translator of the XLII has altered, even significantly altered, the English text of the XLV. It is trusted that this as-it-were anachronism and illusion will not cause any difficulty.

Where there is no difference between the Latin of the XLV and the Latin of the XLII, there has been no systematic consideration of whether the English translation of the XLII is the most felicitous. The translation of the XLII is sometimes quite free or fulsome, though that does not necessarily mean that it is wrong.

Spelling and orthography

Cardwell's English text of the XLII suggests that the original was simply punctuated, with a tendency towards long sentences often simply divided by commas. In the present translation, spelling and punctuation have been modernised, but not language.

Numeration

From Article XXIX onwards the numeration of the XLV and the XLII differs: the numeration of the XLV has been followed, and the numeration of the XLII has been given in square brackets in the right-hand margin.

Detailed notes

Where the Latin of XLV and XLII is the same, but the translation of XLII has not been adopted

Article II, nn. 2 & 5
Article VIII, nn. 3, 8, & 9
Article XVII, n. 7
Article XXII, n. 4

Article XXVIII, n. 3
Article XXX, n. 2
Article XXXVII, n. 4
Article XXXVIII, n. 2

Examples of where the English of the XLII translation is fulsome

Article VIII, n. 1	Article XXXII, n. 2
Article XVIII, n. 18	Article XXXV, n. 4
Article XXII, n. 4	Article XLII, n. 3
Article XXX, n. 2	Article XLIII, n. 6

Vocabulary usage

- *Regenerated / born again / new birth*

Article VIII –
in renatis ('born again'): 'in them that are regenerated' (& in XXXIX)
in XLII: 'in them that are baptized'

renatis et credentibus ('them that are regenerated and believe')
in XLII (& in XXXIX) 'them that believe and are baptized'

Article XIV –
regenerati: 'born again'

Article XXVIII –
regeneratio: 'new birth'

- *Church / Congregation*

ecclesia is usually translated 'church' (but the heading and first occurrence of 'church' in Article XXXVI are renderings of the adjective *ecclesiasticus*).

ecclesia is translated 'congregation' in Article XXIV (three times) and Article XXV (two times).

In Article XX the word translated 'congregation' is *coetus* – 'assembly, gathering, company, congregation'

- *The Lord's Supper*

Coena domini is used in the heading and text of Article XXVI. *Coena dominica* is used in the heading and first words of the text of Article XXIX [but in XXXIX: *Coena Domini*].

Eucharistia is used in Articles XXX, XXXI (heading and text), and XXXII (heading and text). The XLII translated *eucharistia* twice – once in Article XXXI (part of Article XXIX in 1553) and once in Article XXXII (part of Article XXIX in 1553); on both occasions it was rendered 'the Lord's Supper' (which was also the practice in XXXIX). This practice has been followed.

- *Christen / Christened* in the XLII Articles

See Article XXVIII, nn. 3 & 8.

Also Published by the Latimer Trust

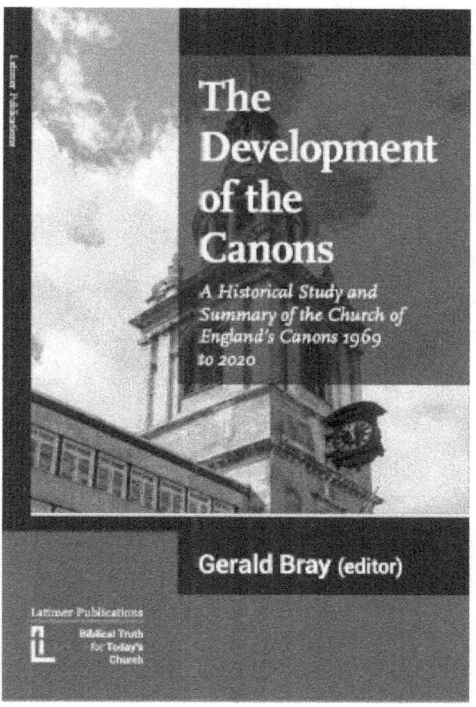

After three and a half centuries of relative neglect, the Church of England embarked on a thoroughgoing reform of its Canons, which led to the promulgation of an entirely new series of them in 1964 and in 1969. A year later, the present General Synod was inaugurated, and since then the Church's canon law has undergone a sometimes bewildering number of additions and alterations.

Keeping track of these developments is not easy, because although the material is available, until now it has not been gathered together in one place or set out in a user-friendly format. This book is a compilation of the 1964/1969 Canons with all their many modifications in the first half-century of their existence. It has no legal authority of its own, and those wanting to know what Canons are currently in force will need to consult the official publications of the Church of England.

This edition is a reference work aimed to clarify how the Church has developed its Canons over the past fifty years. As such, it will be of great benefit to historians, and to lawmakers in the Church who want to find out what has happened to the Canons in the recent past, even as they make new ones for the future. It is a snapshot taken in 2020 that provides a template for the study of a work that is still in progress, even as it continues to reflect the principles and practices that have guided its development since 1970.

From our Christian Leadership series

Bishops – A Concise Study summarises the key points of the argument of Martin's major study 'Bishops Past, Present and Future' (Gilead Books 2022). It is designed to meet the needs of those who would like to know more about bishops, but who would balk at tackling the 800+ pages of the original book.

This concise study is published in the hope that will help many in the Church of England, both ordained and lay to think in a more informed fashion about how bishops should respond to the challenges facing the Church of England at this critical point in its history as it considers how to move forward following the publication of the Living in Love and Faith material.

In our St Antholin lectures

The Puritans wished to live godly lives in heart and thought as well as action. One of the tools they utilised in training their hearts and minds was the practice of diary-writing. In this short overview we see the theory of Puritan diary-writing as worked out by John Beadle, and the inspiring example of the sixteenth-century Puritan Richard Rogers writing about his life.

www.ingramcontent.com/pod-product-compliance
Lightning Source LLC
Chambersburg PA
CBHW022111040426
42450CB00006B/661